S0-ASM-166

Teaching Tough Kids

This book is dedicated to Lucy, an inspired and young aspiring writer in our family. May you find what I have. I have had the privilege to work with an extraordinary group of adults over the years who taught me how precious it is to nurture the hearts and minds of children. They are teachers. A unique group of unsung heroes who understand the kinds of messages kids need to receive. Their passion is responsible for mine, and I hope mine inspires yours.

Teaching Tough Kids

Simple and proven strategies
for student success

Mark Le Messurier

FRANKLIN SQ. PUBLIC LIBRARY
19 LINCOLN ROAD
FRANKLIN SQUARE, N.Y. 11010

Routledge
Taylor & Francis Group

LONDON AND NEW YORK

First published 2010
by Routledge
2 Park Square, Milton Park, Abingdon, Oxon OX14 4RN

Simultaneously published in the USA and Canada
by Routledge
270 Madison Avenue, New York, NY 10016

Routledge is an imprint of the Taylor & Francis Group, an informa business

© 2010 Mark Le Messurier

Typeset in Bembo and Franklin Gothic by
Florence Production Ltd
Printed and bound in Great Britain by
MPG Books Group, UK

All rights reserved. The purchase of this copyright material confers the right on the
purchasing institution to photocopy pages 203 to 227. No other part of this book may be
reprinted or reproduced or utilised in any form or by any electronic, mechanical, or
other means, now known or hereafter invented, including photocopying and recording,
or in any information storage or retrieval system, without permission in writing from the
publishers.

British Library Cataloguing in Publication Data
A catalogue record for this book is available from the British Library

Library of Congress Cataloging-in-Publication Data
Le Messurier, Mark.
  Teaching tough kids: simple and proven strategies for student success/Mark Le Messurier.
    p.cm.
  1. Problem children—Education.   2. Effective teaching.   3. Academic achievement.   I. Title.
  LC48001.L4 2009
  371.93—dc22   2009008206

ISBN10: 0-415-46060-3 (pbk)
ISBN10: 0-203-86199-X (ebk)

ISBN13: 978-0-415-46060-6 (pbk)
ISBN13: 978-0-203-86199-8 (ebk)

Contents

About the author

Mark Le Messurier

Mark Le Messurier is a teacher, author and conference presenter. His background spans twenty years in schools and includes special education, adult education, child-centred education and community education projects. Mark is a recipient of the prestigious Australian National Excellence in Teaching Award. He is a passionate educator.

Mark works in schools and in private practice at Fullarton House with children and adolescents he affectionately refers to as the 'tough kids' – kids whose lives are compromised by the unpredictability of their functioning, or by the capricious nature of their home life, or by both. Consequently, they find life much tougher than most and in the process make life tougher for those who care for them and educate them. They comprise a challenging population of students who are increasingly being identified with underlying executive functioning delays. Without adequate executive functioning capabilities kids lack the ability to delay gratification, listen and filter out distractions, process new information, remember, plan, persist, adapt to change, keep track of time and self-regulate emotion and behaviour. Mark provides practical and therapeutic interventions to strengthen the performance of the tough kids. *Teaching Tough Kids* encapsulates the work he is engaged in.

Mark regularly presents at conferences for public and independent schools, parents and interested groups throughout Australia and Australasia. In 2007 he was a Keynote Speaker at SPELD New Zealand's International Learning Difficulty Conference. His presentations relate to mentoring, ADD and ADHD, Asperger syndrome, specific learning difficulties, developing emotional resilience, successful parenting and teaching children with challenging behaviours.

In 2004 he wrote *Cognitive Behavioural Training: A how-to guide for successful behaviour*. This popular resource was written for special education coordinators, teachers, teachers in training, school support officers, counsellors, psychologists and health professionals and is now distributed throughout Australia, New Zealand, the United States and the United Kingdom. It addresses common problems that students face: organisation, remembering, self-awareness, motivation and emotional resilience. Mark has also completed a training and development film on learning difficulties,

Reflections on Dyslexia. The package, which also contains a staff development hand-book, is available to individuals, schools, colleges and tertiary institutions.

In 2007 *Parenting Tough Kids* was released. It is a book for parents, parent resource libraries, teachers and school counsellors, in fact for anyone with an investment in children. It has also become a popular book in Australia. In 2008 Mark and Lindy Petersen's *STOP and THINK Friendship DVD Package*, first released in 2000, was revised and reprinted. This social skills development resource is also distributed to schools, educators and clinicians throughout Australia, New Zealand and Europe.

Mark is also the architect of the unique *Mentoring Programme* currently building capacity in South Australian Catholic schools. The programme provides opportunities for interested staff members to develop skills so they are equipped to mentor students who are experiencing learning, social or behavioural difficulties. These students, aged from six to eighteen years of age, often do it tough and benefit from the ongoing friendship and encouragement from a caring adult working within the school system. Mark describes the programme as truly inspirational and will tell you what a privilege it is to work alongside such passionate staff. Already, in a short space of time, a number of highly skilled school personnel are taking extra care of some of the most vulnerable students in schools.

About Bill Hansberry, co-author of Chapter 2

Bill Hansberry lives in Adelaide, Australia and divides his work week between being a classroom teacher, a consultant in restorative practices in schools as well as an educator and mentor to young people in private practice.

He has spent the last fifteen years working in primary and secondary schools in Australia and the UK and has specialised in the area of school counselling and whole school approaches to behaviour management. Bill has worked at both school and district support levels within the South Australian public education system and has taught within the Catholic education system.

Recently, he has had the privilege of mentoring many, many committed educators in the area of behaviour management through workshops, online forums, and international conferences where he has shared his knowledge and experience in restorative practices in schools. He is passionate about helping young people to discover (or rediscover) their potential.

Bill believes that relationships and learning are inseparable, and that without a focus on strengthening relationships in schools, quality learning is a casualty.

Foreword

by Stephanie Newland

I am one of Mark's 'tough kids' and at eighteen years of age I'm probably his longest serving project! I'm challenged by mild cerebral palsy, dyslexia and more recently severe clinical depression.

High school was not a happy place for me. My differences were obvious and because of these I became a target for silent bullying, gossip and humiliation. Needless to say I never graduated into teen girl world. Naturally, with my physical and learning disabilities it was a struggle to keep up with my peers and with the work. I constantly battled fatigue. Dealing with all this at such a young age was too much for me and by the time I reached fourteen I was caught in a downhill spiral of severe clinical depression. Despite the hardships I faced at school I was incredibly blessed to be surrounded by a few extraordinary teachers. Amongst these teachers was my beloved special education teacher, who became my biggest supporter, defender and dear friend. Whenever necessary she went into battle for me, convincing teachers to see things in a different way, or to put a little extra time and effort. She set up a desk and chair dedicated to me in her classroom and we spent a lot of time together, especially when I first started high school. She listened to all of my fears, worries, disappointments and ranting. She comforted me when I cried and never stopped helping me with my school work. My biggest issue has always been my shocking organisation and planning. I'm sure it is a part of my condition. My special education teacher understood this natural challenge and she constantly showed me how to break tasks down and get them done.

Even though I have faced hardship and injustice my story to date is one of triumph. I am grateful to the amazing teachers who saw my potential and wanted to care for it. They made me feel that it was okay to be me, and did not judge me or write me off because of my differences. They fought for me when I could not fight for myself and because of their work and belief in me I managed a score of 90.45% in my final year of secondary school!

The tough kids are real kids, their problems are real and they depend on teachers to draw strength, reassurance and direction from. Dealing with us is never easy. We tough kids can be gruelling work, but we can be inspirational too. We can annoy you and we can delight you. We can give you the worst or best teaching years of your life, but if you choose to let us in we will touch you and leave our gentle footprints on your heart forever, and you will never ever be the same.

Teaching Tough Kids captures the essence of what it is really like for a child to live with a difficulty or disability, but it never loses sight of the spirit and untapped capacities we have. Mark's book communicates his experience and contagious passion to mentor kids with unique differences. It also expresses his enthusiasm to find practical ways to help kids discover success and meaning in their lives despite the roadblocks they face. I encourage every educator to join Mark's quest to make a difference to each of the tough kids that come your way.

Acknowledgements

The following people are gratefully acknowledged for their support and contribution to *Teaching Tough Kids:*

Anne Carolin, behavioural educational consultant, Catholic Education Office
Benita Ranzon, psychologist, Fullarton House
Bill Hansberry, teacher, mentor and consultant in restorative practices in schools
Carol Nicolls, artist
Cathy Sires, behavioural educational consultant, Catholic Education Office
Charlie Stone, student and friend
Chris Rampazis, teacher, Catholic Education, SA
Debra Lutze, teacher, Waldorf School
Dylan Lundy, student and friend
Glynis Hannell, psychologist, presenter and author
Helen Hall, teacher, DECS
Jane Buckman, teacher and speech pathologist, Fullarton House
Joe Blefari, acting deputy principal, Catholic Education, SA
John Hall, special education teacher, Fullarton House
Lindy Petersen, psychologist and my mentor
Lisa Harris, educational support officer, Catholic Education, SA
Lee Carter, teacher, Catholic Education, SA
Leigh Burrows, learning difficulties, DECS and lecturer at Flinders University of
    South Australia
Madhavi Nawana-Parker, behavioural therapist, Fullarton House
Marney Yeates, speech pathologist, Director of TALK
Melissa Mun, educational support officer, Catholic Education, SA
Mike Proctor, teacher, Catholic Education, SA
Noni Le Messurier, enthusiastic personal assistant
Pamela Holmes, educational support officer, Catholic Education, SA
Pennie Hazelgrove, student
Sam Hage, teacher, Catholic Education, SA
Sharon Diglio, school counsellor, Catholic Education, SA

Sharon Palm, wife and the keeper of morale
Stephanie Newland, student and friend
Sue Walker, teacher, DECS
Suzie Mackie, client and mother of Tim
Tania Masters, teacher, Catholic Education, SA

I also wish to acknowledge each and every educator who has, over the years, taught me how precious it is to nurture the developing spirit within the children and adolescents we teach. Those who enjoy being with kids, who see value in forging relationships with them and see potential in young people. I am blessed to be part of an exceptional profession who strive to make a meaningful difference for kids. Your enthusiasm is entirely responsible for mine.

Intellectual property

Determining absolute intellectual ownership of many of the ideas presented in this book is easier said than done. It's frequent to see one idea evolve into a new concept depending on the situation that presents itself at the time. This is just the way it is. Wherever possible, the obvious sources are acknowledged. If, by chance, an original source has been omitted, I apologise. The overriding motivation is to add to the repertoire of practical strategies that will benefit our children.

Online content on the Routledge website

The material accompanying this book may be used by the purchasing individual/ organisation only. The files may be amended to suit particular situations, or individual learning needs, and printed out for use by the purchaser. The material can be accessed at www.routledge.com/education/fultonresources.asp.

01 think strip
02 star chart
03 catching helpful behaviours
04 student monitoring
05 chunking tasks
06 mini daily timetable
07 after school timetable
08 my weekly planner
09 my four week planner
10 progress charts
11 progress train
12 my checklist
13 the islands of competence inventory
14 success plan
15 ABCs of behaviour
16 my way to do it
17 blast off! tracking chart
18 go fly your kite! tracking chart
19 you can count on Winston's segments! tracking chart
20 staying on track with my dragon tracking chart
21 staying on track with my duck tracking chart
22 being different is ok
23 my team
24 break card
25 my happy face collector

Introduction

Who are the 'tough kids'?

These are the kids whose lives are compromised by the unpredictability of their functioning, or by the capricious nature of their home life, or by both. As a result they find life much tougher than most and in the process make life tougher for those who care for them and educate them. They comprise a worrying and growing population of students in schools (Russell 2008).

These are the kids we take home in our thoughts most days, over weekends and on holiday breaks. They are complex kids living complex lives who present us with great challenges. Many, often boys, are inclined to explode and let their hot-headed feelings run away for all to witness. When things don't go their way they overreact, refuse, disrupt, avoid, threaten and clash with peers and authority figures. In contrast, there are those who deal with their feelings inwardly. They learn to mask feelings of worry, shyness, shame, sadness, isolation, despair or inadequacy. They struggle, but hold their very private feelings inside and do their utmost to keep them invisible. What we often see at school is just the tip of the iceberg. They teeter on the brink of unravelling, imploding or giving up. Sadly, a few quietly slide into anxiety, introversion and depression before our very eyes. Yet, they are also inspiring kids to teach. They compel us to confront what we do and why we do it, and whether our actions are truly helpful. As they take our patience, persistence and endurance to the outer limits they prompt both our personal and professional growth. And, in those moments when something clicks for them, or a few years later when we hear about their success, it reminds us that we are all in this together. They teach us about the value of connectedness and the depth of human spirit.

This book is written to enrich the ways we think about the tough kids and fortify the work we do with them in our schools. It celebrates the real heroes in schools – educators who dig deep everyday to regenerate the spirit within kids so they can stay connected to school, to learning and to their dreams. *Teaching Tough Kids* is a collection of ingenious understandings and ideas, inspired by the resourceful practices of my colleagues aimed at maintaining the buoyancy of students with diverse abilities.

So, how is a tough kid best defined? No one description adequately tells all. Perhaps the best way to explore this is to offer a series of personal snapshots that may bring you closer to understanding the complex lives many of the tough kids live. As you will discover, unpredictable home lives, disability, misfortune, ridicule, tragedy and disadvantage often feature in the lives of these kids.

Case study

SNAPSHOT: *'My mum doesn't tuck me into bed at night anymore'*

When she comes home from work she goes straight to her laptop in her bedroom to do her Facebook. She doesn't even say, 'Hi, how was your day?' I wish she could just get off the laptop and do some stuff with my brothers and me. A few days ago it was nine o'clock at night and I asked for dinner. She said she didn't have to get it because I'm a fat little boy and I've eaten everything in the house anyway. Mum has not cooked for so long now. She just orders pizza. I like it, but it's not good to have every day. When I stacked the pizza boxes out the back one on top of the other they were higher than me. The way it's going I don't like mum at all. She blames dad for everything. He blames her for everything. She says she'll leave if dad doesn't stop doing what he's doing. I don't know what he's doing.

Max, 10 years

Case study

SNAPSHOT: *'You can't help me mum. I'm never going to learn to read.'*

Our Timothy had been very flat for most of the summer holidays, but the last couple of weeks were particularly hard for him. He had cried a lot about having to go back to school. A day did not pass without him questioning why he had to go. With a week of holidays left the tantruming subsided, but the tears continued. It seemed he had resigned himself to return to school.

His younger brother and sister were asleep, Timmy was watching the television and I was in the kitchen.

'Thud.' A couple of seconds passed. 'Thud.' A few more seconds passed. 'Thud' is the only way to explain the sound. It was deep and powerful like nothing I'd heard before and recalling it makes my heart jump to my throat.

'Thud.' It got the better of me, so as good mothers do, I went to investigate. Not often did I need to check on Timmy, we had been blessed with a calm, thoughtful child. I made my way into the lounge, stepped inside and looked. There I saw Timmy doing a tall handstand on the couch.

'Timothy how many times have I told you and your brother?'
'Thud.'
'No. No. No. No. Stop!'
It all hit home. He was lifting himself up as high as he could with his hands on the back of the couch, and then jerking his hands away so his head

crunched into the couch seat below. The 'thud' was his feet hitting against the wall helping to propel him with all the more force into the seat.

I grabbed him and pulled him onto my lap.

'You could break your bloody neck if you keep doing this!' I screamed.

'I know,' he calmly responded.

'If you know why on earth are you doing it?

'I don't want to be here.'

Innocently, I said, 'That's fine. If you're bored don't stay here. Go and do something else.'

'No. I don't want to be here. I want to die,' he said staring up into my eyes.

He continued, 'I don't want to feel this way anymore and if I am dead I won't have to go to school.'

'You can't help me mum. I'm never going to learn to read.'

I hugged him and sobbed. I couldn't let him go.

Timothy had spent eighteen months in preschool, eighteen months in reception and twelve months in Year 1. After four years of formal education he had stalled on the readers from the orange box. Each of them had just a word or two to a page. His best friends were beginning to read the Harry Potter books. A few months later Timothy was identified with a learning difficulty, dyslexia. That helped to explain why he has such confusions, but it hasn't changed the way he feels about it.

I love our son. I hate our lounge. I still can't think of our beautiful desperate little boy bouncing on his neck because he didn't think there was anything else he could do. Timothy was seven and half when he tried to escape the world because he couldn't read.

Suzie, Timothy's mother

Case study

SNAPSHOT: *'My life has been about me and my mum surviving it.'*

I know my life is different to most kids. I live with mum and gran. Mum doesn't work and drinks white wine most afternoons. I hate her doing it and every afternoon at school I start to worry about how she'll be when I get home. When she does drink I lock myself in my room until she falls asleep. Gran is old and bossy and mum says she's lost it. We live in her small house and because she has more money than mum and I she makes the decisions. I don't have a lot of things and there aren't many places I've been to that I can brag about. I've never been on a plane and I've never been out of my city. My life has been about me and my mum surviving it.

I don't know my dad because he's never wanted to know me. I don't know any stories about him and we don't have photographs of him. For a long time I thought there must be something wrong with me and that was why he couldn't be bothered staying around. Now I think my dad is the one who's missed out on me. I know I'm okay now, but it still hurts sometimes. When I was younger I was pretty crazy though. Everyone tells me that when something went wrong at primary school I'd chase kids yelling and screaming and swinging my fists or a cricket bat at them. I'd chase them around the yard trying to get even. I got so mad. I was too sensitive. I've learned that I always want things to be fair. Mum says I've got justice problems and I think she's right because I still feel so bad when things aren't fair for me or for others.

My life has shown me that I'm probably a nerd. I like computers, video games and know a lot about them. I'm good at them too. If that makes me a nerd then I am a nerd.

So you can see my life has been different compared to most fourteen-year-olds. I've learned some things about myself, and after three years fighting anorexia nervosa, I've learned that I like myself. I'm a good person and don't want to fall into the slot of mediocrity. I want to be me, but it's hard to be true to your beliefs.

Dom, 14 years

Case study

SNAPSHOT: '*No wonder I hated school so much.*'

Late last year on my birthday I found out I was dyslexic. I'd never heard of it before, and finding out about it has answered so many questions for me.

Having dyslexia was like carrying a huge weight on my chest, and it hurt. It made me feel so dumb each day in front of everyone I was growing up with. These days I know that I just learn differently than other people. Now at sixteen I have decided to accept it, but it has left me with low self-esteem. Finding learning hard caused my low grades at school and meant teachers had to witness me giving up and complaining that the work was not worth the trouble. And, my family and friends have had to tolerate me being happy one minute and upset the next.

What's the worst thing a teacher ever said to me? That's easy to remember. My maths teacher told me in front of the class that I would never amount to anything. That was just last year. After she said that I found it even harder. Her words jumped into my mind whenever I didn't understand the maths. Looking back, I can't believe she made me blame myself for something that isn't my fault. To calm my anger at her, or when I couldn't get something in maths, I'd sing a song I liked over and over in my head. Then she left the school, and now I can't listen to that song without crying. But to this teacher I say, 'I'll succeed in life. I'm much more than you ever thought about me.'

How can teachers help? The most important thing is for them to be positive. To praise the work I do so I know I'm going in the right direction. But the most important thing is the support I have got from teachers this year now they know I'm dyslexic. I feel so relieved. I don't have to go through this by myself anymore.

Now I know I have to work on accepting my disability and that means honestly accepting that I'm never going to be as fast or accurate as the other kids in maths, pop quizzes, reading or writing, but being dyslexic will not stop me from what I want to achieve.

Pennie, 16 years

SNAPSHOT: *'I love Aidan very much, but he is a struggle every day.'*

I have thirteen-year-old Aidan, who is nearing the end of Year 8 and has a history of aggressive behaviour towards people in authority. He has always refused to do homework and that's always caused problems with school and at home. The deputy principal at his new high school speaks about him as a young teenager at high risk. His teachers are worried about his anger, swearing and lack of control. I knew it was just a matter of time before things would fall apart at this school too and it breaks my heart.

Aidan has two sisters, ten-year-old Shelly and four-year-old Jodie. His father, Stu, was diagnosed with paranoid schizophrenia when Aidan was nine. Soon afterwards he was hospitalised and became convinced that Aidan was the devil incarnate. Stu later committed suicide by hanging himself in the backyard for all to see. Sadly, Aidan and Shelly found him with me. At the time I was four weeks pregnant with Jodie.

Two years ago his primary school helped me to transfer Aidan to a new school. They did this because they felt there was nothing more they could do. At first the change seemed positive. The erratic, argumentative and angry behaviours subsided. In that same year I remarried, but Aidan was strongly opposed. He still struggles to accept his stepfather and pushes Eric to the limit. Eric is actually a saint to him. After about three months the teachers at his new primary school began to see a rise in Aidan's bad temper and opposition. Soon the feedback that I dread came. Aidan's teachers and school counsellor said his behaviour was outside of their expertise. Since then I have tried to see counsellors, psychologists and a psychiatrist with Aidan, but he either refuses to talk or swears non stop at them. He has seen it as a game he has to win.

This year Aidan started at high school. In the first semester he was suspended twice, had detentions and has had many 'rest days' to help him calm down. Most of the angry incidents have been over trivial events with teachers and with older kids. He has a few friends, but it is up and down.

He has now started a learning support programme at school and this gives him opportunities where he can be supported with his schoolwork and homework. The school psychologist recently assessed him and his intelligence came in at two years above his age. However, as you would imagine, Aidan's school reports have never reflected his intelligence. He has struggled to start tasks, to complete work and pass most subjects. The psychologist is about to write a report and told me that Aidan will be identified as a student with ADHD and with oppositional and obsessive behaviours.

I love Aidan very much, but he is such a struggle every day. He's hostile towards his sisters, and says he hates them because they get more than he does, and he truly resents my husband. In between, when Aidan is in a good mood, he is a beautiful kid whose company everyone enjoys. As for his future, we all deeply worry.

Mardi, Aidan's mother

SNAPSHOT: '*This was one of the times when I hated my cerebral palsy and myself.*'

My cerebral palsy (CP) is called hemiplegia and it has badly weakened one side of my body. My arm and leg on the left side of my body don't work very well. It was discovered when I was six months old at a check-up because I refused to pass a ball from my right hand to my left. This alerted the nurse, who referred my parents to doctors and a string of therapies and treatments.

I remember not being very keen about starting school because I was worried what everyone would think of my weak arm and leg. I spent ages as a young kid trying to find a way to do my shoelaces up by myself, but never sorted it out. It made me so mad. Looking back I realise I spent a lot of time at school worrying about what people thought about me. As I progressed through school I became a keen tennis player and at one of my specialist appointments I showed a doctor how I could throw the tennis ball into the air with my left hand, which surprised her. I was determined to learn how to serve a tennis ball so I spent hours and hours practising. Yes, it's amazing what a bit of determination can do, but you have no idea of how many hours I had to put in to do this one supposedly simple thing.

When I started at high school I remember becoming the target of two very clever bullies. They were both much bigger and stronger than me and had the class under their spell. In front of the other kids, when the teacher wasn't in the room, they'd drag me across the floor and lift me up and down under the blades of a rotating ceiling fan. It was terrifying and impossible to defend myself because of my lazy arm and leg. This went on for quite a while and was one of the times when I hated my CP and myself. I felt so useless. It destroyed me emotionally for a while, but the teachers at my school acted quickly once they found out and the trouble stopped.

Cerebral palsy affects each of us differently. Most will tell you it takes us a lot longer to do things, such as type this for Mark. For me, I get tired because I have to use my right hand and right leg for everything. I have had times when kids were cruel, but I think this can happen to anyone who is different. At eighteen years of age as I look back I think that having CP has made me who I am today, and that's okay. It has also made me more understanding of the visible and invisible disabilities of others.

Jack, 17 years

SNAPSHOT: '*He has been emotionally scarred by our family life.*'

My boy Teale is thirteen years old. Yesterday he was involved in throwing rocks into a tree to retrieve a football and later climbed the tree to get it. Once again he's in trouble at school.

I feel caught between trying to understand whether my son misbehaves because he is basically bad or whether his impulsive behaviour and poor choices are genuinely difficult for him to control. He says he cannot, at times, control what he does. As well, my mood has been pretty flat for the last twelve months and I have tried antidepressants, but reacted poorly. Money is very tight and I'm facing financial difficulties with the Child Support Agency. I think this is the trigger for my depression. I have moments when I think Teale would be better off living full time with his mother.

His life has been hard for a long time. Since my spiteful marriage breakdown nine years ago Teale has lived with his mother one week and with me the next. However, his older brother and sister have always remained with their mother and will not speak to me because of the continuing bitterness between their mother and me. When Teale stays with his mother he's treated like a second rate citizen. He knows that to have a difference of opinion with her is pointless. Harry, his older brother, recently told him that he does not have the same rights as they do because he does not live there full time. Teale continues to want to share his life with his mother, but it comes at a dreadful cost. The cost, I think, is that he has been emotionally scarred by our family life, and I wonder whether his failure to deal with typical day-to-day stress situations is messed up as a result.

I love my son and it hurts to see the way he behaves and gets into trouble at school. Yet, he is also caring and can be a pleasure to be with. He is my greatest joy and greatest worry.

Malcolm, Teale's father

Teaching Tough Kids places a spotlight on a broad group of kids who have much more in common than we may first think. They are the kids usually challenged by poor executive function. Let me explain.

Researcher, Elkhonon Goldberg, has described the executive functions as the conductor of the orchestra (Goldberg 2001). They take place in the prefrontal regions of the brain and supervise various complex mental processes providing an individual's capacity to sustain goal directed behaviour (Ardila 2008). As educators, we are acutely aware how students struggle when they lack the faculty to listen and filter out distractions, process new information, get started, persist, adapt to changes in routine, keep track of time and multi-task (Meltzer 2007). With a scarcity of this valuable personal resource it is difficult to delay gratification, strategically plan, self-regulate emotion and behaviour and retrieve information stored within memory that would be helpful (Martinussen *et al.* 2005). The healthy functioning of this set of mental processes is the basis for success and when it is not working the way it should most aspects of an individual's social, academic and personal worlds suffer. Our fallback position is to remain ever watchful for practical and therapeutic ideas to encourage and strengthen their performance, and this of course is the mission of *Teaching Tough Kids*.

Poor executive function is associated with a number of developmental problems, psychological disorders, difficulties and disabilities: Asperger syndrome, learning difficulties, ADHD, oppositional defiant disorder, Tourette's syndrome, obsessive compulsive disorder, traumatic brain injury, depression, epilepsy, cerebral palsy and so on (Bradshaw 2001; Reiter *et al.* 2005; Salimpoor 2006). And, there is a significant (and unexplained) increase in the numbers of children being diagnosed with these conditions (Russell 2008).

In recent times another group of children and adolescents with executive functioning difficulties have begun to emerge (Silins *et al.* 2007). These are the kids who have endured anxiety provoking and traumatic life situations. Kids who have suffered the disadvantages of neglect, abuse, deprivation, stress and uncertainty display the classically related symptoms of hyperactivity, hyper vigilance and impulsive behaviours ('Bad behaviour' 2008). We know that when young human beings are stressed within normal limits their physical performance is enhanced by the release of natural chemicals in their bodies. First the adrenalin kicks in, providing the increased heart rate just in case they need to escape a frightening situation or stand up to a terrifying bully. However, in the event that the threat continues, the signal is for their body to remain on high alert. To sustain a high alert state a hormone called cortisol is released by the adrenal gland to increase blood pressure and blood sugar. As this stress hormone surges into the brain it severs access to the rational, thinking, memory and immune system parts of the brain. For a child who is continually stressed these parts of their brain actually become pruned. As a consequence, their reactions and decision making become trapped in the emotional part of their brain to a point where new experiences are interpreted as a threat rather than a tempting challenge or something that may evoke curiosity. While the brain continues to grow and has a desire to increase its connections this scenario seriously affects the way a child's brain actually grows. The wiring to the rational, thinking, memory and immune system doesn't set up as strongly and most of the action is switched to the emotional part of the brain.

> What we've seen from the 1950s onwards is a steady rise in rates of mental health problems, particularly for children and adolescents. We know that some of the major predictors of mental health problems are the levels of stress and social support for the parents and the kids.
>
> ('Bad behaviour' 2008)

The verdict is in. The link between too much stress in a young person's life for too long and mental health problems is now well established. No one would deny that the landscape of students in our care has become, and is becoming increasingly complex. In recent years children's behaviour has attracted serious concern in schools and in the wider community. Zito *et al.* (2000, 2003) in their study found a 300 per cent increase in prescriptions for children under the age of five years with behavioural difficulties and disabilities between 1987 and 1996. In fact, medication treatments for youth in the 1990s virtually reached adult utilisation rates. Child health researchers are confirming what educators in schools have seen for some time. The rise in broad-based emotional, behavioural and mental health problems in young people is alarming. Professor Fiona Stanley, Director of the Telethon Institute for Child Health Research and Chair of the Australian Research Alliance for Children and Youth, presents evidence that emotional and mental health problems in kids are currently running at about 14 per cent (Stanley 2008). She says we are witnessing ominous warning signs for our children and their future.

There are a worrying number of threats to children's health in today's society. They are worrying because they are very burdensome and many of them are increasing. They are worrying because on the whole they are getting more complex and occurring at younger ages. Behind the statistics that I talk about are the tragedies of kids who aren't going to make it.

(Stanley 2008)

Stanley's investigations reflect data collected by an eminent group of health researchers from The Australian College of Educators in 2007 (Silins *et al.* 2007). They looked at the incidence of emotional and mental health problems experienced by children aged from five to thirteen years in South Australian schools. Teachers indicated that close to 11 per cent of students displayed what they considered to be emotional/mental well-being difficulties. This translates to about two or three students per class, and most teachers believed the issues not only had a significant impact on their learning and socialisation, but impacted heavily on the learning and interactions of every student in their class. Cahill's earlier Australia-wide research proposed that 20 per cent of children and adolescents are affected by emotional and mental health issues. These include, disturbed conduct, antisocial behaviour, depression, suicidal behaviours, eating disorders, self-harm and the abuse of drugs and alcohol (Cahill 2000; Cahill *et al.* 2004).

Why place a spotlight on the tough kids?

Unless our response and interventions match the rising complexity and intensity of student needs there will be too many kids from this population of vulnerable kids that will not make it.

These kids are dependent on the quality of our collective wisdom and care. While it may be more challenging to influence change within the group I affectionately refer to as the 'tough kids', we have the advantage of being an influential group who understand the kinds of structures and messages all kids need to receive. As many of us have witnessed and experienced, it is too easy to respond abruptly or unhelpfully to the problematic behaviours of the tough kids, and as this happens, these kids are quick to absorb the negative messages they hear about themselves. They become convinced that the problem they have just encountered reflects what they are, and what their future must hold. Soon they begin to fulfil a role – the clown, the joker, the victim, the runaway, the avoider, the disrupter, the aggressor or the outsider. By the time some begin middle primary they have developed reputations. Soon they disengage from school and look towards shadow groups who stroke their ego and welcome them. Before they reach high school some say, 'It doesn't matter anyway', 'You can't make me' or 'I don't care'. Their reputation spreads and the beacon of transformation latent in every spirited child begins to dim. Indeed, we play a potent part in deciding the trajectory they are likely to take.

Everything we do ought to relate to enhancing the life chances of the kids we teach: developing their self-esteem by talking and making plans with them, consciously delivering thoughtful feedback, sharing ideas, celebrating achievement, delivering evidence of care and acceptance, and engaging them in relevant curricula.

Relevant curricula and flexible programmes are fundamental to the success of all kids, but the way teachers actually think and respond to students carries just as much weight.

It's vital that those who seek to promote high academic standards and those who seek to promote mental, emotional and social health realize that they are on the same side. Social and affective education can support academic learning, not take time away from it.

(Weare 2004)

This is the moment to recall that our best work has always taken place inside relationships with kids. It is in relationships where we learn how they think and understand what they do is part of their unique functioning. Our work with them has to begin by engaging at a truly personal level because it sets the scene for the best chance of connection, best learning and acts as a strong protective factor against alienation, depression, hostility, frustration, school violence, leaving school prematurely and ill health.

Essentially, as we get our thinking and practice right to work more successfully with the tough kids we will reach many more kids, and schools will become better places for everyone.

What is our job?
To accept we are potent agents of change

As educators, we have the capacity to influence transformation within students. We can fill them with inspiration, dread, dreams, confidence or deep feelings of failure or resentment, and history tells us we are very good at it. Whether we know it or not, the mark we leave on every student who comes our way is absolutely enabling or disabling to them.

The results from Dr. Pamela Snow's recent Australian studies remind us of something many educators might predict, and wish for. Snow emphasises the dynamic influence educators have on the young people they interact with. She encourages teachers to think of themselves as public health professionals – holding each generation's future emotional, economic, mental and physical well being in their hands (Snow and Powell 2008; Snow 2008). Snow's research strongly suggests that the longer educators engage students in learning, the longer teachers can sustain vibrant emotional connections with students and the longer students remain at school with a willingness to learn the healthier and wealthier their life expectancy will be. Similarly, New Zealand researcher John Hattie tells us that 'teachers make the difference' (Hattie 2009). He says we have little control over what kids bring to us at school because 50 per cent of their variance in achievement is contributed to by genetics, personality and background. Our role is to teach them all, whether they happen to be large or small, eager or reluctant, fast or slow, red or blue, compliant or otherwise. The next largest variance in achievement for students is associated with the potent influence teachers have on them. Teacher influence accounts for about 30 per cent. Hattie believes it is what teachers know, what they say, what they do and how they show they care. They have a big impact on the climate of a school and the perception the community holds of a school. Teachers are powerful.

The young learners who are at the heart of this book are reliant on teachers who continually question and adjust what they think, say and do with kids in classes, in both the good and bad moments. Options to build the emotion, behaviour and learning of these kids require hard work, persistence, flexibility and faith. Rarely is there a silver bullet, and believing it is possible to measure some of the fabulous transformations seen within students in the same way literacy and numeracy levels are scored misses the spirit and depth of an educator's work and influence.

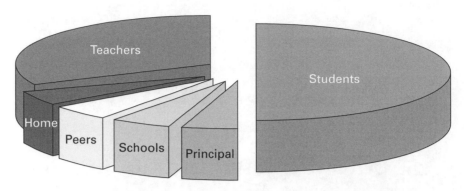

Figure 1.1 Percentage of student achievement variance (Hattie 2009)

These students are dependent on our clever abilities to place an emotional lens on our work while delivering quality curriculum (Thornton 2008). The best any of us have to offer is a willingness to connect with students through a quality emotional lens. It is the only thing that will ever go close to providing any sort of inclusion that is remotely authentic.

So before leaping into grand plans to encourage any student to lift their organisation, care, motivation, mood or responsibility let's review what we have to offer: the depth of our personal resources and our understandings. A periodic stocktake helps us to resist the temptation to blame students for their poor functioning or under-performance. Without this awareness, the constructive influences we may be able to generate are likely to be erratic at best.

Take a look at a few guiding ideas that can help young learners, tough or otherwise, find success.

Your personal checklist, take the challenge and reflect

Do you offer relationship and engagement to students?

Engagement is an emotionally based experience and relationship is the catalyst. However, not all educators understand it or want it.

Nothing is as effective as real, everyday connections. They bubble to the surface as a smile, a wink, a silly face, a nudge, a dare, a joke, the zombie walk, a friendly eye roll, a thumbs up, a kind or a reassuring comment. They allow cooperative attitudes to be reinforced, stretched, reshaped and improved. What is more, the benefits arising from a trusting relationship provide the scope for everyone to make mistakes without a catastrophe ensuing. Without relationship and engagement with students all we have are a few flimsy tricks to deliver a little temporary control. Our best work is always done inside relationships with kids because as we truly get to know students the wonderful advantage of being able to read them so much more successfully begins to surface. It becomes easier to gauge changes in their emotions and we begin to know when to pull back and change tack. As relationship strengthens there is the scope to develop privately understood signals that convey vital messages between both. A look, in these circumstances, is worth a thousand words.

Experience alerts us that the first interaction is the one that really counts. It's the one that becomes imprinted on their social memory, and is likely to be drawn on as trust in difficult times. Recovery from negative first impressions is always difficult. One of the best tips is to start by reading the student's file before meeting them: anecdotal notes, reports, reviews and assessments. Skilled educators build on the judgements of those who have previously worked with students. Their collective opinion is valuable in appreciating the student's journey and places an educator in a far more proactive position.

Do you ask kids,

> 'What will help?',
>
> 'What can I do to help you?'

When a student's performance is awkward or challenging they are almost always aware of the difficulties too. They know that their short concentration, impulsiveness, bossiness or emotionalism triggers tricky situations. When asked, a surprising number of kids know what could help and are prepared to trial ways to help. Others won't know, but don't despair because it's not the idea that tips the balance. More often it is the act of asking and participating that makes the greatest difference. Make time to talk and listen. Let them know that many fine human beings have had difficulties and low motivation about school and schoolwork. They may, at the moment, find it difficult to embrace the school culture, but reassure them they are 'normal'. A critical step is to normalise their functioning. Begin by teasing out what they enjoy and what they feel good at. Work to create balance so interests are rekindled and feelings of success are aroused.

Reflect on your own school days.

- Can you recall the teacher who had a positive impact on you?
- What did they say or do?
- How did they gently build your belief in yourself?
- How did they plant optimistic seeds?
- How did they approach the tough conversations with you when they needed to?

In all probability the teacher that made a difference was the one who made quality relational connections with you.

Between teacher and child: what sort of emotion do you radiate?

I have come to a frightening conclusion.

I am the decisive element in the classroom.

It is my personal approach that creates the climate.

It is my daily mood that makes the weather.

As a teacher I possess tremendous power to make a child's life miserable or joyous.

I can be a tool of torture or an instrument of inspiration.

I can humiliate or humor, hurt or heal.

In all situations, it is my response that decides whether a crisis

will be escalated or de-escalated, and a child humanized or de-humanized.

(Ginott 2003)

A teacher who radiates an emotional tone of acceptance, openness and enthusiasm creates an atmosphere where there is always potential to fine-tune the emotion and behaviour of students. Kids of all ages quickly gauge a teacher's emotional character and make a decision whether they will trust and enjoy, or challenge and react against the teacher's manner. As a student assesses their teacher they run through a set of questions.

- Does my teacher like me?

- Is my teacher moody?

- Is my teacher short-tempered?

- Does my teacher like me?

- Is my teacher predictable?

- Does my teacher shout?

- Does my teacher like me?

- Does my teacher get agitated by some of the kids too easily, too often?

- Does my teacher prefer the smart kids?

- Does my teacher admit when they are wrong or have made a mistake?

- Does my teacher like me?

- Do the rules keep changing?

- Is it safe for me to make mistakes?

- Does my teacher like me?

- Is it safe in my classroom?

- Is my teacher fair?

- Does my teacher speak to me in the same way they speak to my parents?

- Does my teacher like me?

Just beginning the day on a positive note can make a big difference to the quality of energy circulating within the classroom. A rise in classroom energy can be induced by reading a joke or two to the class from a joke book and having the kids score the quality of the joke. For others with a touch more technical expertise, they prefer to show a strange or funny sixty-second film clip on their interactive whiteboard as an energising start to the lesson or the day. There are oodles of these available ready to be played directly from www.youtube.com. Another way to help maintain buoyancy is by introducing a positive saying each day or week to the class. There are a multitude of these and it's surprising how some students seize hold of a saying and use it to persevere with. The best sources are from inexpensive books often found on the sale table at the local newsagency. If none of the above fit with your style just meeting and greeting students with a smile, a little energy and a positive comment can go a long way.

Think about the entry procedure you have constructed for your class or classes. What happens as students enter the room? Are you already prepared? As they enter do they see the lessons and the materials required written on the whiteboard. Do you regularly begin the day by having a question, a quote, and a fact displayed on the board ready for students to solve? Try it. Primary and secondary students alike adore it. Do you hold up your mobile phone, turn it off and ask your students to do the same before beginning the day or lesson? Do you help the more energetic kids make the distinction between outside play time and classroom learning time by settling them outside the classroom by chatting with them before entering the classroom?

To get off to a good start at the beginning of the year some teachers are quick to write an engaging letter about themselves and tell their incoming students and parents what is planned. Teachers who supply their school email address and make a point of gathering phone numbers and the email addresses of parents send a reassuring message that communication is welcomed. A few begin the year by sending home a questionnaire that asks parents to clarify their child's strengths and challenges. This immediately gets parents onside as it assures them that the teacher wants what they want. A friendly idea comes from teachers who, after the first few weeks of school, send a short letter home to parents outlining how their child has settled into their new class. Contained within the letter are several humorous snippets that illustrate the student's personal, social and academic triumphs. There is also a range of responsive, connecting ideas used by educators who value engagement with parents. Those who are particularly savvy recognise the worth of advertising what is genuinely on offer by:

- Regularly distributing a class newsletter

- Sending positive, newsy group emails or texts to parents

- Commenting on something especially uplifting about a student in their diary

- Writing a generally positive message in a student's diary

- Writing thoughtful letters to parents

- Sending home uplifting work samples

- Making sure certificates and awards are sent home and distributed evenly

- Phone hugs: making a positive phone call home to share an encouraging story about their child

- Deliberately catching a parent after school and spending several minutes chatting

- Occasionally sending home a helpful article, a television programme to watch or a useful website

- Holding an evening, a weekend event or a breakfast with parents and students

- Offering an extra interview to those few parents who are likely to find solace from it

- Going 'high-tech' and setting up a class website or class blog.

If you do not have sophisticated ICT skills, commission your ICT person (or an ICT savvy student) to get this up and running for you. Websites and blogs have the capacity to convey all manner of things from teaching philosophy, breaking class news, fabulous images from lessons and class events, due dates for assignments, interesting website links, homework help and email contact. Just a few years ago most of us would have baulked at the idea of using email so freely with parents, now it is commonplace. I'm sure this is the destiny for class websites and blogs.

For ideas to raise the energy within the classroom take a look at Chapter 7, 'Designs to lift moods'.

Do you look after yourself?

Teaching is a profession with an insatiable appetite. For teachers there is always so much to do: curriculum requirements, system demands, the preparation of engaging lessons, responsibility to committees, maintaining student harmony, mediating parental concerns, extracurricular activities, finding time for training and development workshops and individually mentoring students to ensure their dignity remains intact to mention just a few. And, the expectations seem ever increasing! Teaching today demands high level input, commitment and ongoing skill development in an environment that is bursting with energy and activity. To be candid, a sustained effort in the classroom and in schools can come with personal costs to a teacher. No one is immune.

Occasionally each of us needs to come up for air and reflect on why we continue to teach, what we have to offer and what we want from teaching. How long is it since you reviewed the depth of your personal resources? Sometimes, when we have long been absorbed in the fray our objectivity and sense of humour become casualties. It is wise to understand the extent of our personal resources because as they become depleted our optimism also becomes patchier. Knowing where our limits lie and how to pace ourselves, helps us from succumbing to the vortex of chaos that often surrounds the tough kids we teach.

To help place your weariness or enthusiasm into perspective, reflect on these questions:

- Why do you continue to teach?

- What really motivates you?

- What is it about teaching that stimulates you and makes the passion bubble to the surface?

- What was your last kind act? When?

- How long is it since you took stickers, certificates, vouchers or uplifting messages out on playground duty, and shared them with students?

- How long since you joined in a game with students while on playground duty and challenged the notion of 'policing'?

- How do your colleagues, students and parents describe you? Is it the way you want it?

- Do they see you as balanced, approachable and safe?

- What is it you do so students and parents know you care?

- Is there something you consciously offer to students? Do you set individual goals for vulnerable students and find ways to help achieve them?

- What legacy do you want to leave your students with?

- Do you find ways for vulnerable students to locate and achieve goals?

- How do you maintain communication with parents?

Over the past two decades increasing attention in the literature has been given to teacher weariness, stress and burnout. As well as having serious adverse effects on the teachers, stress and burnout can appreciably disadvantage students' growth and learning (Evers *et al.* 2004). Although the signs of burnout are always uniquely personal, they are generally 'lack of' type symptoms: lack of energy, joy, enthusiasm, satisfaction, motivation, interest and zest. The top stress and burnout factors cited by teachers usually concern difficult and threatening interactions with students, angry parents, heavy workloads, lack of recognition, poor long-term career prospects, and inadequate school discipline policies (Hastings and Bham 2003). As we all know, the consequence of teacher burnout is exhaustion, dissatisfaction and high staff turnover.

In the absence of winning the lottery, being awarded significant pay rises or having additional support staff here is a plan to keep your life in good balance.

1 Cultivate a group of good friends to have fun with, to complain to about school, and to be caring towards you.

2 Arrive at school 15 minutes earlier each day. You know what it's like. If you're at school early and something has a fifty/fifty chance of going wrong, it won't. But, if you're chasing time you can be sure it will go wrong!

3 Recognise what you can and can't control, what you want to be part of and what you can let go. Many teachers are perfectionists and forget that no one else will ever know when they haven't quite met their goal.

4 Learn to say no. It is not unusual to see the highly motivated and committed teachers involved in many aspects of school life. They are on curriculum committees, management teams, running their own specialised student

well-being programmes and are very active professionally. If you fall into this category make it a point to understand where your true limits lie and work to these.

5   Always ask for help when you need it.

6   Gravitate to the enthusiastic staff members. These are the people to sit with at break or lunchtime, at staff meetings and to work with on various projects. They are the best group to develop a solid professional relationship with because they engage in a professional dialogue where the talk is professional, helpful, upbeat, and even zany when required. This will keep you energised and passionate!

7   Never teach alone. Develop a small team or find a buddy to creatively share work with. Plan together and share resources and ideas when you can. If there is a topic you enjoy, and have developed abundant resources for, arrange to do it in the class of a colleague as well as with your own class. In return, ask them to present topics in which they have expertise to your class.

8   Consciously discover the things you can do that will renew your energy and spirit. It helps to know, because once energised we place ourselves in a much better position to make the most of setting ourselves, and those around us, up for success. Here is a brief selection of ideas:

- make a regular time for fun, family and friends;
- join a choir, a hiking group or an art class and let that hidden talent shine;
- put a regular time aside each week for dealing with school matters, rather than allowing them to progressively encroach into your home life or leisure time;
- make a regular time, if it helps, to talk to a trusted friend or a health professional;
- listen to your favourite music and escape!
- join or start a book club, movie club;
- start model building;
- deliberately build better relationships with a colleague or principal;
- start a breakfast club and go out to breakfast each week or fortnight with friends;
- join a garden/building group or keep your own garden/building project underway;
- get to the gym, start eating right and build your physical self;
- get home and, two or three times a week, take a 'nana nap';
- play 'Second Life'; a 3D virtual world where you can become anyone you dream. Second Life currently boasts an inhabitance of three million people from around the globe. Go to www.secondlife.com;
- treat yourself to a hair cut, facial, a massage, a manicure or pedicure;

- enrol in a course to learn something new: woodcarving, belly dancing, cooking, stained glass, painting, politics, floral design, etc.;

- decide on which two days of the week you will turn your mobile phone off;

- enjoy a meal and a movie with friends each month;

- occasionally take a day off from school and do what it takes to relax;

- find a walking partner and walk together a few times a week;

- take a long soak in the bath;

- go and find a mentor, someone you admire and trust (perhaps someone who is in a more senior position), who is able to keep you focused on your career and encourage you as you work towards your next set of professional goals.

To continue to motivate and inspire students, teachers need opportunities to find fulfilment and happiness for themselves.

Do you remind students they can change and get smarter?

Very few achieve success through the use of smoke and mirrors. We've long known that successful individuals, with or without difficulties, do not find success by accident (Raskind *et al.* 1999). Success is sparked by a desire (even an embryonic one), by planning, setting goals, reviewing and persisting. Numerous studies and experts over the years have concluded that the immersion of young people in encouraging environments is what makes the greatest difference (Seligman 2002).

Students need to know that from the very beginning the cells in their brains are miraculously organising themselves into networks that communicate with each other, store and process information and learn new things. And, teachers need to know that we are part of this miracle. What we say and do in class on a day-to-day basis has a direct influence on how our students' brains develop. The brain research is clear, when teachers provide the right learning experiences brain development is enhanced and accelerated (Hannell 2004). That's right, new learning actually causes intelligence to grow! Striving to learn something new every day, persisting at tasks, reflecting on social encounters, thinking about choices and giving things a go promotes transformation as this dynamic organ changes, grows and makes new connections with use.

Your brain is like a muscle. The more you use it, the more you can use it. Every time you learn something new, your brain makes a new connection. Learning enhances blood flow and activity in the brain. If you go for long periods without learning something new, you start to lose some of the connections in the brain and you begin to struggle more with memory and learning. New learning actually causes increased brain density and weight. Strive to learn something new every day even if just for a short period of time.

(Amen 2002, p. 4)

This flies in the face of the traditional view that each of us is born with an IQ virtually set in concrete, and that IQ is what will make the greatest difference. Knowing that the brain continues to develop through consciously choosing and reflecting should make a world of difference to a student's optimism. As students learn how their brains work, the realisation dawns that it is possible to progressively rewire and improve on their innate brain circuitry. Nothing aids transformation as well.

How conditioned are you by your inheritance?

Responding skilfully to the inevitable troublesome emotions and behaviours of tough kids begins with appreciating our long history in schools to punish and pay back students who have erred. Once upon a time in schools teachers demanded respect and got it. They commanded instant reform from students and got it, even if it meant ordering a student's parent to help out to extract discipline. The power balance between teachers and students was so great that the teacher always had the final say. After all, the prevailing attitude was that kids had to be controlled because innately they were bad, or at least unruly. Today the power balance between teachers and students has shifted, and what used to work to discipline students and manage behaviour doesn't work as well any more.

It is, however, tough to escape our history to punish because our conditioning runs deep. Think about it. The control and punishment design we have inherited from scores of years of maintaining control in institutionalised learning settings continues to flourish in pockets of our school systems. There is still an edge in a number of classrooms where it is more convenient, and perfectly acceptable, for a teacher to address a student's mistake, or annoying behaviour automatically with a time-out card, a behaviour management report, a rethink slip, a reflection contract, a co-management slip, red ink, a red slip, green slip, yellow slip or pink slip. The recent complaint of an assistant principal, who incidentally is a delightful person and fine secondary school educator, epitomises just this.

> 'Mark,' she explained, 'the detention system doesn't work any longer for students in our school.'
>
> 'Halleluiah,' I thought to myself, someone who is beginning to see new dimensions in assisting students to work with their emotion and behaviour.
>
> Before I could pay tribute to her revelation she continued, 'It's hopeless. Teachers can't send a student for an immediate Saturday detention at the moment. The system is so overloaded with student numbers that there's a three week wait to get them in!'

But there is worse. 'You've got a penal' is what the students who attend a prominent private school in my city hear from teachers to address mistakes and misdemeanors they make. A penal is a 20-minute session held during lunchtime. Students take work with them or complete a task set by the supervising teacher. They work independently and in strict silence. Perhaps the term stems from the word penalty. However, penal, according to the 'Ask Oxford: Oxford Dictionary' (2008), 'relates to the punishment of offences under the legal system. Extremely severe'. What an enlightening example of outdated language completely misplaced in an otherwise progressive school. The problem, of course, is that punishment first language is more likely to encourage a punishment first response from a teacher.

Both examples underpin the notion that the thoroughly active promotion of positive behaviours of students in schools continues to be an emergent concept in education. For a long time the experts have insisted that the best way to influence new productive behaviours in kids is to catch them doing well, and comment on it (Webster-Stratton *et al.* 2004; Lannie and McCurdy 2007). As we openly acknowledge the positive behaviours we see in students they gain an insight that their strengths are valued by us. This sort of attention leaves kids feeling less defensive, less reactive and more willing to explore new prosocial ways. While time-outs and detentions still have a role, their nature is limited as they are formatted by forces of coercion and control. A reliance on this format reinforces to students that someone or a process, not them, will take responsibility for their behaviour. Sadly, when kids become locked into battle with this process for too long, indifference, contempt and retaliation become the masters of behaviour. Ideally, the teacher who is in the relationship with the student should be the one directly managing the process, rather than the deputy principal or 'behaviour management personnel' steering it from a distance. Our challenge lies in reprogramming ourselves to do more of what we know really works with kids of today, and to resist the attraction to believe in the fanciful perfectness of human beings. What we actually do, and how we handle each issue at hand, is what matters most.

Today when contemporary educators speak about behaviour management an increasing number are beginning to frame strategies within a healthy social and emotional context. They broadcast the benefits of a well-being approach, a quality of care that is not veiled, strained or fake. Approaches to school discipline work best when they are genuinely educative in nature and where the focus is on creating, maintaining and improving relationships between people. Chapter 2 explores the essence of the restorative spirit. This is a practical paradigm shift emerging in a few of our innovative schools. It subscribes to practices that skill kids to repair problems and conflicts by discussing them, listening to others, exchanging ideas and finding ways to compromise.

How do you control?

- How would you describe your leadership style at school?

- More to the point, how do others describe it?

Historically teachers have been urged to control the behaviour of their students, and control still remains a crucial element for all teachers today. However, the focus is rapidly shifting away from blatantly demanding it. Rather than spitting out emotionally charged phrases as 'you should', 'you will', 'you must', 'you won't', 'you can't', 'I want' and 'do it now!' there is a focus on the quality of control expected from educators. What continues to grow, ever so gradually, is a far broader repertoire of how we go about exercising control in schools and in the classroom.

It is professionally awakening to reflect on our need to control and how we exercise this. The Social Control Window (Figure 1.2) is a handy tool to help us to examine

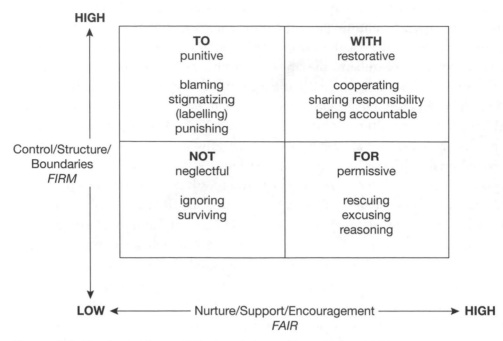

Figure 1.2 The Social Control Window (adapted from Glaser 1969)

our leadership style: how we work with others, how we use our authority and what our style really looks like.

By way of an overview, the vertical axis presents a continuum of firmness. This axis concerns how we set boundaries, clarify expectations, impose limits, hold others accountable and provide structure for those we work or live with. The horizontal axis displays the levels of nurture, support and encouragement we offer to those within our influence. In truth, we each spend time in different parts of the Social Control Window. On good days, most of us manage to strike the balance of being high on both continua, and work within the restorative quadrant. The length and intensity of our visits to each quadrant is largely governed by our emotional states: moods, motivations, engagement, levels of anxiety or stress, how fresh we feel and so on. Despite these varying emotional factors, each of us have a quadrant that we naturally gravitate to or 'live in' most of the time.

- Do you know which quadrant you 'live in'?

- Do you know why?

- When the pressure is really on, which quadrant do you snap into?

- Does your current style work for you and for your students?

Living in the TO quadrant, being punitive

The TO quadrant is reserved for those who must control. These individuals are demanding and rely on the delivery of the traditional phrases of 'you must', 'you will', 'I want', 'I am in charge' and so on. These teachers are strong on power and authority, have to be the boss and will do whatever it takes in the name of right, respect and responsibility.

As for the students and parents in their care, they see this teacher as overbearing and threatening. Think of your most frightening experience with a teacher or a principal as a child. There is a fair chance they lived squarely within this quadrant. Their oppression left little room for you to freely express yourself and may have probably brought out an urge to rebel or find a devious way around them.

In reality it is gruelling for teachers to work with this mindset because they are compelled to find new rules to keep in front of the ever emerging responses of students. They feel as though they only just manage to stay on top of things. They believe that if students are not controlled they will become uncontrollable. Such teachers cannot share power with students. When things go wrong, as they do, the focus is on what happened, who is to blame and what the right punishment should be. They overlook how individuals or relationships have been affected and how they might be repaired. Fairness and justice is seen as treating everybody the same and bringing rule breakers to justice.

The TO quadrant is an uneasy place for a human being to exist. In this place students reach down to the expectations of their controlling teachers and behave irresponsibly for two obvious reasons. First, there is great entertainment value for students to wind these teachers up and watch their perfectly predictable explosive reactions. Second, students learn quickly that the centre of control for their behaviour lies away from them and is always with the teacher who is in charge, so they do not need to take charge. In these circumstances bullying behaviour between students tends to flourish because, let's be honest, what students experience from their teacher is the essence of bullying behaviour.

Living in the NOT quadrant, being neglectful

Teachers residing in the NOT quadrant offer too little support and nurturance, and have too few expectations of the students. Consequently boundaries are poorly or rarely set. For one reason or another individuals in this box are not doing too much at all. This is where neglect, disregard, avoidance and survival scripted behaviours live.

To be fair, most of us spend brief periods in this quadrant. It is very normal to do so, and may be the result of weariness or disappointment and the need to call for time-out. As we retreat to this quadrant we notice the loss of our humour, the loss of permission to play and the passing up of positive dreams for the future. When this spirals too far out of control it can manifest itself into exhaustion, dissatisfaction and a desire to be anywhere else except at school.

Teachers who spend occasional moments in this quadrant, and who are aware of this, are not the focus of our concern here. Of serious concern are educators who spend more than fleeting moments in this corner and are not aware of this or unable to move from it. We have each been a bystander to a colleague who has spent enough time in the NOT quadrant to cause us to worry about them and those in their care. Sometimes they may carry feelings of ineffectiveness, even ineptness. Such feelings may have grown from poor skill development, a lack of confidence or difficulties in managing those they are responsible for. These colleagues require our attention, compassion and sensitive intervention.

When teachers work fairly consistently in this quadrant classrooms tend to degenerate into unstructured and chaotic places. Discernable boundaries are absent. More often, the teacher can be found at their desk browsing at a newspaper or at the computer, doing all they can to hide from an ever unravelling group of students. Conflict or harm between students goes unaddressed and students are left to fend for themselves when upsets occur. In these classrooms students make the rules and rule! They do as they please, often putting their safety, and the safety of others around them, at risk. Not surprisingly, bullying can also be rife in this environment as students adopt the 'might is right' philosophy. If questioned about the disruptive and unruly behaviour of their students this teacher's reply is, 'what can I do given the backgrounds these kids come from?'

Living in the FOR quadrant, being permissive

Here live teachers who offer elevated levels of support and encouragement, but lack the capacity to set adequate structures and expectations. Much of what they do is fair, but lacks decisiveness. They have a tendency to serve students and are likely to apply an approach that is easy going, popular and lenient. The way these teachers are treated by students is very predictable. Essentially, they get walked over. Students in the care of these teachers push and shove at them to determine where the boundaries lie and how far they can stretch them. Student behaviours become increasingly outrageous as they keep looking for that illusive line in the sand to be set by their teacher.

Typically, when this teacher is pushed too far their style is to snap into the TO box and become perfectly punitive. When this switch occurs students are initially confused. A little later, when the punishments are dished out to students they become resentful and angry because they are too severe. A characteristic response from students after the switch has occurred is, 'What? We didn't see that coming' or 'What's wrong with him/her? That wasn't fair'. Colleagues begin to see the same see-sawing emotional switch as well. One moment things appear fine, and then suddenly, those same students who this teacher puts an excessive amount of time into rescuing, excusing and putting up with are being sent to report to the office. And, this isn't the end of the cycle either. A few minutes after the explosive switch the teacher will complain to colleagues that these kids just don't seem to appreciate all the effort they have put into them. Next day, once their emotion has settled, they feel as though they may have acted too hastily and too harshly. So to make things right they return to being permissive, sometimes delivering an apology for their actions to the class. And, the cycle begins to build again. The grey arrow running diagonally between the TO and the FOR quadrants in the Social Control Window illustrates this very typical pattern.

Living in the WITH quadrant, being restorative

On good days most teachers spend time operating in this zone. Here, high levels of understanding, encouragement and quality feedback are offered, as well as making expectations clear by providing appropriate limits, structures and boundaries. This is the moment when a teacher feels they are able to read their students. It is the moment when the class seems to be interacting well, and this feeling is affirmed as students reciprocate with warmth and mutual respect. During these times, even when a problem occurs, it can be dealt with so the student is left feeling comfortable about the redirection. In fact, the act of redirection may even strengthen connections. This is where we find restorative teachers.

These are teachers who recognise that respect has less to do with their position, and much more to do with their relationships with students. They understand that problems and conflicts are inevitable, but can be seized upon as valuable learning opportunities as they crop up. Class meetings, regular class circles and activities that bring students face to face are a regular part of the week regardless of the age of the students. The goal is to involve students in day-to-day decisions so their sense of connectedness and community progressively broadens. During the process words and phrases such as 'us', 'we', 'the group', 'our group', 'the community' or 'our class' are used by teachers and students alike affirming that cohesion is valued.

With their radar finely tuned to the social climate of the classroom, the teacher in this quadrant is likely to use social measuring devices as sociograms to keep abreast with the dynamic social connections of students. Discussions as a whole class or with small groups about how to keep one another included are frequent, and because of this, when a student is struggling to stay socially connected it is possible to pull together teams of students to quietly look out for the welfare of another until they find their social footing again. Similarly, the teacher is mindful to regularly change class seating arrangements to ensure that each student has a chance to build a relationship with each class member. This is also a preventative measure against bullying as it gently works to minimise the impact of exclusive cliques. In actual fact, many of the practices often seen in the first weeks of the school year in classes – the establishment phase – continue all year long. These teachers simply never let up on activities and tasks that build a more united group.

Finally, teachers within this quadrant develop visible classroom behaviours and agreements with students to ensure that rights, relationships and property are protected. These are constantly revisited, adapted and enforced in an open and emotionally steady manner. Dialogue is always centred on ways to find improvement and make things right again when students have fallen short of agreed expectations.

The Social Control Window provides a fascinating and revealing insight into how we lead, view authority and use it.

- Have you decided on which quadrant you live in most of the time?

- Do you know why?

- Do you live in the same quadrant at home, or do you reserve it for school?

- Is your current style working for you and your students? Is it what you want?

- Which of the quadrants do you default to when exhausted, fed up or under pressure?

What is our core work?

It was an early morning meeting at a large Reception to Year 12 school and I sat at a table with a dozen educators. Before the meeting got underway the principal observed how much easier teaching used to be, and how much easier it would be for teachers if they could get on with the core work of teaching. She continued, 'All we seem to do is crowd control and ease the emotional eruptions that spring up between kids and parents.' Bravely, a young talented third year teacher timidly answered, 'Isn't what we do every day our core work?' Ella, the principal, shot her an intimidating glance, but acquiesced with, 'Hmmm, you're right. Perhaps I'm being nostalgic.'

The truth is no teacher has ever delivered the next batch of great curriculum in a perfect social vacuum. Teaching has always been hard work because it is a profession so deeply immersed in the close encounters of humanity. Some days are easier than others and some schools are easier than others for some, but every school and its community has peculiarities and challenges.

The healthiest and most grounding starting point is to recognise that every one of our students is in absolute rehearsal. That's right, they are young and clumsy, learning, gathering experience and bound to make poor judgements. It is what young learners do. In fact, despite the sanctity of school rules, and the tranquillity we so desperately crave in our classrooms, most students have to make mistakes in order to grow. There always has been, and always will be conflict and tension between individuals in schools. There has to be, because the nature of schools is to pack together so tightly, so many young developing individuals in the name of education. Almost thirty years ago Carol Weinstein passed comment on the artificial environments we have created called schools, 'No where else, but in schools, are large groups of individuals packed so closely together for so many hours, yet expected to perform at peak efficiency on difficult learning tasks and to interact harmoniously' (Armstrong 2000, p. 82).

What is the real work, our core work? Not surprisingly, it is centred about the everyday work we do with students, planned and incidental, connecting the domains of curriculum, social and emotion because this is where the learning need exists. Since conflict between students are certain, a big part of our core work is to resist taking the moral high ground, and instead, help kids to discover the skills to live more harmoniously in a complex, tightly knit community. Unless we actively live this approach it is all too easy to fall victim of memory distortion, where the not so fond memories of past drop out and are replaced by some sort of dreamy embellishment of times or a place that must have been better. Once we give in to this it is easy to lose sight of our core work.

Perhaps Socrates' time honoured statement about the youth of his time provides some comfort and a little inspiration.

Our youth now love luxury. They have bad manners, contempt for authority; they show disrespect for their elders, and love chatter in places of exercise. They no longer rise when elders enter the room. They contradict their parents, chatter before company, gobble up their food and tyrannize their teachers.

(Socrates, 469–399 BC, quoted by Knowles 2001)

Stay on guard, because a reliance on nostalgia or mythology may be comforting, but it will surely hinder our capacities to see and tap into what is real.

Do you promote what you do to parents?

Most teachers want the very best for their students and work tirelessly week in and week out to achieve this. However, those of us who work with the kids whose learning, emotion and behaviour is tough, know that their parents can be unaware of the abundant amounts of time, worry, help and resources we gather to support their child. Teachers frequently say to one another, 'Those parents just don't appreciate what we're doing to help their child. They don't give us enough credit for bending over backwards to help.' I agree with them! But, there is more to this puzzle than meets the eye. What usually occurs is that the educators get busy doing what good educators do: doing good things quietly. They assemble all sorts of flexible supports and interventions for the student, but overlook adequately informing the student's parents about what they have pulled together. The result is that parents often don't know or are unclear about what is happening (Lock 2008).

This is the time to parade what we do so well to parents (Russell 2008). It is the time to immerse them in the process inclusive educational practice (Forlin *et al.* 2008). A wise starting point is to create a small team who can support the student, one another and implement review meetings. Review meetings offer a forum to talk, make adjustments and plan. It can also be uplifting for students to meet with their team from time to time to see and hear their teachers' care and participation. The creation of a team helps to stabilise one another's efforts because frustrations in these situations are bound to crop up.

All states in Australia offer a learning plan in the form of a Negotiated Education Plan (NEP) to students who are eligible for special education support (www.decs.sa. gov.au). An option for students experiencing difficulties, but who do formally meet the very stringent criteria for funding or support, is to actually use the formal plan as a structure to establish goals, meet the needs of students and report to parents. It is an ideal mechanism to determine priorities and transmit to parents that their input is valued.

This is also the perfect time to help parents unravel some of the mysteries and misgivings they have about what their child 'should be' entitled to (Williams 2008). What always transpires is that most are not fully conversant with what is on offer because the rules, criterion, guidelines and jargon for eligibility for support keep changing at the system level. It is of value to plainly explain this, and make it clear that the healthy alternative you have created is based on goodwill. Perhaps one day it will become commonplace to podcast some of the fabulous lessons, super interventions and wonderful interactions we have with kids so parents can appreciate how we truly differentiate the curriculum for students as we endeavour to meet their needs. In the meantime, we will need to keep talking to parents and make time to show them our expertise and willingness to help.

Do you offer steady support to families?

Teachers are the natural interface between students and parents, and parents often look to educators for emotional steadiness and advice. From time to time they will seek you out to offload irritations and to discover help or hope. At other times you will become caught up in their fury as they defend their child from the indefensible.

Avoid taking the moral high ground or absorbing their fiery approach too personally. This is often the result of a parent's utter exasperation. It can be their way of saying 'I don't know what to do'. Reassure them that raising any child is hard work and most parents find themselves out of their depth every so often, but raising a child with a challenge is always tough. In fact for some, it can be a very isolating experience. It affects everyone in the family because it places pressure on parents, brothers, sisters and on the extended family as well. In these situations nothing should ring truer than the maxim, 'It takes a whole village to raise a child'. And, of course, teachers and schools have the potential to be a big part of their village. The simple act of providing a parent with practical information from a journal, magazine, newspaper or directing them to websites or television programmes shows we care. The action acknowledges that we understand it's tough for them. Sometimes connecting a troubled parent with a compassionate, levelheaded parent who has dealt with similar issues is therapeutic.

For a few parents the pain of having a child with a chronic difficulty, challenge or disability will never go away. The loss of their original dream is tremendous. Parents can remain bitter or in grief for years. To understand the grief that regularly surrounds a parent raising a child with a difference, Emily Perl Kingsley wrote *Welcome to Holland* in 1987 (see p. 29). It is worth reading and sharing with others and was written as a catalyst for healing and finding constructive ways forward.

Make no mistake – being a steady, positive influence in the lives of parents and kids is a precious gift.

Teaching Tough Kids offers a broad set of sensible strategies for educators to draw on to bring about positive changes for the students who do it tougher than most. It delivers realistic ideas to help students with memory, goal setting, organisation and planning, concentration, problem solving, socialisation, persistence and task completion. The tough kids that are far more dependent on our clever abilities to support them find healthier patterns of thinking, emotion and behaviour. The approach keeps the focus on the possibilities of change and transformation rather than seeing the student as an intractable problem child.

The best advice I can offer when looking at the range of ideas offered in the book is to:

- Appreciate that no technique is a substitute for real warmth and real relationships with students. Understanding how these kids 'tick' at an intrinsic level outshines dipping into a loot bag of stand alone emotional or behavioural modification tricks.

- Make sure the approach is appropriate to the age and abilities of the student. Goals and possible outcomes always need to be optimistically loaded in the student's favour so they quickly see changes and feel reassured.

- Use your good sense about how much change, and how quickly, is realistic for your students. The overriding goal is to normalise emotion and behaviours.

- Concentrate on the strategies that work and with which you feel comfortable.

- Be patient, and be mindful that it is the everyday things we do that make the greatest difference to the development and happiness of our tough kids.

WELCOME TO HOLLAND

When you're going to have a baby, it's like planning a fabulous vacation trip – to Italy. You buy a bunch of guide books and make your wonderful plans. The Colosseum. The Michelangelo David. The gondolas in Venice. You may learn some handy phrases in Italian. It's all very exciting.

After months of eager anticipation, the day finally arrives. You pack your bags and off you go. Several hours later, the plane lands. The stewardess comes in and says, 'Welcome to Holland'.

'Holland?!?' you say. 'What do you mean Holland?? I signed up for Italy! I'm supposed to be in Italy. All my life I've dreamed of going to Italy.' But there's been a change in the flight plan. They've landed in Holland and there you must stay. The important thing is that they haven't taken you to a horrible, disgusting, filthy place, full of pestilence, famine and disease. It's just a different place.

So you must go out and buy new guide books. And you must learn a whole new language. And you will meet a whole new group of people you would never have met.

It's just a different place. It's slower-paced than Italy, less flashy than Italy. But after you've been there for a while and you catch your breath, you look around . . . and you begin to notice that Holland has windmills . . . and Holland has tulips. Holland even has Rembrandts.

But everyone you know is busy coming and going from Italy and they're all bragging about what a wonderful time they had there. And for the rest of your life, you will say 'Yes, that's where I was supposed to go. That's what I had planned.'

And the pain of that will never, ever, ever, ever go away . . . because the loss of that dream is a very, very significant loss.

But . . . if you spend your life mourning the fact that you didn't get to Italy, you may never be free to enjoy the very special, the very lovely things . . . about Holland.

Emily Perl Kingsley, 1987

With the above in mind, collect up the ideas you find appetising, enjoy the case studies and make use of the worksheets presented at the end of this book. If you wish to further individualise the worksheets they can be accessed at www.routledge. com/education/fultonresources.asp.

A restorative spirit
Giving kids the skills to listen, discuss and repair relationships

I wish to acknowledge Bill Hansberry as the co-author of this chapter. While I am greatly indebted to him I also enjoyed the friendship that grew through the collaboration. It is our hope that this chapter will strengthen the idea you may have about working restoratively with students. It not intended to be a comprehensive guide, its purpose is to light the fire of possibilities for restorative justice processes in schools.

The one thing Bill and I want you to take from the chapter is that everything that happens in schools hinges on the quality of relationships between people. When considering an approach to discipline, educators do best when they challenge their actions with the question: 'Does my disciplinary approach support relationships between members of the school community or does it erode relationships?'

Naturally, making the mind switch from a power over to a relational and educative process is a tricky leap given our punitive past, but research and experience now clearly illustrates restorative climates can transform student behaviour. 'Schools are not buildings, curriculum timetables and meetings. Schools are relationships and interactions among people' (Johnson and Johnson, cited in Dalton and Boyd 1992, p. 68).

Kids today are socially savvy. They demand the 'human stuff' from teachers and peers and sometimes, to get it, they'll push buttons to capture the full range of human emotion. This is particularly so for students whose social bonds with teachers and peers are weak or strained, and lack a sense of belonging. When things go wrong, attempts by teachers to suppress emotions and to discipline these kids in cold, clinical, disconnected ways can make things a lot worse. These kids need colour and life in their dealings with teachers and with each other. They need real interactions, where everyone receives a hearing and is given the opportunity to take responsibility, to plan with others and to make bad situations better. Kids nowadays will not stand to be treated as mere organisms to be manipulated through excessive behaviouristic approaches. Their response tells us this.

We need to read the signs, and draw on the moments stored in our memory that reassure us our best work is done inside relationships with kids, and nowhere else. Relationships in schools have never been so important. We now know as well as setting the scene for better learning, good relationships also act as a protective factor against school violence (Morrison 2007).

Make no mistake: there is a link between school discipline and criminal justice

Traditionally, punishment in schools has mimicked society's response to infringements to law and order (Marshall *et al.* 2002). The quasi-judicial practice and philosophy to manage student misconduct has been modelled on existing western systems of criminal justice (Thorsborne and Vinegrad 2002b). As a result, punishment remains an uncompromising shadow of control in many classrooms and schools.

As a society, the response to poor behaviour, wrongdoing and rebelliousness has been to create laws that restore the balance that has been disturbed by the wrongdoer. In this way the rights and safety of the majority were protected, and victims of crimes were recognised. By reacting punitively and treating all people the same, fairness within communities was thought to be achieved. There is quite a history where those who err must 'get their just deserts' through some form of suffering or pay back in order to restore balance to the scales of justice. Over time, as society's attitudes have ebbed and flowed in its understandings and tolerance about crime and conflict, there has been a tug to find a balance between two competing concerns: those for the welfare of individuals who have found themselves on the wrong side of the law, and those for the welfare of the larger law-abiding community.

Schools have also reflected these broader trends, and have vacillated between a focus on the rights of individual students who have struggled to do the right thing at school, and the rights of the rest of the rule-abiding student population to learn without undue disruption. However, one inescapable truth remains for school administrators and teachers today – what used to work to discipline students and manage behaviour doesn't work nearly as well any more. The world has changed. Teachers who once commanded, caned, coerced or humiliated students did so because it was a job that was expected of them. Today, he or she would be seen as a brute, negligent or thoroughly incompetent. Clearly, what was once a state of art practice in school discipline is now considered obsolete and damaging.

The light of hope

In recent times progressive educators, particularly those working with complex students, have responded to the evidence that punishment as a principle means to control the behaviours of students does not stop the recurrence of antisocial behaviours (Sugai and Horner 1999). What the overuse of punishment does is to train students to self-protect at all cost by blaming, lying, minimising and disregarding the impact of their behaviour on others. We also know that continued exposure to harsh disciplinary regimes such as zero tolerance can provoke oppositional behaviours, hatred and mental health issues in young developing human beings, as well as placing them at greater risk of entering the criminal justice system (Morrison 2007). The realisation has emerged for some of us who work with kids that even young children are capable of owning their conflicts, identifying their needs and coming up with solutions when given guidance to do so. A simple discussion between kids about the harm caused can often do away with the need for punishment because nothing is as effective as those involved in the conflict wanting to put things right. And, the healthy bonus delivered to kids in such circumstances, are the priceless opportunities for them to see and hear the impact of their mistake, to learn how to forgive, accept forgiveness and recover from a mistake.

The light of hope is an emerging understanding that punishment does not fix the inevitable problematic behaviours influenced by deficits, delays, disorders, disabilities, syndromes, neglect or abuse in children and teens. Nor will it fix or prevent bouts of healthy exuberance and impulsivity from students who get caught up in the moment.

Description, the restorative spirit

Restorative practice is a constructivist learning-based process that distinguishes between managing behaviour and managing relationships. Based on the principles of restorative justice, restorative practices assume that the best way to deal with a problem is to teach individuals how to discuss, listen, share and exchange ideas about it.

The restorative spirit rejects poor behaviour, but endeavours to understand it, repair the problem and find agreement on what needs to happen to make things better. The needs of those who have been harmed are central in these decisions. Those who have caused harm are enabled to make amends and find a way to continue their positive engagement in school life (Moxon *et al.* 2006). The restorative message to those who have behaved inappropriately is, 'You're okay, but that behaviour isn't'. This is a world apart from the traditional disciplinary message, 'You've acted badly, so now you will be treated like a bad person'. Mistakes and wrongdoing are seen through the lens of how they affect others, and consequences always focus on what needs to happen to mend the harm caused. Those who have caused a problem are encouraged to show care and take responsibility. The group (including the teacher) also commits to re-accepting the wrongdoer once they have acted to right their wrongs.

In practice, an entire class or group of students may be found sitting in a circle arrangement discussing a particular issue at hand. Class meetings or group circles bring students face to face to clarify what happened and how others have been affected. Consequences do not come any more real than hearing first hand from those who have been hurt or upset by a behaviour. Steve Biddulph (1994) in his book *Manhood*, captures how adults and young people can communicate within a restorative paradigm. In essence he writes about effective communication. He states that the spirit of effective communication with young people, particularly boys, is to get engaged, eyeball to eyeball, and to be definite so that children can state their case but also be made to listen to the case of others (Biddulph 1994). He asserts that this approach is necessary, and is the opposite to techniques of distancing and isolation that 1950s psychology dished up. Biddulph drives the understanding that children today do not need more remoteness – they need us to get involved with them and to help them to get involved with one another.

The restorative approach invites students to accept responsibility for their behaviour despite facing adversity. First, kids are engaged in a dialogue concerning how their behaviour affects others and impacts on their rights. Second, with guidance and structure, we ask them to take an active role to put things right again. We immerse them in talking and listening to others – hearing first hand the impact the behaviour had, whether this be from a peer they have bullied or from a teacher whose class they have continually disrupted. What arises from discussion is a sense that we care for them and want to maintain engagement and relationship.

At worst, a student may choose not to take up the invitation for restoration. Instead, they may decide to use other processes the school has in place to address problematic behaviours. In contrast, when a student takes up the offer of restoration they have a chance to face the people their behaviour has harmed, and to fix things. They can deal with guilty or shameful feelings about the incident, remaining secure in the knowledge that their relationships can remain intact as long as they are willing to take responsibility for their behaviour. Feeling connected to the group and wanting to save relationships is a strong incentive to make positive changes. The alternative, when students reach the point of feeling isolated, hated and as though there is nothing left to save, can be catastrophic. Any human being who reaches this depth of desolation is a danger to themselves and those around them. Look no further than the spate of High School and University shootings as evidence of how dangerous these young disconnected human beings can be when they feel as though there is no other way.

What is emerging from the restorative process is an irresistible sense of fairness from all involved.

There is now abundant growing empirical data to show restorative practice, with its spotlight fixed on rights and relationships, fair process, and a clear focus on relationship building and healing, which actually invites growth in student behaviour and well-being (Cameron and Thorsborne 1999).

Control

Lessons to be learned from the Social Control Window

Before reading on, it is best to reflect on the leadership style you automatically draw on to manage the students in your care. To refresh your understandings, turn back to the section titled 'How do you control?' (p. 21 onwards).

The Social Control Window is a valuable tool to help us understand our leadership style: how we work with others, how we use our authority and what our style really looks like. Where we sit in the window influences our readiness to accept restorative principles. For some, the idea of restorative practices challenges the very core of their paradigm. Yet, those who already spend time in the restorative window, or are working hard to spend more time in it, are inclined to find the transition easier. All the same, the restorative teacher doesn't run a utopian democracy. They are prepared to assume responsibility for the classroom climate and use their power to veto class decisions when necessary. The distinguishing feature of the restorative teacher is a clear desire to share the power in decision making with students, knowing that this will lead to improved learning, responsibility and group unity.

One way to examine where you sit in the social control window is to consider the leadership characteristics of others. Two case studies follow. Can you identify which quadrants John and Matt work in, or work between? Why is it that one of these teachers could adapt, accept new learnings and put them into practice, yet the other could not? As you gather an appreciation of their styles and responses also reflect on your own attitudes, values and pedagogy. As you read, let these questions resonate within, 'how adaptable am I?' and 'would moving from my present leadership style surrender my right to be assertive or in charge?'

Case study

Big John

Big John had taught continuously in four country schools over twenty-three years. Outside of school he had long been a tireless worker in depressed rural communities helping to manage and staff recreation centres for youth and work on projects to support the disadvantaged. He had received many accolades for his generous contributions over the years. John had recently started as a Year 7 teacher in a new school, and while the year level was familiar, this new placement was very different to what he knew.

John believed his strength was his delivery of a rigorous preparation for secondary school to Year 7 students. He saw himself as a fair teacher who valued a straight forward, no nonsense approach to discipline and curriculum delivery. He believed he had the right to use his authority to demand students change to what he thought were more desirable ways. From his viewpoint, teaching was not about winning popularity with students. The bigger picture was education, control and preparation for the future. His ability to meet the challenges of his young adolescent students head on, and win, had made him a popular choice with parents in the past.

To maintain order he relied on his position and quick tongue to cut students down to size. And, given Big John's impressive size, his verbal tirade always got the result he wanted. It was intimidation enough even for the biggest of farm boys! At the beginning of each school year, John presented his twenty-two classroom rules to students and told them his consequences of breaking them. Those rules had remained unchanged throughout his career. Big John liked to use didactic driven lessons that centred about lengthy instruction, exhaustive explanations and always incorporated 'his' life examples. Following this, students were expected to complete exercises with little or no discussion.

For students who found it difficult to work hard, be neat and show responsibility, John withheld warmth in the relationship and deliberately distanced himself from them. He maintained this tack until kids finally saw value in changing their ways. Break time and after school detention was reserved for the students who Big John termed, 'repeat offenders'. In fact, much of John's vocabulary when referring to unruly students was of a criminal justice flavour! When these tactics didn't work, John bundled the repeat offenders off to the front office. There, the deputy principal usually dealt with them, and unless these students displayed instant repentance their parents were called and suspensions dealt out. This was the beginning of a slippery slope to exclusion. Mostly, these kids were boys living complex lives that affected their emotion and behaviour. Some didn't see their fathers at all and were being raised by their mums or grandparents, and it was tough for all concerned. John referred to these students as 'hard nuts' or 'blow throughs'. In other words, they were destined for trouble and wouldn't be around for long.

John's new appointment was to a primary school of about 350 students. The area was once rural, but the school had recently been re-zoned as industrial/urban. As he continued to survey his new class a realisation was awakening within him. The unmanageable student, who occasionally blew through in the past, seemed to make up a critical mass in this class. Of John's thirty-one students seven had some form of learning difficulty, three had been formally identified with ADHD and four others displayed obvious social difficulties. School assignments were either handed in late or not done at all. Sometimes students behaved so badly during tests, that the class couldn't complete them. John stopped phoning some of the parents about his concerns because he believed they had no control over their kids. He was tired of aggressive parents challenging him about how he was dealing with their kids.

More to the point, John was dealing with dreadfully disruptive classroom behaviours from a group of girls. As soon as they walked into class their bickering and nastiness started. It was never long before their tit-for-tat remarks escalated into sulking, tears, note passing, swearing, walkouts and arguments over who would work with whom. Their conflicts, which also drew in a group of boys, seemed endless. Their loathing towards one another seemed to occupy their minds, leaving no room for anything else.

It was difficult to deal with. John had never resorted to sending so many students to the office. However, at this school, sending students to the office didn't work. If the truth be told, the high number of students he sent to the office had attracted disapproval from the school's leadership team. He was totally bemused when his principal, Jenny, suggested he might think about introducing a social skill programme or sit down with his students to help them talk through and sort out their problems that were resulting in so much lost learning time.

Jenny also offered to work with John to run class meetings where problems could be raised by students and discussed, but John declined as the proposed time would fall during the weekly maths mental quiz. All John wanted was for Jenny to send a clear message to these students by suspending them. Conversely, Jenny's experience had taught her that escalating suspensions would result in angrier and more disconnected students, as well as losing the support of parents. Jenny continued to raise the concepts of 'relationship building' and 'different learning styles' in meetings with John, but increasingly, he felt devalued and abandoned by her lack of decisive support. John felt the word relationship was thrown around all too much in this school. He believed all 'relationship' did was to take the focus away from efficient behaviour management.

Things hit an all time low yesterday for John.

During silent reading, Bradley swore at Jayden because of a disagreement over a game at lunchtime. John bellowed at Bradley to get to the office. Bradley leapt from his seat in tears protesting that Jayden had called his mum a name that he couldn't repeat. John held his ground and pointed at the door. Bradley picked up his chair and hurled it at the window, cracking the glass. He ran out, crying and abusing John.

Case study

Matt

Matt plays football on the weekends and enjoys time with friends. He's a teacher with four years of experience. This is Matt's second school and he is nearing the end of his contract. The school is in a tough part of the city and is classified as highly disadvantaged. Here he teaches a Year 6/7 class. Matt thinks they are the most complex group of students he has taught to date. Many have home lives that aren't so good. Many of them think they can't learn, others refuse, explode or won't attend school for periods of time. A few are worriers, some have relationship issues and one or two plainly detest authority.

Needless to say, this year had been very demanding. Although he is a young developing educator, he has started to pull together some key ideologies about teaching. At the moment Matt believes:

- in his relationships with kids: for him, it's vital to talk with students and listen, to share his interests and try to laugh with them;

- in being a positive male role model to young people, and above all to the boys: he knows that what he projects is a stark contrast to the male modelling a few of the boys receive at home;

- that to genuinely engage students in learning, the learning has to be real. As much as he can he uses a collaborative approach. To help make learning real Matt runs a unit of enterprise education for a term where students create a fantasy company and produce a product, or range of products, to market and sell to the school community. Real money changes hands and according to the feedback from parents and students this programme is a 'huge hit';

- never to accept disrespect or rudeness from students: he continues to refine the elusive art of when it's best to confront or walk away from a cranky young teen. He learned early in his career that when tempers heat up and emotions become stretched results can quickly become disastrous. Matt has learned that so many of his students are reliant on his composure, his respect, his calm tone of voice, and giving them time to respond;

- in the failsafe delivery of weekly class meetings;

- in the value of 'mood lift' and 'team building' activities a couple of times each week as part of circle time: he believes that virtually any unifying activity invites kids to belong to the group and see value in being together;

- in assisting students to build a sense of belonging to the wider school community: to this end, he builds opportunities for his group to participate in listening to junior primary students read, being rostered to help in the canteen, organising the gym for assemblies, running lunchtime activities for younger students and so on.

Peter, the Indonesian teacher, is in his twelfth year of teaching. He is new to the school this year and has been curious about Matt's style with his class. Peter works with them twice a week and has gleaned that when these students experience conflict, they're often proactive in quietly solving their issues. He was recently impressed when Kira and Sharleen, two of Matt's students, approached him during a lesson and asked if they could have 5 minutes together to sort a problem out. At first Peter was suspicious. He suspected they were trying to avoid work, but when they quietly re-emerged a few minutes later and resumed work, he knew something very positive had just occurred.

A few days later during a quiet moment with Matt's class, Peter decided to ask Kira and Sharleen a few questions to satisfy his building curiosity.

'Girls, what goes on with your class? Most of you spend more time on task than other classes, you sort your problems without too much drama and basically you get along well most of the time. Why's that?'

Kira and Sharleen grinned.

Kira said, 'It wasn't always like it looks now. In first term we were a bad class!'

'Really?' replied Peter.

'It was a big mess. We fought, kids got really angry with each other and stuff was being stolen from tables and the art cupboard. There was a lot of trouble,' told Sharleen.

'So how did you get to where you are now?' quizzed Peter.

'Sue [the school counsellor] ran a big class meeting with Mr Richards [Matt]. Everyone had to talk about what they had been doing and how they felt about stuff. Heaps of people apologised and nobody got into trouble and some people even cried!' Kira explained.

'Yeah . . . then we made the class agreement about what needed to change in the classroom and how we would fix things up if people upset one another,' added Sharleen.

'And people stuck to that agreement?' asked Peter.

'Most of the time they do. Sometimes people break it, but that's mainly because they forget. If they do, someone else will say, "hey, you're breaking the agreement" and they'll remember it again,' said Kira.

'We talk about how the agreement is going every week in class meeting,' added Sharleen.

'What happens when people don't follow the agreement?' asked Peter.

'People get a chance to talk about it if they think they've broken the agreement or if they think someone else has broken it,' said Kira.

'Yeah, the person that's broken it has to say what they were thinking at the time and explain it to the class. Then they need to make things right with the person or people they might have upset,' added Sharleen.

'That sounds tough,' said Peter.

'In a way it is. But, everyone in the class tries to make it work. Most try not to break the agreement,' replied Kira.

As the girls returned to their seats, Peter's eye caught the 'Year 6/7 R Class Agreement' pinned to his classroom wall. He recalled two students from Matt's class asking if they could put it up in his room during their first lesson with him at the beginning of the year. He didn't take much notice at the time, but now it made much more sense. These were the revised class rules – the behaviour agreements the class had agreed to follow after that decisive class meeting, and that's why Matt wanted copies up wherever his class went. Peter remembered thinking at the time that this was just a little too diligent of Matt.

Matt's method started to crystallise for Peter. For him, this was a new way of connecting with students, and he was keen to find out more. Finally, Peter found time to speak with Matt and Sue.

'Matt, I want to know more about the big class meeting you had in first term with Sue to sort out class agreements.'

'Who have you been talking to?' Matt replied playfully.

'A couple of your girls,' Peter said with a smile, 'So what's happened with your class since first term?'

'Talk . . . just talking . . . that's all,' replied Matt with a smirk.

Sue chuckled, 'It's restorative practices, Pete. We've worked with the class to teach them how to fix things up with one another when things go wrong instead of going straight to disciplinary style consequences.'

'We still use regular school consequences and sometimes we still suspend, but this doesn't get in the way of what the kids call, "doing the real stuff", or "cleaning the mess up",' continued Matt.

'It's been working pretty well with Matt's class. Ever since our first "No Blame Classroom Conference", they've been a different group, much more settled,' commented Sue (Thorsborne and Vinegrad 2002a).

'Is this stuff new?' enquired Peter.

'No, good teachers have been doing this with students since the day dot,' quipped Sue, 'It's about behaviour management "with" the students, instead of doing it "to" them.'

'It's about getting students to discuss what's happening, to listen to others and decide what needs to be done to improve things,' said Matt, 'Things that would usually only be the business of a few becomes the business of everyone. It's humanised my classroom. Some of the kids have really changed the way they interact with others and that's what's so powerful.'

'What about confidentiality, you know, with the business of a few becoming the business of many?' enquired Peter.

'We discuss that issue with the kids every time we do a circle or conference and they seem to respect that what we discuss in a circle is sensitive. We have a saying: what is said in the circle stays in the circle,' responded Sue.

'Yeah, it's really blown me away how well the kids actually respect confidentiality,' added Matt.

'And when they don't they'll find themselves in a circle the very next day and have to face 29 other irritated kids over the issue,' quipped Sue.

'And it won't be us who will request the circle to deal with it either,' added Matt.

The restorative spirit, a practical start

The way in which we deal restoratively with an issue always falls at some point on the restorative practices continuum (Figure 2.1). For the most part, our day-to-day dealings with students occur at the less formal end by way of affective statements, affective interactions and small impromptu conferences. Typically, these will be used in the classroom and play ground when dealing with small conflicts and incidents. These are techniques to skilfully redirect or challenge student behaviour. Taught to students, they are also powerful ways for students to confront one another on harmful behaviour. At the far end of the continuum is the formal restorative conference. This style of conference is usually called to address an incident where significant harm has occurred. It frequently involves extensive preparation where participants are identified, invited and individually interviewed so the facilitating teacher can understand their stories, needs, feelings and the outcomes they hope will result from the conference.

Evidence indicates that as teachers become adept at using affective statements, affective interactions and small impromptu conferences, the need for large group and formal conferences diminishes. As you might imagine, when problems are handled more effectively at the less formal end of the continuum, they tend not to explode into large incidents that require a more formal restorative intervention.

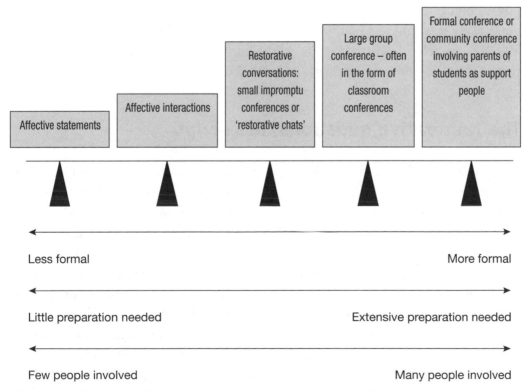

Figure 2.1 The restorative practices continuum (adapted from Wachtell and McCold 2001)

A little theory behind the restorative questions

The restorative questions were developed by Terry O'Connell and colleagues in the early 1990s in the New South Wales Police Service as a scripted set of questions that restorative conference facilitators could ask to youth offenders and the victims of their crimes to assist dialogue between the parties. These scripted questions worked so well that extensive research was subsequently undertaken to find out what made the restorative questions so consistently successful. A range of theories and approaches emerged to explain the effectiveness of the scripted questions. Some of these were Socratic questioning style, 'reintegrative shaming' (Braithwaite 1989), 'fair process' (Kim and Mauborgne 2003) and 'human affect theory' (Nathanson 1992). The restorative script provides a fair and respectful framework to support those harmed and reintegrate those who caused the harm, and can be adapted as a preventative intervention as well. For comprehensive examples of such prosocial adaptations, see *Restorative Practices in Classrooms: Re-Thinking Behaviour Management* (Thorsborne and Vinegrad 2002a). In school settings teachers who regularly employ restorative strategies appear to be educators who intrinsically value empowerment, honesty, respect, engagement, voluntarism, healing, restoration, personal accountability, inclusiveness, collaboration and problem-solving (Morrison 2007). Nevertheless, the restorative questions are fundamental helpers. They guide educators, especially when under pressure, to remain within the 'with' quadrant of the Social Control Window, and find constructive ways forward.

Educators who do best understand that a restorative practice is not a quick fix – nor is it a map to tell how things should be done. More than anything, it is a compass, continually pointing us in a restorative direction in our dealings with others (Zehr 2002). Every school's context and needs will be different and this is why restorative justice must truly live in the hearts and minds of its practitioners.

The restorative questions, the script

To ensure the effective use of the restorative questions in a variety of contexts, commit the script to memory. That's right, practice saying the questions! Liken the restorative script to a car! To 'drive them' we need to have some knowledge about how they work so we can accelerate, slow down, change direction or, if necessary, hit the brakes fast and reverse. Once mastered, a confidence will grow allowing you to become creative with the wording of the questions so they match the situation and students you are dealing with. While the wording of the questions can vary, the order they are asked in must remain as presented below. There are many different examples of these, and in some instances, schools have created their own cards to assist staff. With the script firmly in mind, you'll be able to listen to the responses of students and work through the problem, rather than having to work hard to recall the questions. The truth is that the basic pattern of questions is very easy to remember as they are strongly connected to common sense. And, that's just as well because you will quickly appreciate just how attentive you have to be during a restorative intervention, especially when individuals are upset. Occasionally, managing your own emotions and remaining as impartial as possible will be a challenge too!

Whether you are a novice or a veteran, a restorative intervention does not always go to plan. Sometimes students are too upset or are not willing to take part respectfully, and sometimes you may not have the time to do the process justice. When this happens, try not to be overly critical of yourself or give up on the process. Persist, and soon you'll develop your own confident restorative style. And remember, if you sense things are beginning to go wrong there are always the options to:

- postpone the conference/chat until everyone has cooled down and there is time to deal with the issue – it's much wiser to slow the process down than try to expedite a restorative process;

- refer the issue to another staff member who has more experience or more time available to facilitate a restorative intervention;

- decide against using a restorative intervention and use a formal school consequence instead (this is often the only alternative left if students choose not be respectful, won't take any responsibility for their behaviour or engage agreeably in a conference).

The restorative questions, in summary

1 The questions to a student who has done something to hurt/upset somebody else:

(a) What happened?

(b) What were you thinking/feeling at the time?

(c) What have you thought about since?

(d) Who do you think has been affected by what you did? In what way?

2 Questions to the student who was affected by the actions of the wrongdoer:

(a) What did you think (feel) when you realised what had happened?

(b) How have you (and others) been affected by this?

(c) What has been the hardest thing for you?

(d) What do you think needs to happen to make things better?

3 Question to a student who has done something to hurt/upset somebody else:

(a) What do you think needs to happen to make things better?

4 Question to the student who was affected by the actions of the wrongdoer:

(b) If this doesn't happen/our agreement is broken, what do you think should happen then?

5 Question to a student who has done something to hurt/upset somebody else:

(c) If this doesn't happen/the agreement is broken, what do you think should happen then?

Often you can finish with:

- Before we finish, is there anything else anybody wants to say?
- Do we need to make this a formal written agreement?
- Are we agreed?
- Do we all know what needs to happen now?
- Thanks for being respectful and mature enough to sort this out.
- Well done, you've come to an agreement.
- Thanks everyone.

Affective statements

Affective statements are frequently used by intuitive teachers who understand the importance of separating the behaviour from the student when addressing problem behaviour. Affective statements assist teachers to redirect a student's behaviour. Also, teaching students themselves to use affective statements with one another is an incredibly powerful alternative to the often ridiculed 'I statement'. The three components of an affective statement are (Laycock 2007):

1 identification of something positive about the person whose behaviour has caused harm or upset;

2 identification of the act that has caused harm;

3 identification of the harm that has been caused.

Example: an affective statement between a teacher and a student:

'Mark, you're a friendly person and I really enjoy having you in my class (1) but I'm disappointed about the way you constantly called out this afternoon (2). It made it really hard for me to teach (3).'

Affective interactions

An affective interaction involves a third party who witnesses a harmful act and decides to ask an individual (or a group) to think about how their behaviour may have affected another. Affective interactions are powerful approaches that can be learned by teachers and students. The aim is to raise the instigator's awareness about the effect of their behaviour.

Case study

'Everton supporters are losers!'

A teacher is walking down the corridor when he hears Greg (a Year 9 student) say in passing to Travis that all Everton supporters are losers. Travis, who is wearing his Everton football scarf, looks up with a hurt expression and storms off in the opposite direction. Noticing that Travis is upset by Greg's hurtful comment the teacher casually approaches Greg.

> Teacher: 'Greg you're normally a pretty fair person, but I just heard what you said to Trav. How do you think he felt when you said that?'
>
> Greg: 'I dunno. I was just mucking around.'
>
> Teacher: 'I'm sure you were Greg, but I saw the look on Trav's face. I think what you said upset him.'
>
> At this point Greg has been made aware that his behaviour may have caused upset and that a teacher is aware of this.
>
> Teacher: 'Greg, this isn't major stuff, but maybe you could smooth things out a bit when you see Trav next?'

At all stages the teacher was friendly, direct and affirming with Greg. The elements within 'affective interactions' are similar to those in the 'affective statement'. They are:

- affirming the person whose behaviour has caused harm or upset;

- point out the act that has caused harm;

- point out the harm that has/may have been caused.

Affective statements and interactions are skills worth teaching to students as well. They help kids to support one another and confront harmful behaviour in peaceful ways that can actually improve the situation. As you know, students often have the best of intentions, but in their zeal to fix things they will use an inept or spiteful comment to challenge the behaviour they observed. An important part of restorative practice is showing students how to resolve and restore, not punish the wrongdoer with the same kinds of hurtful actions or words used in the first place.

Impromptu restorative conferences

The impromptu conference is the most frequently visited point on the continuum. It is an 'on the spot' conference called to address a problem, and is the entry point on the restorative continuum where the scripted questions are employed. Although these conferences usually deal with less serious issues and are less formal, they require the facilitator to have the restorative questions memorised and have experience enough to be able to adapt the script to suit the situation. There is often little time for the facilitator to really work out what happened, or to talk with students separately, before bringing them together for the conference. The aim is to restore relationships.

Many teachers and school administrators are looking for alternative responses to giving time-outs. They know that an over reliance on it actually triggers quite a few kids to become angrier and more resentful. It is not unusual, particularly with boys, to see time-out as a punishment that is an inconvenient interruption. Consequently, the very problem that attracted the teacher's attention will reoccur as soon as students have finished time-out. If the truth be told, the time-out period is used by some students to plot revenge on those with whom they originally had the conflict with, or on the teacher who referred them. The impromptu conference offers so much more than the limitations of time-out.

> Schools need to review their pastoral care and disciplinary procedures so that the current pre-occupation with punishment changes to natural consequences for misbehaviour. Children who are punished often have revenge fantasies that interrupt true remorse for what they have done. Girls and boys who are quickly punished by our school systems are not given the opportunity to make amends for what they have done, as punishment clears the ledger and allows boys to re-offend in the future without attendant feelings of guilt.
>
> (Lillico 2004, p. 23)

Of course there is a place for time-out when students continue to escalate their behaviour and do not respond to less intrusive forms of teacher direction. Time-out can be a perfectly reasonable consequence, but should only ever be part of an intervention to address inappropriate behaviour. Time-out is counterproductive as an isolated punitive sanction for unresponsive students. Used well, time away is a powerful prelude to a restorative conversation as it gives upset students a moment to gather themselves so they can engage more respectfully with others to resolve issues.

In a rush, a powerful professional learning tool

The following case study illustrates how a teacher, experienced in impromptu conferencing techniques, can use restorative questioning to help students restore peace following an incident. So often, incidents in schools are triggered by an accidental act that is misread by another. Working from a restorative framework allows everyone to see that mistakes occur rather than immediately assuming they are the victim of a hurtful intent.

First, a word to the wise! If you begin to feel uncomfortable, or angry, as you read of Jill's (the teacher's) approach to the event in the role-play, it may be because your core beliefs about managing the behaviour of others are being challenged. This particular scenario does not intend to make light of the very serious issue of violence in schools. Its purpose is to raise a style of intervention that can reduce the likelihood of further violence in the wake of an unfortunate event.

As you progress through the case study, remain mindful of Jill's skill and style with the boys. Ask yourself:

What would I have done if I were Jill?

Would have I dealt with it differently? If so, why?

Quiz yourself and reflect:

What kind of response does my approach normally attract from students in situations similar to this?

Does it achieve the outcomes I really want for young developing human beings?

Does my process advantage them and support their emotional growth?

Finally, imagine the outcomes if Jill had simply lectured the boys about fighting, written time-out or detention slips and sent them off to their next lesson.

Feel free to use this scripted role-play in your own workshops with groups of educators. Be prepared though, as it will be entirely provocative for some. Some will argue that a formal conference is more appropriate to deal with an incident of this nature. A few may argue that suspension was needed before any type of conference was held. Others will feel that Jill's approach was by far the most effective. Always allow plenty of time for collegial conversation afterwards as the role-play is intended to draw out robust conversation. An excellent resource with processes to facilitate professional learning conversations can be found on the *Professional Learning On-Line Tool* website (www.plotpd.com.au).

See 'In a rush, the role-play', pp. 47–50.

Large group restorative conferences

The large group restorative conference usually takes the form of a whole class conference or a group circle. One such process is 'The No Blame Classroom Conference', described comprehensively in Thorsborne and Vinegrad's manual, *Restorative Practices in Classrooms: Rethinking Behaviour Management* (2002b). This process can be used to address unacceptable levels of harassment and dysfunction in classes by bringing grievances and conflicts between students out into the open. Large group conferences are used when:

- conflict has caused widespread upset;

- concerns about the behaviour or troubles of particular class members need to be shared;

- the disruptive behaviour of students, and the affect it is having on the class and teachers, needs to be addressed;

- harassment or bullying need to be dealt with in an open forum;

- harmful behaviour (such as theft, graffiti or damage to property) has occurred and the wrongdoers are unknown, but students (and teachers) have been affected and would appreciate the opportunity to air their thoughts on the matter.

In a large group conference all participants are given the chance to talk about what has happened, how they and others have been affected and how an individual or group might repair what they have done. These formal conferences work best when the physical setting has been intentionally structured to create an area where everyone can participate (i.e. placing chairs into a circle formation). This is highly recommended, because with no physical barriers between them, each student can appreciate the full flow of verbal and non-verbal communication. Without question this heightens the dynamic of restorative interactions and contributes to the sense of 'we', 'us' and 'ours' that is crucial to building community.

Sometimes the purpose of a large group conference is to expressly address an issue of wrongdoing. When an incident, or set of incidents are being addressed, emphasis is placed on:

- sharing information;

- giving time for students to air their thoughts and feelings;

- encouraging everyone to tell how they have been affected and how they think others have been affected;

- achieving a fair process for everyone, including those who have been called to account for their behaviour;

- providing scope for the group's general feeling about what has happened to materialise, so no one feels alone about what has happened;

- creating opportunities for students to take responsibility for their behaviour, and if the behaviour caused harm, to make amends to those harmed;

- students finding ways to help and support one another;

- looking at ways to share responsibility and share in the repair process;

- re-establishing guidelines for acceptable behaviours;

- generating new expectations for behaviour, and this may be specified as a written agreement or a change to the existing student behaviour agreement;

- ensuring the physical and emotional safety of everyone (including staff).

This process can be steered to give the quieter majority a voice. As we have all experienced, much of the talking time in class can be taken up by the more popular, extroverted, charismatic or troublesome kids. The silent majority also have thoughts, feelings and needs, and drawing out their voice brings a greater depth of shared ownership to the emotional environment of the group. One idea to support this is the use of a talking piece. The talking piece is part of indigenous practice modelled on North American First Nations people. It is used with the understanding it will be passed around the circle and people may only talk or respond when holding it. Everyone else has the responsibility to listen, to hear and gain from the thoughts of others. Students also have the right to pass the talking piece without comment or challenge from any member of the group, including the teacher.

As you may already appreciate, the large group conference works best with older students who look to peers as significant others in their lives. As the developmental blinkers that keep younger children largely self-centred begin to come off around the age of eight years, the benefits of this conferencing model intensify. At this point kids really want to be part of a group. However, large group conferencing is still effective with younger students, but requires obvious adaptations.

In a rush, the role-play

Narrator

It has been a double lesson of maths for 9C and the bell finally sounds. Bill is in a rush to get to PE. Hurriedly he throws his books into his bag, jumps up from his seat and runs at the door. As he attempts to jump an upturned seat near the door, his foot gets caught on one of its legs. Bill scrambles to regain his balance and he clips Mark's broken arm, which is in plaster. Mark yelps and reels in shock. He sees it was Bill who knocked into him. Mark, a burly fourteen-year-old, known to have a fast temper, glares at Bill. Bill freezes with a smirk on his face and says nothing. The two stare intently at one another for several seconds. Bill's smirk widens. Mark explodes calling Bill 'stupid' and punches him in the side of the head with his good hand. Bill recovers and screams, 'What the hell was that for!' Students gather around the two of them and Chris, a bystander, starts to chant, 'fight, fight, fight, fight, fight'.

Jill, a teacher, hearing the commotion calls out, 'Bill, Mark . . . STOP.'

She navigates her way through a forest of excited students. She repeats her instruction, 'Bill, Mark . . . STOP.'

Both boys retreat. Jill says, 'Boys, I need a word with you in the classroom. As for the rest of you, off you go'. Jill is thankful that she knows both boys by first name. There has been a whole staff push to learn and use more students' names over the semester – a learner well-being initiative that has just paid dividends! Jill suspects that being able to use Bill and Mark's names at the critical moment may have made the difference between them stopping or escalating the conflict to a full blown hallway fight. Jill takes a deep breath. She is fully aware that she needs to calm herself before having any chance of calming the boys.

Chris returns from his locker where he grabbed his phone and sent a text to twenty of his friends about the fight. He is unaware that Jill has interrupted the conflict. As he approaches the group he chants, 'fight, fight' pumping his fist in the air. Abruptly he realises that he is the only person making any noise. Tactically ignoring him, Jill directs Mark into the classroom first and then follows with Bill behind her. Jill asks a nearby student to let the PE teacher know that she's helping Mark and Bill sort a problem out.

Jill, watching the boys carefully, phones Sandra, one of the assistant principals. She asks if Sandra can keep an eye on her Year 8 class for 10 minutes, briefly explaining the situation. Sandra, relieved that she doesn't have to deal with the issue in her office, gladly agrees to watch the class.

Jill: OK boys. Bill, are you OK?

Bill (angrily):   The idiot hit me because I accidentally bumped him.

Mark (angrily):   You're just lucky my punching hand is in plaster you loser.

Jill (firmly):   Bill, Mark, you're here to talk through what just happened. That's all. You'll both get a chance to tell your side of the story. If you won't cool down, this chat ends. I'll refer you to the year level manager and tell her you didn't want to handle this with one another. You both know how the school will handle it then don't you?

Mark & Bill (mumble):   Yeah.

Jill: Mark, are you OK?

Mark: Yeah, I've got a sore shoulder where he rammed me.

Jill: Do either of you need ice on anything before we deal with this?

Mark & Bill:　Nah.

Jill (with a grin):　OK boys, can you sit with me to work this out without hurting one another . . . Mark?

Mark:　I suppose.

Jill (looking at Bill):　And how about you Bill?

Bill:　Yeah.

Jill:　OK, boys, pull a seat over.

Both boys grab a seat (with attitude of course). Jill sits down with them; the formation loosely resembles a triangle with the boys facing one another.

Jill (softly):　Do you guys think that a fight is the only thing that will sort this out, or can we talk it out? Mark, do you want to fight?

Mark:　Nah, but if he's going to start on me, I'm ready for him.

Jill:　Bill, do you want to fight?

Bill:　Not really, I didn't want one in the first place.

Jill:　OK . . . so what I'm hearing is that neither of you actually wanted to fight – is that right?

Mark & Bill (quietly):　Not if he doesn't want to . . .

Jill (light-heartedly):　OK, neither of you want a fight. Well, there's hope then! Mark, we're not here to decide who is good or bad or who is right or wrong. I'll ask you both some questions about what happened, how you've been affected and what you think needs to happen to clear this up. Bill, I'll ask you the same questions.

But, for this to work we need to take turns, be respectful and be honest. I know you're both worked up, especially you Bill, but does that sound fair?

Jill checks with both of them by looking at them

Mark & Bill:　OK.

Jill:　Mark, I'm going to start with you. What happened?

Mark (agitated):　I was going through the door and he charged at me for no reason. He knocked my broken arm, which killed. I didn't say or do anything to him.

Jill:　Did you see him coming? Were you guys having a problem at the time?

Mark:　I didn't see him coming, he came from behind. We weren't having a problem, I hardly know him.

Jill:　What happened next?

Mark:　Well after I got up, he was standing there ready to start on me – he was even smiling at me!

Jill:　Keep going Mark . . .

Mark (righteously):　Well, I wasn't going to put up with that, so I punched him in the head with my good hand.

Jill:　What were you thinking when you hit him?

Mark (righteously):　If he was going to start on me, I'd get the first punch in.

Jill:　You honestly believed Bill was starting on you . . .?

Mark:　Yeah. Why else would he ram me and then smile about it?

Jill:　Now that we're having a chat about it, what do you think about how you hit him?

Mark:　I suppose I shouldn't have, I just lost it because my arm hurt after he knocked me.

Jill: Who here's been affected by what you did?

Mark: Him I suppose (pointing at Bill) – because I punched him.

Jill: OK, thanks Mark. Is there anything else before I ask Bill some questions?

Mark: No.

Jill: Bill, what did you think when Mark hit you?

Bill (defensively):   It happened so fast. I didn't know what to think. It was just an accident. I didn't mean to knock you. I tripped on a chair.

Mark suddenly looks uncomfortable

Jill: *(enquiring)*:   So, you didn't charge Mark on purpose, you tripped and fell into him?

Bill: Yeah, I was in a hurry to get to PE.

Jill: Mark said you were smiling.

Bill: I didn't mean to be smiling, I was just shocked, I didn't know what to say, and he looked like he was going to kill me!

Jill (enquiring):   So you weren't smiling because you were happy about running into Mark.

Bill (urgently):   No!

Jill: Mark, are you hearing this?

Mark nods.

Jill: Bill, how has this affected you?

Bill (distressed):   My face hurts where he hit me!

Jill: Bill, what's been the worst of it?

Bill: I dunno, that he punched me in front of everyone.

Jill: Mark, you just heard Bill's side of the story. Is there anything you want to say?

Mark (regretfully):   I thought you were having a go at me. I wouldn't have hit you if I'd known it was an accident. You should have said something!

Jill: Bill, what do you think needs to happen to fix this?

Bill: For him not to hit me again!

Mark (to Bill):   I won't.

Jill: Is there anything else you need from Mark?

Bill: Just for him to say sorry I suppose.

Mark (quickly):   Sorry.

Jill (slowly):   What exactly are you apologising for Mark?

Mark (to Bill):   For hitting you.

Bill: That's OK I suppose . . . sorry for running into you!

Mark: Yeah, all right.

Jill: Boys, how are you with those apologies?

Mark & Bill: OK.

Jill: Well boys, there's a school full of Year 9s and 10s excited about watching you two have a fight, with their mobile phones ready to put you two on the net. What are you going to do?

Mark: Just tell them it's sorted.

Jill: How's that sound to you Bill?

Bill: Sounds OK.

Jill: So when you both walk out of here you're going to tell your mates it's sorted?

Mark & Bill: Yeah.

Jill: You guys know there are people who will probably try to start something between you just to see a fight. How will you deal with that?

Bill: Not believe them.

Jill: Mark?

Mark (to Bill): If someone says you're talking crap about me, I'll come and ask you straight.

Jill: So you both agree that you won't get sucked into fighting and if there's a hassle, you'll talk to each other instead of believing rumours. Is that a deal?

Mark & Bill: Yep.

Jill: You both know I have to write an incident slip about this. Even though you'll avoid a punishment this time, this will be kept on record in case there's another problem between you two. I will write in the report how good you both were with working through the problem.

Mark: My dad is going to go crazy over this at me.

Jill: Sorry Mark, there's not much I can do about that other than let your dad know in the note home that he can give me a call if he's got any questions. Bill, what's likely to happen for you about this at home?

Bill: Mum's going to be cranky that I got hit, but I'll tell her it's sorted. Can she call you if she doesn't believe me?

Jill: Sure, she'll also get the incident report from me telling her what happened. Boys, it's really important you are straight with your parents about what happened and your part in it and how we dealt with it, especially you Mark.

Mark & Bill: We will be.

Jill: One of the school counsellors will see the incident report and may be in touch with you both about a meeting together in a week to check in on things between you.

Mark: Why do we need another meeting?

Jill: Just to check in with you both about how things have been since today. If you are called in for the meeting make sure you go.

Jill: OK boys, we've all got places to be. Thanks for letting me help you sort it out without you hurting each other!

Just as the boys are about to move away, Jill signals for Bill to stay behind.
Mark moves off.

Jill: Bill, how's your face where he hit you?

Bill: A bit sore – I'll be fine.

Jill: I'm sure it will, but I want you to go and get it looked at anyway.

Bill: OK.

Jill: Bill, are you sure you're OK with how that went?

Bill: Yeah, if he'd just got into trouble he would have come after me because he thought that I was starting on him. Things would have got worse.

Jill: What do you think about how we settled it?

Bill: I'm fine with it.

Jill: OK – don't forget to ask Mum to call the office and leave a message if she's worried. I'll call her back. If she's really worried, we'll do that meeting thing I mentioned before.

Bill heads off towards the office to get his face looked at.

'My stuff's been stolen!'

The issue

A whole class conference is called following the disappearance of property from several students' (Sam, Kieren and Renee's) bags and pencil cases. It is unclear as to who may be responsible.

The process

A class circle is formed and the following restorative questions asked by the teacher.

The teacher thanks the students for coming together to help deal with a problem that has caused upset to people in our class. Everyone is reminded that there will be no naming, blaming or shaming during the conference and that if anyone wishes to take responsibility for missing property they can do that during the conference. Students are also reminded that if they have anything they want the teacher to know about the missing property that involves using people's names it is best they talk with the teacher privately after the conference.

Two questions are asked to the class using the go-around process. The go-around process gives each student in turn the opportunity to respond to the questions that are asked. A talking piece is often used in this process.

- Who knows about what is missing?

- When you have had something taken, how did you feel?

Then, Sam, Kieren and Renee are invited to speak.

- Sam, Kieren and Renee, could you tell us what is missing and how this has affected you?

- What has been the hardest about this for you?

Finally, the teacher asked three questions to the entire class. After asking each question the go-around process continued using the class talking piece.

- What would you think if it was someone from this class who has taken Sam, Kieren and Renee's things?

- What would you want the student who has taken their property to understand about what they have done?

- What can we do as a class to make things better for Sam, Kieren and Renee even if we don't get the pencil cases back?

Although a few stolen items turned up in the classroom soon after the conference, those responsible were never identified. There were, however, no more thefts following the conference. At a subsequent conference the teacher and students discussed what was more important – the thieves being caught and punished, or the stealing stopping. All agreed that whoever had taken the pencil cases now knew about what the rest of the class thought about theft.

In the beginning, a lot of teachers worry about the amount of time group conferences are likely to absorb. Soon, even the sceptical discover conferencing actually offers a healthy dimension to classroom functioning, and students learn to do it with increasing skill and ease. Certainly, teachers who commit to an ongoing restorative approach will tell you how much more productive the learning environment becomes and how the 'feel of the class' changes. As for students, they talk about being able to 'get things off of their chest'. In essence, whole class restorative conferences, in combination with ongoing circle work, mark the emergence of a far more relational classroom focus.

Formal restorative conferences

Large group and community conferences are called to address serious incidents or serious ongoing conflicts. Schools of course make their own policy decisions about what types of incidents warrant the use of formal conferencing and this will vary from school to school.

While a formal conference is best held as soon as possible after the incident, there is a great deal of work for the conference facilitator to undertake. Formal conferences involve extensive preparation where participants are selected, invited and interviewed either individually or in small groups – whichever is more appropriate. The facilitator is required to understand the facts before the conference begins. In this way, the facilitator can understand people's stories and feelings, and focus on the outcomes hoped to be achieved by participants. In reality, facilitating a formal restorative conference is not for everybody. Schools often prefer to train a small group of staff to work at this select level. On occasions a trained facilitator may be invited from another school or outside organisation to facilitate a formal conference, particularly if there is a conflict of interest for the trained staff within the school.

Formal conferences typically conclude with a formal written agreement that is signed by all present. The agreement is a record of what was agreed to in the conference. Upon completion of these conferences, all participants are encouraged to stay and share refreshments. This symbolic gesture of breaking bread helps to restore relationships and socially reintegrate wrongdoers (Braithwaite 1989). In the busyness of a school it is very easy to neglect this aspect, but letting it slip appears to reduce the potential effectiveness of the conference.

Now and again, as the facilitator begins to call together those involved in the incident, the school principal may believe that for the safety of students and staff, or to allow individuals time to deal with the emotional fallout from the incident, suspensions are required pending the conference. In this context it is important to appreciate that the goal of the suspension is not to punish, but to allow time so the chance of a successful restorative outcome is maximised. This of course raises the issue of the interplay between restorative practices and the traditional punitive responses of stand-downs, suspensions and exclusions. There is a mistaken belief that restorative practices do away with these measures. Even though these measures may not be viewed as ideally restorative in nature, used judiciously, there is a place for them. In fact, in conferences a decision is occasionally made by participants to go ahead with a formal consequence such as a suspension or exclusion: it is the clarity and transparency of the 'fair process' that matters most.

Students participating in formal conferences are encouraged to invite a person to support them (a family member or an adult in the school they have a good relationship with) and to sit with them during the conference. Frequently, a student's parents will have a number of questions about why the school believes a formal conference is the preferred approach. Another compelling reason loved ones are invited to formal restorative conferences arises from 'reintergrative shaming theory' (Braithwaite 1989). Braithwaite's empirically supported hypothesis holds that when a wrongdoer hears from their victims about the impact of their behaviour in the presence of loved ones, conditions are created where they more readily feel and show appropriate levels of shame and remorse. This in turn creates conditions where required actions to put things right can be discussed and agreed upon by wrongdoers, those harmed and the loved ones of both parties. In this context the process of reintegration has the very best chance (Braithwaite 1989).

Naturally, support people are bound to ask what will happen, which questions will be asked to whom and what they are expected to do. The facilitator will give support people the opportunity to speak and be listened to about the impact of the harmful behaviour(s) before the conference. It is well worth showing patience during this phase because demystifying the process often provides emotionally constructive ways forward for participants. It may be wise to take the key conference participants through the scripted restorative questions that will be asked so they have time to think about and prepare their responses.

When appropriate, the facilitator may choose to share some information with participants that they have gained in other pre-conference discussions. An example of this is to let those harmed know that the 'other side' have admitted to their involvement and are keen to try to put things right with them.

The usual practice is that the school will proceed with a formal conference providing:

- everyone involved agrees to do so;

- the wrongdoer(s) have admitted their involvement; students who fail to own their behaviour are poor candidates for this process. Their total denial of the incident, or hurt caused to others, will only make things worse for those harmed by their behaviour. Enforced involvement for wrongdoers should be avoided.

In summary, the formal conference involves the wrongdoer(s), those harmed by their behaviour(s), chosen support people and others who were affected by the incident. The process guarantees all participants have the opportunity to tell their stories about the incident(s) and respond to what other participants have said. Allow as much time as necessary for those involved to agree on acceptable outcomes. A good rule of thumb is to allow a minimum of two hours for formal conferences in schools, and always state from the outset that more time is available. Avoid giving in to the temptation to rush a formal conference. If no time is left and there is more to do, then reschedule.

Formal conferencing questions

Important note

The script below is an abridged version of the full formal restorative conference script. The full conference script gives clear guidance on questions to pose to wrongdoers as well as those affected, in addition to helping support people of both parties. There are many available adaptations of the formal restorative conference script.

Formal training in large group and community conferencing is highly recommended.

To the wrongdoer(s)

- What happened?
- What were you thinking at the time?
  (What was going on in your mind?)
  (What was happening for you at the time?)
- What have you thought about since?
  (How have you felt since?)
  (Looking back on what you did, what do you think now?)
- Who has been affected by what you did? In what way?
  (Do you think anyone was hurt by what you did? Who?)

To those harmed and other affected persons

- What did you think when you realised what had happened?
  (What was going through your mind when this was happening?)
  (Tell us the story.)
- What impact has this incident had on you and others?
  (What has it been like for you since it happened?)
  (What sorts of things have been going on in your mind since . . .?)
- What has been the hardest thing for you?
  (What's been the worst thing for you from of all of this?)
  (What's been the most difficult thing to cope with?)

To those harmed and other affected persons

- What do you think needs to happen to make things better?
  (What do you think should happen now?)
  (What do you think needs to happen to make things better for you?)

To the wrongdoer(s)
- What do you think you need to do to make things better?
  (What do you think should happen now?)
  (Can you think of anything that might need to happen to help . . . ?)

To those harmed and other affected persons

- If the agreement is not completed what do you think should happen then?

To the wrongdoer(s)

- If you do not do what you have agreed to do, what do you think should happen then?

Conclusion: looking to the future

As the balance of power between teachers and students, and between schools and communities, continues to shift, the emotionally healthy spirit of restorative practices is gathering momentum. Most school administrators and teachers are grasping the realisation that the way they manage discipline issues today either strengthens or alienates their connections with students and the school community. One thing is for sure: the traditional control paradigm is fast becoming impotent and counter-productive to the problematic emotion and behaviour experienced by kids and teens in schools today.

Certainly, the way we have handled conflict, harm and wrongdoing in schools in the past has mirrored the largely unsuccessful ways of our criminal justice system. The punitive approach may be an old, comfortable and organisationally convenient tool, but used largely as a stand alone instrument it is more likely to incite young individuals and teach them to cover their mistakes, threaten, pay back or blame mistakes on someone else. It is not a legitimate behaviour change instrument.

Students who have started their restorative journey will readily share the benefits. They warm to the transparency of the process where they can learn about their behaviour, the behaviour of others, their forgiveness and the forgiveness of others. Students of all ages warm to the sense of community that forms within restorative schools and classrooms where a strong sense of 'we', 'us' and 'ours' emerges. This feeling of belonging to a community is in itself a protective factor against harmful behaviour in schools. Students will tell that hearing directly from those who have been hurt by a behaviour, witnessing the emotion in their voice, seeing the looks on their faces is an integral part of deciding what needs to happen to put things right and to restore community. Make no mistake, the restorative process holds kids accountable, often in a far more potent way than the traditional, emotionally removed processes that typify many systems of school discipline.

As for teachers who are pioneering restorative principles: they each share something very special. They believe the quality of relationship management is at the core of behaviour management.

Teachers reveal, even in the early stages of implementation, that the restorative approach is a far more satisfying way to work with the big and the small issues. They often remark how quickly students see the forum as fair and just, how willing kids are to talk, to reflect and come up with plans to improve a range of situations. Most teachers working within restorative environments say that having a clear, interactive mechanism to deal with disputes actually results in fewer impasses and helps school to become a safer and happier workplace.

It is not by accident that this challenge comes at a time when student academic achievement in schools is worryingly poor, student retention is in decline, and suspensions and exclusions for difficult, dangerous and violent behaviours continue to rise at an alarming rate. This of course is especially so for boys as an increasing number disengage from school because they perceive it as an alienating experience (Trent and Slade 2001).

There is no single answer to 'fix' these matters. What the restorative spirit does offer is a vitality to connect young developing individuals on a basic human level where they can feel a sense of belonging and where relationships are valued, and above all else, feel valued themselves. What schools don't need more of is increased formality of process to protect people from one another. Schools need now, more than ever, an injection of emotional intelligence and human connectedness.

A restorative culture immediately places kids on a far healthier trajectory. What could be any more real, connecting, teachable or sustainable than offering a pro-social mechanism to sort through the real issues that matter and occur every day in the lives of kids?

> We live in a world that is becoming increasingly disconnected. We all experience constant exposure to graphic scenes on television involving violence, incivility and rejection of authority. More and more young people who experience isolation and alienation are turning to alcohol and drugs to medicate their pain. Yet, very few of us understand why violence is endemic in our communities and sadly, in our families.
>
> (Nathanson 2004)

Refer to p. 189 for useful websites and further reading.

CHAPTER 3

Inspiration to improve concentration and task completion

Inside tough kids with poor attention and impulsive behaviour

This chapter is dedicated to the kids who battle relentlessly busy minds, intrusive thoughts, impulsive acts and endlessly restless bodies.

Case study

The need for speed

It was Wednesday morning shortly after morning break when I observed twelve-year-old Troy in his classroom. Each of the students were, more or less, writing and illustrating their narratives. Suddenly Troy made his entrance. He had just returned from taking a piece of 'excellent work' to the principal. He whooped out his own fanfare and held his exercise book open above his head for all to see. Everyone stopped to look. They knew the cue! Troy glided across the room turning in slow circles so everyone could view the principal's award in his book and witness his very cool hip-hop moves. He finished off the display with a short, humorous song that poked fun at himself. Everyone laughed and applauded. He bowed. Then out of the blue, he dropped to his knees and begged his teacher to let him go back down to the office again as he had thought of something else he could show the principal.

Quietly, his teacher redirected this urge and encouraged him to return to his desk and to complete his sketch. She handed him his workbook. Troy acquiesced and moved away, but he didn't return to his desk. Instead, he bounced around the classroom looking for something to draw with. Finally he chose to stand and draw near the window, placing his paper on the window sill. His drawing took all of twenty-two seconds to complete. Then, he bounced back to his teacher to show her, also managing to show it to at least nine others on the way. She praised his work and directed him to another activity in the classroom. He appeared delighted with this, however quietly seeped from the room to investigate the noise coming from a group of students engaged in an art activity in the hallway. Troy happily chatted and wandered about the group. His interaction was energetic, chaotic and very good natured.

After a while his teacher called him back. Once again he obliged, yet as soon as her attention was taken from him, he slipped back out of the classroom again. Then, as luck would have it, a school support officer who often worked with him arrived. Troy was happy to see her and skipped ahead of her twirling around and around as he went. As she brushed past me she commented that he'd had one of his 'very busy mornings'. She thought his teacher, and the class, may appreciate the break.

These kids will tell you as they get older how unbearable it is to live with noisy, impulsive thoughts in their heads. Just think how hard it must feel to have to run at one frenetic pace all the time? It is not the way they choose to be. The choice is not theirs. As one of my clients explained, she came home from work with some calming chamomile tea for Ally. Like me, she enjoys a cup of tea and lately they've been experimenting.

'Great,' she said, 'I just wish there was a "think before you do tea".'

The chapter is also dedicated to every educator who works tirelessly to educate these kids in a school environment that naturally overstimulates and overwhelms their senses.

Overview: attention deficit disorder (ADD) and attention deficit hyperactivity disorder (ADHD)

ADD and ADHD are neurological development disorders '. . . characterised by developmentally inappropriate degrees of combinations of severe and persistent inattention, hyperactivity and impulsivity' (Darby 2002). The conditions are thought to affect about 5 per cent of the general population (Barkley 2006). This translates to about one or two students per class.

ADD and ADHD, according to Russell Barkley's widely accepted Unifying Theory of AD/HD, involve a disorder of the brain's management system linked to the operation of executive functioning (Barkley 1997). The executive system regulates thinking, organisation, planning and starting, maintaining and completing behaviours.

1 Consequently, AD/HD is seen largely as a disorder of inhibition. Deficits in inhibition interfere with the consistent carrying out of thoughtful responses that would usually be appropriate to the situation.

2 AD/HD is a disorder of working memory. Working memory permits information to be retrieved from long-term memory. It assists each of us to remember what we need to remember and return to tasks following interruptions. It also prompts us to get back to the job!

3 AD/HD is a disorder of self-regulation that leads to impulsiveness. Self-regulation helps us to think before we respond. It helps us to adjust our responses and carry out the 'boring' tasks imposed by someone else.

4 AD/HD is a disorder of internalisation of speech. Think of internalisation of speech as the ability to create self-talk. We use it to assess and direct our behaviour. The sort of self-talk used by students identified with ADHD tends to be less task oriented and far less efficient than that used by others.

5   AD/HD is a disorder of performance. What this means is that kids identified with AD/HD can't use what they should have learned from their past experiences at the very moment when they really could use it (Barkley 1997). Quintessentially, this is the disability.

Barkley's longitudinal studies have determined a delay-gap of 35 to 40 per cent existing in the areas of inhibition, impulsiveness, planning and organisation in kids and young teens identified with AD/HD compared to others the same age. This is an insightful rule of thumb for educators. To clarify this, a ten-year-old with AD/HD may well look like they are performing at the age level of what we would expect from a seven-year-old. In the same way, a sixteen-year-old, in the increasingly exacting middle school environment, is likely to be performing at about a twelve-year-old level. Indeed, AD/HD results in a serious performance delay.

AD/HD is also a co-morbid condition. This is to say that about two-thirds of primary school aged children identified with AD/HD also have a learning difficulty, or a psychiatric or emotional disorder such as oppositional defiance, conduct, sleep, anxiety, obsessive compulsive, mood, depression, bi-polar and Tourette's (Brown 2008). The co-morbid nature of AD/HD creates deep layers of challenging difficulties for educators to work with.

Attention deficit disorder (ADD)

When a student receives a diagnosis of ADD it alerts teachers to their highly inattentive functioning. The behaviours of these kids are, as a rule, described as vagueness, dreaminess and highlighted by poor performance at school, both academically and socially. Their natural tendencies are to drift off, stare into space, mishear and forget to plan or be organised. Despite the student being in the classroom on a full-time basis, the truth is that they are only available to listen and process information on a very part-time basis.

Naturally, teachers worry over their reduced written output as this is a major component in assessing a student's quality of learning. When these students get off to a good start they can still lose the thread before finishing up. At other times starting work can be difficult: they are not sure where to start, appear unsettled, uncertain of instructions, unsure which resources are needed and where they might be. Teachers often comment, 'He seems to be in a world of his own' or 'She never seems to know what's happening'. Quite often their desks, lockers, schoolbags and bedrooms are in disarray, which completely mirrors their internal disorganisation.

Mostly, these kids are passive, immature and impressionable, but every so often in stimulating situations impulsive behaviours are triggered as well. In the over-excited mode, they find it difficult to make the link between their actions and the likely outcome. They cannot independently apply the breaks and wait their turn. Instead they will blurt out their thoughts. They become judged as poor team players because they just cannot wait their turn and have to come first. When they don't win their temper explodes and a tantrum is unavoidable, even if it is in public and they are fourteen years of age.

Their global inattentiveness also impacts heavily on organisation, remembering and socialisation. Friendships are often compromised as their lack of attending inhibits keeping up with the pace of interaction. Soon they find themselves discarded and on the outer. The luckier ones build friendships with quieter children who over time appreciate their individual style. In my view, one of the saddest aspects about the impact of both ADD and ADHD is the insidious secondary damage done to confidence and self-esteem through social alienation.

Attention deficit hyperactivity disorder (ADHD)

In contrast, the kids with ADHD are those whose behaviours truly grab our attention! They are inescapably active. In fact, so active that they can struggle to sit still even when eating their favourite meal at dinner. They're hyperactive! They are 'in your face', loud, 'over the top' and reckless. And, because they are so 'full of beans' they cannot look and listen. Consequently, they miss vital cues that help most find academic, social and personal success. These are the kids and adolescents who touch things they were asked not to and say things they later regret. They don't mean to, it's just that with emerging levels of inhibition they find it hard to regulate what they say and do. They cannot find their breaks and apply them when they should, and are likely to do the same act again the next day.

Kids living with ADHD are forever sidetracked by spontaneous thought interruption. New thoughts and ideas constantly crash in on them. Teachers find them wandering the classroom fiddling with the belongings of others and engaging half a dozen students on different topics in the space of a minute or two. As soon as they want something they'll call out insisting their need be met, even if asked to wait their turn a few minutes before. Little imagination is required to understand the devastating impact this innate behaviour has on planning, persistence and meeting deadlines.

Teachers can't help but notice their extraordinarily short attention spans. They finish tasks soon after they start. They have what is referred to as a low boredom threshold. Being the first to finish every time is important to them, even though they make the same careless mistakes in their work each day. These kids work erratically, finding it tough to monitor and improve the quality of their work. When teachers raise this behavioural pattern to parents they are often quick to defend their child's concentration span insisting they can play video games, surf the net or watch DVDs for hours. Later, when they grasp the true measure of concentration, the idea of sticking to an imposed task that may not be a stimulating personal choice, parents begin to understand.

Poor peer relationships and rejection is common. Peers avoid them because of their immature, bossy and unpredictable behaviours. Some of these kids jump impulsively from one 'friendship' to another looking for someone who might be more interesting or is a risk taker just like them. On the other hand, those who are shyer tend to isolate themselves working well within their own set of narrow interests. Others will latch on to a friend and as the relationship grows it becomes lopsided. Consciously and unconsciously the friend is used as an emotional steadier or caretaker, but receives little back in return. Eventually the friendship collapses through resentment and an intense emotional overreaction is likely to occur.

Medication and alternative therapies

The delay-gap between what students with AD/HD can deliver and what is expected by teachers is a major point of contention in schools. These kids do not have the natural capacity to meet the typical sets of expectations independently. They are reliant on educators to change expectations and alter curriculum delivery to maximise their chances of success (Carter *et al.* 2009). The onus falls to us, as educators, to actually understand their challenge. With this in mind, this chapter presents dozens of realistic options to help the genuine inconsistencies students identified with AD/HD face.

However, I cannot continue without raising the issue of medication because when working with this group of kids the question of whether a parent should or should not medicate is usually asked of educators. Responding to this question is truly a dilemma for teachers. First up, we do not have a medical degree and whatever we offer to a parent is little more than an educated opinion about medication. It is wise to make this patently clear to the parent. This brings home the relevance of where each of us gets our information about AD/HD and the merit of medications. Reflect: how long is it since you read a referenced article on the topic in an educational periodical or journal? How long is it since you visited a well regarded website on AD/HD and spent some time with the information? Where are you sourcing your information from? How do you know it is up to date and accurate?

Every parent wants to do the right thing for their child, but invariably they have seen sensationally driven television programmes, magazine pieces and internet sites that warn of the poisonous effects of pharmaceutical medication. The families of medication used for the treatment of AD/HD have been systematically discredited by the media and various organisations over the years. Understandably, most parents become confused. Some are fearful, but want to cautiously proceed. Others are plainly terrified and will avoid it at all cost. Interestingly, relatively few parents in studies realise that there is a range of other treatments (psychological, educational, counselling and family support) available as well as medication. While medication can deliver advantages in supporting a child or teen with AD/HD, it was never intended to be a separate, one size fits all, frontline approach (Prosser 2006).

A most useful question to ask parents is: do you see medication as a first or last option? The urgency in their answer to this question is always telling. Sometimes kids with AD/HD crave for quietness that they cannot achieve without medication. Their predisposition for tremendous overactivity and uncontrollable thought interruption will either eliminate or greatly reduce the value of other interventions. Medication is frequently reported to help these kids find quietness as it temporarily normalises the underlying problem. However, medication will not solve their academic and friendship problems per se. It simply provides a chance where other interventions, remediations and care have a chance to make a difference.

This is the perfect moment to raise the outcomes from a study conducted by the National Institute of Mental Health (2000). To help families in the United States develop a better understanding about the effectiveness of treatments for kids with AD/HD, the National Institute of Mental Health funded a study known as the Multimodal Treatment Study of Children with Attention Deficit Hyperactivity

Disorder. The study included 579 primary school students with AD/HD who were randomly allocated to one of four treatment programmes:

- medication management alone;

- behavioural treatment alone;

- a combination treatment (medication management and behavioural treatment);

- generalised community care.

The results indicated that long-term 'combination treatment' and the 'medication management alone' were the most effective. An advantage of the combined treatment was that children could be successfully treated with lower doses of medication, compared with the 'medication management alone' group.

It is always best to encourage parents to make an appointment with a personable psychologist, general practitioner, paediatrician or psychiatrist well regarded in AD/HD so they can have their child assessed, talk about the possibility of medication, find out about side effects, explore related issues and discuss various interventions. Try to be open, flexible and responsive. This is such a difficult journey for families.

Parents are also likely to ask you about the abundance of alternative preparations and therapies on offer. An uncontrolled and unregulated alternative therapy industry has grown around the treatment of AD/HD. Many fall well outside of proven, mainstream treatments because they lack evidence-based efficacy. You may need to assist parents to understand the great divide between alternative therapies, evidence-based systems and the charlatans. However, integrative medicine is becoming more widely adopted. This is a design where an emerging complementary therapy is combined with a mainstream approach based on solid scientific evidence. It is vital for parents to discuss this design with both practitioners to ensure both treatments are compatible. Encourage parents to be open-minded, but cautious in the search to improve their child's condition. A logical way to support a parent is to suggest they ask any practitioner offering a treatment programme the following questions (Hannell 2004):

- What are your professional credentials?

- Could you provide me with copies of your qualifications and registration?

- Could you provide me with copies of articles published in reputable journals about this treatment?

- Could you explain to me what your treatment does, how it works and how we will know it has worked?

- Will this treatment cure?

- What are the limits of this treatment?

- May I ask my child's teacher (psychologist, paediatrician) to evaluate my child before we start treatment and then after you have finished?

- What are the side effects of your treatment?

- May I have a copy of your indemnity insurance?

- Could you please show me results of clinical studies that show what you are doing is safe?

- If we start treatment and I find it unsuitable, am I able to stop without further cost?

- If the treatment does not work is there a money back guarantee?

- Can you put me in touch with others who have used your treatment and can recommend you?

- Can you provide written information about the treatment as I would like to discuss it with our doctor (or psychologist, teacher, etc.)?

Ideas to ease physical restlessness and impulsive choices

Many students identified with ADHD experience difficulty being quiet, being still and being able to stay in one place. Hyperactivity is a physiological problem and needs to be appreciated in this light. As tricky as it is, try to avoid making physical restlessness into too much of an issue. All sorts of ideas exist to support physically restless students. Let's explore a few.

Legal movement

Develop several legal places in the classroom the student may move to providing they deliver a cue before moving. In other words, moving is fine, but they need to stretch their appreciation of what works for you as well. Sometimes letting them stand at a desk or a bench to work can help to sustain concentration a little longer.

Tall desks

Some teachers arrange for one or two desks in the classroom to be modified so they have tall legs. In this way the restless student can stand at the desk and work. Everything from their shoulders down tends to move, yet surprisingly this movement seems to strengthen the length of their concentration and help with work output. A further option is to replace a couple of student chairs with medium-sized fitness balls. It sounds unconventional, but once again the need to gently and constantly reposition their body on the ball seems to be enough to take the edge off their restlessness.

X marks the spot

When you want kids to sit on the floor one idea is to stick a piece of masking tape as an X on the floor for your wriggly students to sit on, or give them their own personalised cushion. Rubber cushions inflated with air called 'wiggle cushions' can be purchased for this purpose as well. This approach needs to be negotiated and handled sensitively though.

Coloured tokens and raffle tickets

An idea to support the physical restlessness of students, and to help stretch their self-awareness, is to give them a red, green and yellow token that is kept in their pocket, on their desk or on yours. All three tokens can be used up during the day, but when they are gone, they are gone! Each colour describes what the student wishes to do. For example, a red token may indicate a need to go for a quick drink, a green token may represent the need for a drink and toilet stop and a yellow one might signal the need for a brisk run around the school to burn off some energy, or a 10-minute visit to a buddy class or friendly teacher. On a similar note, to help students monitor the number of breaks they required from the classroom, an ingenious middle primary teacher gave his hyperactive students ten raffle tickets each at the beginning of the week. They were asked to hand over a ticket each time they decided to take a short break from class. Knowing that each raffle ticket would have a monetary value assigned to it on Friday afternoon was reason enough to ration their breaks. On Friday afternoon the tickets could be cashed in at the canteen in return for a treat.

Class monitors

Set up vigorous classroom tasks to compensate for the student's physical restlessness: allow them to clean the whiteboard, sharpen pencils, organise displays, collect or distribute books, run errands and so on. Keeping these kids constructively on the move helps them to compensate for their inbuilt need to move. Sometimes giving them leadership opportunities, or important jobs to do, helps them feel a part of things. Again, the approach may help to channel their physical restlessness.

Plan to burn energy

Find acceptable ways for these kids to leave the classroom and burn off their surplus energy. Send them on a message to avoid the inevitable, even if it is just getting them to take a note in a SEALED envelope explaining to a colleague or two that you need a 15-minute break. This is so much healthier than both climbing the walls together!

Organise for double PE or sport lessons

Energetic exercise throughout the day helps many of these kids to burn off surplus energy. Apparently vigorous exercise triggers particular neuro-chemicals and this stimulates improvements in concentration (Mulrine *et al.* 2008). Take into account benefits from the fun factor as well! So why not talk to a colleague and organise double PE each day for your physically restless student.

Fidget toys

Providing some form of fidget toy can be helpful during times when you want a student to be focused and take in a lot of information. They are especially handy at those times when you know your instruction will be lengthy or when you need the group's attention for a while. As the student handles or fidgets with the toy (a piece of blu-tak, a small foam ball, a piece of sticky Velcro fastened to the underside of their desk so the student can rub it while they listen, a soft squishy ball, etc.) their physical senses appear occupied and their restlessness gives away to improved concentration.

Think strips and wrist bands

Find worksheet on page 203

Many of the kids with AD/HD wrestle with lightning reactions. Their natural style is to 'do' rather than stop and think first. The think strip and wristband are two tactile tools outlined in my previous book, *Cognitive Behavioural Training: A How-to Guide for Successful Behaviour* (Le Messurier 2004). They offer students a way to make stronger links between how they feel, what they can do and what is likely to happen.

Think strips can be fastened to school desks, to rulers, placed on pin-up boards – anywhere to help strengthen the decision-making process. When there is a problem to be sorted, the lightning reactions of kids can be slowed by the act of running their finger across the think strip. This buys just enough time to help them to think more clearly. Wrist bands on the other hand, are worn on the wrist. Usually, they are hand made from plaited yarn with three or four beads attached. The idea is for the student to touch or slide each bead along as they think about the best option to choose. Surprisingly, kids like to wear them and talk about the help they receive from them!

Ideas to promote settled, cooperative behaviours

Developing rules and expectations

All kids need to understand what the class behavioural expectations are and exactly how they will work. This is doubly helpful for the students with social awkwardness, memory weaknesses, short attention spans and elevated levels of physical restlessness. The best class rules are those developed through healthy student and teacher discussion. Students are far more inclined to follow classroom expectations when they see themselves as stakeholders in their development. The best set of class expectations works around being simple and minimal. It is wise to define each rule as well. For example, the class may decide on the rule, 'Students should always listen to the teacher and follow their instruction'. Defining means teasing it out so that students really understand what the rule means in the heat of the moment. A sensible way to define this rule may be, 'Even if you feel angry, stop. Listen to the teacher. Do what he/she says. Trust he/she will listen and help you sort out your feelings.' It is a good idea to do this with each of the key rules. Also discuss what fair and predictable consequences should be when the rules are ignored. Finally, display them in the classroom with the signature of every class member on them. Never hesitate to review and rework them because classroom expectations are all about helping everyone to live more successfully together in the crowded classroom.

Structure

The creation of structure and routine for the kids we are concerned about in this chapter is an obvious link for them to deliver cooperative behaviours at school. Visible, well developed structures offer them the best chance to know what is expected and how to go about fulfilling the expectations. They are far more dependent on timely prompts and having conditions arranged to give them the best chance to function well. Generally speaking, they respond well to the three Rs: routine, reliability and repetition. Chapter 4, 'Strategies to help organisation and memory' details a broad assortment of practical ideas based around routine, reliability and repetition.

Classroom set-up

Students identified with AD/HD benefit from fewer distractions. They are very sensitive to overstimulation. This is why they function better in regular classrooms with four walls rather than in an open unit arrangement. Open units, due to their vastness and increased numbers of students, tend to attract a greater number of visual and auditory distractions for kids.

First, think about arranging the furniture into a configuration that permits you to circulate easily. The ability to be able to move about freely in the classroom is probably one of our best management tools. The more personal and frequent your interaction is with each student the better. Frequently touching base with students helps them to hold their interest and allows you to gently redirect their attention before it fades too far. Even within a regular classroom, the ideal desk arrangement is limited by the available furniture and size of the classroom itself. Seating distractible kids by swinging doors, windows, high-traffic areas and noisy air conditioners is unhelpful. Likewise, seating them permanently in groups can be overwhelming and distracting. As mentioned earlier, develop an understanding with the distractible student that they can work between two places in the classroom. Provide them with a desk near yours, near the board, that's not touching the desks of others when they have quieter, sustained work to do. This makes it easier to monitor them. At other times encourage them to sit with their group. Keep in mind that surrounding them with grounded classmates is useful. The best advice is to keep experimenting and talking to your student about what seems to work best for them.

A study buddy

Kids identified with AD/HD tend to be immature when compared to their classmates. They are still growing and finding their way. A steadying strategy to assist them to persevere is to sit them alongside a naturally grounded buddy. Find a buddy who knows what needs to be done and can do it. Explain to the buddy the role you have in mind for them. As you would expect, a series of buddies during the course of the year may need to be found, but don't worry too much about wearing them out because these are the kids who are likely to become counsellors, social workers, teachers and psychologists. It's great practice for them to start honing their skills now!

Physical proximity

Simply moving closer to a student and lingering a little longer can help them to stay with the task.

Signals

Direct, genuine feedback is a powerful motivator for students. Set up signals so that the student who procrastinates, avoids or has difficulty staying on task receives feedback on what they are doing. As you walk past them in class place two pencils together on their desk. This predetermined signal may indicate, 'You're doing really well with the task'. When things are not going so well agree that you will place an item of some sort on their desk to remind them to stick with the task just a little longer.

Work to music

Increasingly teachers are encouraging students to work in class while listening to music. Once the explanation is done and the instructions are out of the way students are reminded to switch on their iPods or MP3 players and put their earpieces in. Some educators swear by this and will tell you student concentration increases and distractible behaviours decrease.

Become an expert at chunking tasks

Unless we modify for the obvious they will not deliver what is required.

Assisting students to break tasks into manageable pieces guarantees they are able to arrive at the destination, with the task completed, at the same time as others. Without this, the inconsistencies these kids face with concentration, organisation and planning will get the better of them.

- Create an opportunity for the student to talk through how they intend to tackle the task. This supports them to clarify and prioritise. Students with AD/HD rely on verbal planning and written mapping.

- Build a progress checklist. On it outline the individual parts of the task that need to be completed, and assign a due date for each stage.

- Provide the student with a jump-start by organising yourself, an older student, another teacher, a school support officer or a tutor to spend a session or two with them early on.

- Frequently monitor progress. Review what has been done and work on solutions to avoid the difficulties you sense will arise.

- Help to maintain routine. Incorporate the activity into each day, until the task is done. Encourage them to set small tasks to complete, take a short break and then return ready to begin the next task.

- For those lucky enough to have it, home help is really useful. Do what you can to develop opportunities for parents to know what is happening and how to best support their child.

• Never be afraid to lend a hand and model how it looks to stick with a task. Be patient. It takes longer for these kids to gain independent skills. They rely on opportunity after opportunity to watch, listen, discuss and participate in ways to read, research, chunk and present information.

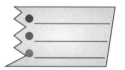

Find worksheet on page 207

A series of practical ideas to support kids who procrastinate and manage time poorly are outlined in detail in Chapter 4, 'Strategies to help organisation and memory'. Worksheets to support the chunking of tasks can also be found at the end of the book (pages 212–14).

Ideas to stretch written output

Reduced written output can be a devastating problem for students with executive functioning difficulties. A few may meet the criteria for a *writing* difficulty termed dysgraphia. These kids are bright enough, but lack the ability to effectively integrate their thinking into a coherent written form. They struggle with the volume of writing, neatness and fluency. They make inappropriately sized and spaced letters and the quality of their handwriting rapidly deteriorates soon after they begin. Basic spelling is often a casualty as well. In less severe cases, students are often able to talk through their creative ideas, but transferring the potency of what is in their heads onto paper is such a challenge. The writing process itself demands layers of continuous concentration so for the kids who have trouble convincing their restless minds to stay focused the challenge to produce print is far deeper than often appreciated.

There are, however, ideas to make the writing process a little easier for them.

• Allocate more time if necessary. These kids take longer to process ideas and information. An extension of time, with guidance, gives a much better chance of completion.

• A classic problem is the students who 'get stuck' trying to pick a topic. They just can't decide and use up their time and energy before they even start writing! Expedite the process and help them make a choice. If they can't decide, flip a coin.

• Teach students how to brainstorm and build a concept map or web (for more information, try www.inspiration.com). Concept maps and webs support kids who cannot easily hold their ideas in their minds for long. Alternatively, introduce the idea of using sticky notes. Teach students to record each idea they want to use in their written work on an individual sticky note. In my experience, this works well for kids of all ages. It also works nicely when students write an idea on a sticky note for who, what, when, where and why as they construct a report or recount.

• Provide a scribe to write the student's thoughts, ideas and opinions.

• Encourage the student to record the information they know. Yes, it is important to explore the references and learn new ideas, but make sure to start with their base knowledge. It is a legitimate source to build around.

- Offer opportunities for students to present information in alternative ways that appeal to their interests and strengths – TV news reports, graphs, cartoons, surveys, concept maps, slide shows, film, interviews, music lyrics, advertisements, flow charts, photographs, CDs and so on.

- Allow the student with poor concentration to tackle the writing task in two or three short bursts, rather than having to stick at it for an entire lesson. This assists them to produce work that is lengthier and of greater quality.

- Be prepared to guide the writing process. When a student looks to be struggling, sit down and help them to short circuit the impasse.

- It is a good idea to avoid making spelling and grammatical corrections while the student is writing. The trick is to let them capture the ideas first and correct and edit later. In some instances it may be best to remove neatness as a grading criterion.

- Encourage students to use the keyboard: a laptop, PC or alphasmart (for more information, try www.alphasmart.com). Teach them how to improve spelling by using the spell check on the computer and don't overlook hand-size electronic spell checkers (for more information, try www.franklin.com/estore/ dictionary/LM-6000B/). They are powerful little helpers.

- Also teach them how to use the thesaurus and synonyms on the computer. It's surprising how few students are aware of these functions and once they discover them, new worlds open up.

Success designs: group reinforcement and feedback plans

Every human being looks for and thrives on positive feedback. The experts have long told us that nothing brings about the cooperative behaviours of another as well as catching them doing well and acknowledging it. When it comes to kids, noticing a helpful behaviour and delivering feedback about it in front of peers immediately highlights their effort and reinforces they are on the right track. This is such a powerful and obvious motivator, yet one that can be easily overlooked.

Kids, just as adults, behave according to the pleasure principle – behaviour that is rewarding to them tends to continue, and behaviour that is unrewarding tends to stop. Group reinforcement plans, totally distinct from awful, ill-founded classroom competitive win and lose systems, can help students to move beyond behavioural habits that do not work for them. While all students benefit from group reinforcement plans, or a personalised improvement plan, for the kids facing executive functioning difficulties these types of ideas are priceless. Don't believe students should be provided with incentives to cooperate and work with unity? Why not? Even within the adult world rewards are commonly used as healthy motivators and to secure loyalty: fair pay for a fair day's work, frequent flyer rewards, banking reward schemes for clients who pay their mortgage repayments early or on time.

Chapter 5, 'Creating the best start for challenging kids', targets the instrumental steps required to build an individual reinforcement plan with a student. This chapter, however, concerns itself with appealing ideas to develop group reinforcement and feedback plans. Before proceeding, two notable points must be made about the construction of individual reinforcement plans and group feedback designs. First, that guiding the emotion and behaviour of another is always tricky. In truth, any programme that concerns itself with skilling others to manage their feelings, and provide practical options for them to think and behave differently will always yield mixed results because we cannot control others. Behaviour management in this sense is truly an imperfect science. Second, the programme most likely to achieve success is the one where a good part of the focus is on emotional guidance and relationship – where the educator actually talks to the student or students, listens, exchanges ideas and is willing to participate with them.

Lucky dips

During lessons students are handed a small sticky note by the teacher as a way of praising them for something they have done well. The student writes their name on it and inserts it into the lucky dip box. For older kids two sticky notes are drawn out at the end of the week and the two winners choose a prize from the prize box. For younger kids the draw can take place at the end of a lesson or at the end of the day. This is a fabulous motivator and positive reinforcer for kids of all ages. Try it and you'll see them making the extra effort!

Star charts

Find worksheet on page 204

Kids of all ages are motivated by well thought-through team building ideas. Attach the star chart at the end of the chapter, or similar, to a student's desk or a group of student's desks. Use this idea to encourage kids to show kindness, improved organisation, better listening, a tidy table, working cooperatively and so on. Each time you notice something noteworthy from the group add a sticker to their star chart. The table with the most stars at the end of the week attracts a group reward. A word of caution: work it so that a group is never obviously disadvantaged by a student who can't do as well as the others. Clever adjustments have to be made otherwise this is a certain recipe for resentment and alienation.

Star of the day

At the end of each day a student is selected to become 'star of the day' for the next day. To start the day 'star of the day' is presented to the class and the teacher acknowledges their dazzling qualities to the class. This creates a deliberate opportunity to give positive feedback to the student. As other students offer their encouraging feedback as well, class cohesion is strengthened. A few teachers take 'star of the day' a little further. They introduce the 'star of the day' by presenting them to the class as a short, 'This is Your Life'. It's fun, and as students are given the opportunity to appreciate a little more about one another, friendships and tolerances have a better chance of success. Some educators ask the 'star of the day' to wear a glittering star and help out during the day.

Wheel of Fortune (and misfortune)

The Wheel of Fortune is a motivational tool with the capacity to:

- provide carefully planned competition and interaction between students;
- generate energy within the class, especially when I wish to review curriculum-based concepts;
- encourage students, who usually keep to themselves, to offer a little more;
- settle and unify the class;
- conclude or introduce a lesson with increased engagement.

The wheel is similar to a traditional 'chocolate wheel'. I've made it from thick riceboard and have attached it to a portable stand. The wheel itself is divided into nine evenly spaced sectors, and there are dollar amounts on most sectors: $20, $10, $5, two sectors of $2 and two sectors of $1. There is also a 'miss a turn' and a 'bankrupt' sector.

I first started using the Wheel of Fortune when I worked as the school's science teacher and worked between many classes, seeing one after another. I found it helped as a stimulus for students to positively manage their behaviour. Consequently, I have used it with students aged from about seven to thirteen years of age, and am sure it could be adapted for older students.

At the moment I use it with my own class and usually keep it teacher-directed. If, for example, I am asking questions and a student answers incorrectly, or hesitates for too long, the question is given to another student. Sometimes there is a short volley from one student to another. However, I have the right to answer the question after a pre-designated number of student tries. In this case, instead of a student taking the spin, I would. The students and I can 'bank' money or leave our earnings recorded, but at risk. Banked money is completely safe from bankruptcy. However, it costs the player 10 per cent to bank, so as they answer the question the decision to bank their earnings or leave them at risk must be made quickly.

The scoring system is simple. I use a grid that contains our names, under which the amount earned from each spin is recorded. Every so often I ask students to tally the amounts. As a rule, I choose two bankers each fortnight to record the money. This works well and delivers some good mathematical discussion.

The activity is a great vehicle to highlight to students just how much they know, and that getting something wrong from time to time is perfectly normal. I have seen students become far more comfortable with making mistakes when involved in this process. The wheel actually presents many teachable moments centred around curriculum topics, respect, helping, humility, current affairs, caring, fairness, organisation and team work. I may, for instance, notice a student helping another and as a way of providing strong positive feedback, invite that student to take a spin.

I suppose you are wondering how students spend their money? We generally brainstorm a series of incentives they might enjoy at the end of the term. In the past I have used pancake mornings and free time allotments that include sports, card games, board games, puzzles, listening to music and time on the computer to mention just a few. Usually, students in the group with the highest combined sum of money have first choice in choosing an incentive activity. However, there are of course many alternative ways to arrange incentive opportunities.

I will continue to use the Wheel of Fortune because the students love to play it. It tends to give whatever we are doing energy and freshness. It puts a sparkle into my students! Feel free to experiment with it, and adapt it to suit your needs.

Tania Masters, teacher

Catching helpful behaviours

A catching helpful behaviours chart can be found at the end of this chapter. Enlarge it on to A3 size paper, ask a group of students to colour it, add everyone's name to it and attach it to the classroom wall. The idea is that a sticker is handed to a student by the teacher as acknowledgement for great work, being respectful, showing a smile under difficult circumstances, good organisation or listening, having a neat desk and for cooperative moments. The student then places the sticker along the line with their name on it. As each student reaches a certain point on the chart, perhaps intervals of five, suggest they are entitled to a small incentive. This visual system works well, but as it is on public display make sure no one lags too far behind and feels disheartened.

Golden time

This is a popular idea used in many schools. Students are eligible to receive six 5-minute vouchers from their teacher during the week that they can trade in for golden time each Friday afternoon. Earning all six vouchers provides a student with 30 minutes of golden time. Golden time is usually play-based and offers a choice for students to play card games, board games and puzzles such as Connect 4, Mastermind, Jenga, Kerplunk or the more traditional games of chess, draughts and backgammon. Activities such as football, basketball, sewing, beading, origami, knitting, indoor bowls, air hockey, reading or listening to music are also popular. There is of course an array of variations teachers use with golden time. For example, each voucher may provide more time than 5 minutes and wild card vouchers, which have a double time value, can be drawn at random. Another variation is that every class member begins the week with 30 minutes of golden time. The idea is that they can lose golden time in 5-minute increments if they ignore reminders and don't do what is expected. Usually, once their golden time has finished students continue with finishing up work or quietly read. Kids of all ages love golden time.

Class superstars

The class teacher selects two students from their class who have shown effort during the week – anything from achieving a perfect score to making a wonderful personal effort. The names of the students are read out at year level or school assembly and each student is applauded as they receive a 'Superstar certificate'. Also accompanying this recognition is that the recipient may invite a friend to come along to a fun session provided by a member of the leadership team once a week.

Timers can help

As you well know, kids with AD/HD have genuine difficulty sustaining attention on tasks. As one of my colleagues mused, 'When he's on task he's hot, but when he's not he's not!' Timers can help students to see that those periods where sustained concentration is required are limited and will pass. Use them as a visual prompt to help a student persevere that little longer. Find different sorts of timers and fill your classroom with them – 3-minute egg timers, sand timers, water and bubble timers, goo timers, stopwatches – and allow students to use them as they tackle a task, leave class to go to the toilet, run an errand, finish off the last few maths problems or wait for lunch. Timers are strong visual reminders and can be enticing incentives to stay with a task for just a little longer.

Self-monitoring

The simple act of monitoring one's own efforts and responses can have a positive effect on behaviour because connections between what is happening and what is wanted become stronger (Reid 1996). The approach has long been used with success to help individuals quit smoking and lose weight. As an example, target just one behaviour you'd like to see a lot more of: saying 'yes', smiling, being emotionally steadier, being a friend, helping, being last, being first, completing tasks, being cooperative, recovering from disappointment, remembering homework and so on. Ask the student to record the behaviour you have agreed to track each time it happens. It's a good idea to run it at the same time of the day, each day, when the behaviour is required. Set up in the right way, self-monitoring invites participation while preserving the student's integrity. The outcome can be stunning, considering the approach requires so little work! The possibility also exists to build on to the process and achieve other negotiated targets and goals. You might also consider attaching incentives – a sweetener can really assist!

Student-monitoring

This is a useful tool for parents, teachers and students because it delivers a quick, systematic way to monitor a student's progress. It provides feedback on:

Find worksheet on page 206

- how well the challenges are being managed;

- the quality of the student's behavioural, social and emotional functioning;

- the student's work output;

- when adjustments to treatments and interventions should be considered.

We have long known that student progress improves when we constructively monitor performance and offer more frequent feedback (Rankin and Reid 1995; Reid and Harris 1993). This style of programme relies on the goodwill of a staff member to coordinate it. Completing the monitoring form only takes 5 minutes or so, and sharing it with the student on a regular basis aids in reflective discussion and stimulates new initiatives. The information collected through the system is designed to provide everyone with accurate baseline data, rather than being dependent on opinion, which can sometimes plummet when a behavioural or emotional hiccup occurs. The data helps everyone to make informed decisions about the effectiveness of management.

Choice of language

Develop your feedback so it is encouraging. If things didn't go so well, try, 'How do you think you might have done that differently?' It's much better than saying, 'You're always the one that upsets things!' Always be mindful of using the sandwich effect when giving feedback: a positive comment, a perceptive statement, followed by a positive comment.

Teach and model looking and listening skills

The kids, who are the focus of this chapter, seem to be chronically bad listeners and observers. They live with highly distractible traits and do not have the natural temperament to look, listen and remember. The consequence of this delay is debilitating. These kids are dependent on explicit and ongoing training that shows them how to do this.

Ideas to improve the looking and listening capacity of students:

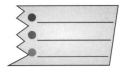

- Share that these are complex skills and without them it is impossible to accurately remember much at all. In fact, teachers and parents often mistakenly describe a student's poor listening and looking skills as poor memory. It all starts with the quality of looking and listening skills.

- Start by encouraging students to brainstorm behaviours that are suggestive of attentive listening and looking. Brainstorm each under the headings of head, eyes, ears, face, voice, arms, hands, body and what they need to look like to give themselves the very best chance to look and listen.

- Get kids to watch others (real or on DVD) and ask them to pick out the qualities they show that makes them great listeners and observers. Even our youngest are up to this.

- Play listening games to identify animal or environmental sounds. Listen to CDs to do this.

- Have fun with musical instruments and get students to copy rhythms.

- Play clapping games and ask students to copy your rhythm.

- Play a quick burst of 'Simon Says'. It can raise looking and listening readiness. Build out the degree of complexity by using three and four instructions such as clap your hands, click your fingers and stamp your feet.

- Read to students as often as you can. During the story, pause and ask various questions to ensure students are listening.

- Play the good fun listening game: 'When I went to the shop I bought some bread.' The next student says, 'When I went to the shop I bought some bread and a pizza.' The next student repeats the previous items and then adds their own, and so the game builds.

Tips for teachers to improve looking and listening readiness:

- Be a good listener yourself. Students model what they see and hear.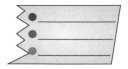

- As you deliver an important instruction hold up a visually impressive object to cue students into knowing that right now is a critical time to listen.

- To make a deliberate impact use a different voice, a different intonation or colourful language. It's strange, but the novelty factor heightens the ability to receive and remember information. Even try whispering!

- Count down from five to zero with students knowing that by the time you reach zero they need to be ready to look and listen.

- Or try, 'Watch the cards I'm holding. They're counting down from five. When zero comes you'll need to be ready to look and listen.'

- Playing a short burst of music or tapping 'tapping sticks' can be useful to tune kids in.

- Remind the student they need to start listening: use their name, or a key phrase you have developed together.

- When you have to, get down on the student's level and make eye contact.

- If necessary, gently touch them on the arm so their attention turns to you.

- As much as is practical, reduce auditory distractions so your voice prevails.

- Break instructions into small parts and keep them short and simple.

- Sometimes get the student to repeat back the instruction.

- Honestly aim to give instructions just once. This is hard because most of us all fall into the trap of repeating because we expect students will expect it. They condition us!

- If they can't remember the instruction, then repeat it, but only use key words i.e. 'maths, book, pencil'.

- Always praise kids for listening and responding well.

Attitude

How important is an optimistic attitude and who is in control of it?
   Discuss this passage:

The longer I live, the more I realize the impact of attitude on life.
   Attitude, to me, is more important than facts. It is more important than the past, than education, than money, than circumstances, than failures, than successes, than what other people think or say or do. It is more important than appearance, giftedness, or skill. It will make or break a company, a church, a home.

The remarkable thing is, we have a choice everyday regarding the attitude we will embrace for that day. We cannot change the past. We cannot change the fact that people will act in a certain way. We cannot change the inevitable. The only thing we do is play on the one string we have, that is attitude.

I am convinced that life is 10% what happens to me and 90% how I react to it.

And so it is with you . . . we are in charge of our attitudes.

(Swindoll 1982)

Self talk and attitude

Self talk concerns the conversations we have in our heads. As you know, sometimes we are able to talk ourselves up so we feel positive and confident, and then at other times, our inner critic begins to dominate and suddenly negative moods and thoughts take control of our thinking.

'Don't ask, everyone will laugh at you.'

'That's too hard for you.'

'It's boring. Do it later.'

'He's stupid anyway.'

'Everyone else's will be better.'

'That must be wrong.'

Explain to kids that swinging self talk is a normal human trait and it takes practice to control it. Play with ideas about how to switch negative self talk off and positive self talk on. It is worth the time because studies reveal that self talk training results in an increase in task persistence and helps to self-regulate learning and behaviour (Clinch 2000). Moreover, we know that students with AD/HD lack intrinsic self talk ability. This of course is why they are less task oriented.

An idea to get students thinking about the impact of self talk is to ask them to fill a page with the sorts of negative thoughts that creep into their thinking. It is best to brainstorm first to help trigger ideas and memories. Then ask them to create a new page of positive things they can say, or wish they could say to themselves, to combat negative talk. Kids of all ages enjoy sharing their thoughts and use the opportunity to add a few of the positive thoughts they glean from others. Finish up by having each student screw up their sheet of negative thoughts and throw it into the bin. Suggest they take the sheet of positive thoughts home and display it in a prominent place as a helpful reminder. Another way to highlight the difference between positive and negative self talk is to ask students to make rose-coloured glasses and black glasses (use cellophane lenses and pipe cleaners for the frames). Next, have students look at images of people facing a challenge. One striking way to do this is to use a gripping image on the interactive white board. Ask them to put on the rose coloured glasses and imagine themselves to be a person in the image. What would they say in their heads or to anyone else involved to positively self talk their way through the challenge? Then put on the black glasses, and discuss the negative self talk that is likely to occur. This is a great way for kids to experience and see the difference. I recall doing this with a group of Year 5 students. I chose Elijah to be the positive voice and another lad to be the negative voice in the activity. I should add that Elijah is highly impulsive, often shows aggression and deals with a pretty tough life at home. They both stared intently at the challenging image and offered a variety of ideas. Both generated a string of creative suggestions, but Elijah's positive self talk was on fire! After we'd finished, he came up to me and said, 'You know . . . I did good didn't I? I ought to listen to that stuff myself!'

A wonderful selection of invigorating ideas to restore and renew a sense of well-being for children is explored in Leigh Burrow's well researched publication, *Recreating the Circle of Wellbeing* (Burrows 2007).

Conclusion: more than knowledge

You've just scanned dozens of practical ideas to help modify for the inconsistencies and performance variability of students identified with short concentration spans, impulsivity and behavioural hiccups. No doubt you have also read books and journals, listened to presenters at conferences on the topic, surfed websites and exchanged information with colleagues and parents, but two central questions remain for you to consider.

First, how many of these strategies have you actually integrated into your classroom practice? In the end, the best way to influence a student's emotion, attitude or habit is to change what we do. Success is more than the acquisition of knowledge. It is placing the information and learning into action. All the best strategies involve setting routines, noticing and rewarding the behaviour we want, artfully avoiding public confrontations and modelling the behaviours we want from students. Second, what value do you assign to these kids? Do you see them as nuisance value, or do you value their potential? There is no doubt about it, working with kids who lack the capacity to apply what they have learned in the past at the very moment they need it is testing.

The wisdom of hindsight whispers it is most productive to see these young people as whole, healthy human beings with boundless potential, albeit less directed at the moment.

Worksheets

01   Think strips
02   Star chart
03   Catching helpful behaviours
04   Student-monitoring

Refer to p. 189 for useful websites and further reading.

Strategies to help organisation and memory
Inside tough kids with learning disabilities

Ask any youngster as they are about to enter school what they want to learn. Most will say, 'I want to learn to read and write'. Of course they do, after all, reading and writing is the mystifying and alluring language of the adult world. It's the place to aspire to.

This chapter is written for all the kids who set off to school intending to learn to read and write, remember and be organised and find success, but falter because of an unexpected and spectacular collection of invisible difficulties. Soon after starting school they realise their learning is not the same as the others. Every day the others read and write with apparent ease and scoot through the glorified reading boxes, while they struggle to crack the print code and burn with humiliation. This wasn't their dream. Shame quickly replaces the dream to read and write, and as it grows every kid ponders the question, 'How can I keep my dignity? What can I do to take the focus away from my learning?'

A few turn their shame inwards and stop trying because it's impossible to fail if they don't try. As the emotional pain grows into baggage too heavy to carry a few will give up and refuse to go to school. Others contemplate the incomprehensible because they see that this may be a better option than dealing with their shame in front of their peers every day. For those who prefer to act out their shame, the script plays out with surprising speed, volatile emotion and errant behaviour. Contrary attitudes are honed to perfection. Not being able to crack the code still hurts, but at least the child begins to gain recognition for something. And all the while, school continues, day in and day out, promoting reading, spelling and writing as the very essence of learning. How is it that any child with a severe learning difficulty can remain emotionally intact when the very heart of learning and recognition hinges completely on having adequate literacy skills?

Gradually educators are intelligently dismantling the traditional notion that students should only access information through the reading of print, and to prove their knowledge acquisition, produce print in essay-type formats. As one middle school student recently complained, 'Doesn't my history teacher get it? If he wants me to write essays all the time then all he's testing is my learning disability, and I'll just keep showing him that I've got a really bad one.'

Overview: specific learning disability

In the case of specific learning disability most teachers expect students to have problems in language and learning. Most know the universal link is the gap between a student's intelligence and the acquisition of their basic reading, writing, spelling and maths skills despite support by sound teaching practice. Most know that the term 'specific learning disability' usually incorporates conditions such as dyslexia (specific reading disorder), dyscalculia (specific calculation disorder) dyspraxia (speech) and dysgraphia (specific writing disorder) and may apply to one or two students in the class group. Arguably, that's about 10 per cent of the student population (Snowling 2000).

Most educators are aware of the associated behavioural characteristics. Early on children are more likely to show persistent difficulties pronouncing longer words and locating the right word when speaking. As they begin, school teachers notice difficulties in students' ability to acquire basic reading, writing and spelling skills. These students appear not to be keeping up and are quickly identified as underachieving. They may be able to spell a word verbally, but be unable to write it accurately: the link between sounds and letters (phonology) does not develop as it does for others. Their reading lacks the fluency and speed we generally expect. They consistently trip over small words, read words that are not there, keep forgetting the same simple word from one page to the next and regularly lose their place, having to rely on their finger to keep track. They sound out syllables as they read, but forget them before they are able to blend the entire word. Classically, they are identified with dyslexia. These are also the kids who can learn for their spelling test and gain good marks, however, when tested on the same spelling words two or three weeks later they achieve poorly. One of the common observations is the misspelling of the same words over and over, year in, year out. A further indicator of a specific learning disability may be their poorly developing written language. Dysgraphia is an impairment to write coherently, despite a student being able to read, think or verbally express their thoughts and opinions satisfactorily. The student may be bright enough, but find combining the complex mixture of tasks needed for a satisfactory written result is remarkably difficult. They are often slow to learn to write; they may experience letter reversal difficulties, produce inappropriately sized letters, mix upper and lower case letters, forget word spaces and produce untidy and inaccurate bookwork despite thorough instruction and opportunity to plan adequately. These students just cannot seem to formulate their thoughts on paper and their teachers often comment on the limited production of written work. Their memory difficulties may not be isolated to reading, spelling and writing, as mathematics can also present difficulties. Characteristic indicators of dyscalculia include regular number reversals (e.g. 37 becoming 73), all too frequent copying inaccuracies and continual misreading of written information so that mathematical outcomes are constantly skewed (Bird 2008). These students battle hard to remember maths symbols, often saying, 'that's an adding sign, isn't it?' They have great difficulty learning and retaining simple formulas, remembering the sequential steps involved in basic maths operations and recalling number patterns (especially the multiplication tables). This difficulty incessantly undermines mathematical confidence and progress.

Yet, a surprising number of seasoned educators are taken aback by the generalised weakened memory, concentration and organisation levels of students with specific learning disabilities. As school life becomes more demanding for students this invisible group of disorders can erode their organisation and prompt avoidance, time wasting, forgetfulness, the loss of belongings and disconnected or disruptive behaviour.

The inconvenience of organisation

'Arrrrgh, she's got a memory like a sieve.'

'She puts it off! She avoids! She forgets! Nothing ever gets done.'

'He loses everything!'

'I'll ask him to get on with it and within a few moments he's forgotten what he's meant to be doing!'

'His desk always looks like a rubbish tip, and worse still the mess seeps all around the classroom.'

Teachers often worry about the poor organisation and planning abilities of kids, especially those with learning difficulty. Unfortunately, engineering thoughtful structures, monitoring progress and reworking routines for students requires hard work (Salimpoor 2006). Some ideas are more effective than others, and most work for a while before they need a facelift to meet a new challenge. The reality is that plans to organise those who do not yet have the natural capacity to organise themselves consumes precious time and energy.

Now and again a teacher's annoyance with a student's continual disorganisation stimulates them to tighten their expectations as a means to initiate improvement. Typical of this was the teacher who became fed up over the organisational shortcomings of a twelve-year-old boy in her class. Will was a friendly kid who had not found much success at school. His dyslexic difficulties in combination with inattentive ADD had convinced him early on that he was 'dumb'. Each year Will's school reports repeated the same inattention and organisational inadequacies highlighted years ago in his psychological assessment. His reports referred to his efforts as lazy, inconsistent, untidy, disorganised and poorly motivated. Little wonder Will had lost confidence and felt disconnected from school. During the conversation with his teacher I gently raised the issue of providing him with a little scaffolding – some reminders and new routines to help him finish off the day so he might have a better chance to fill in his school diary and get it home along with the right books to tackle his homework. However, she bristled over my suggestion. 'Mark,' she said, 'if we do this for him he'll never learn to do it himself. He's old enough to think about what he must do and take the consequences when he chooses not to remember.'

For her, the matter was black and white.

For me, and for many others who know much more than I do, there are shades of grey we need to navigate intelligently, especially when learning disabilities are at play. To settle on this rigid, corrective approach may have been convenient for this teacher, but it offered nothing in the way of developing a framework of structures, tips and ideas to strengthen Will's delayed organisational abilities. What Will's situation illustrates is that it's too easy to misread or misunderstand the underlying causes of memory and planning difficulties. When a specific learning disability exists in isolation it can easily compromise a student's social, emotional and academic domains. However, when a specific learning disability coexists with something else, ADHD, ADD or Asperger syndrome, their impact can be disabling.

Building structures and routines

Most students do not set out to be deliberately poorly organised, forgetful or to fail to do well at school. Some are victims of depressed or chaotic home lives. Some have obvious identifiable difficulties. Others are simply not ready, and because of this, do not yet have the set of higher-order independent organisational skills required to find success. Accepting that all students do best when working in a thoughtfully developed climate of routine, order and structure is the best understanding. Organisationally challenged students rely on us to build and maintain routines to ease their natural confusion. There is no other way! And, the great spark of hope is that tricks and triggers to remind and memory jog are endless. So be creative and seize on anything that helps the forgetful or distracted mind to sort priorities and stay with the task:

- setting timers
- an elastic band around a wrist
- a string on the finger
- the same habits
- establishing a routine
- sticky notes with reminders
- a key word
- a stamp
- a tick on a chart
- an intermittent beep from a CD
- a telephone call
- an email
- a text message
- countdowns
- charts
- pictures
- a look
- a smile

- schedules
- timetables
- checklists
- calendars
- daily or weekly timetables
- fortnightly or monthly planners
- the same repetitive reminding joke
- the same silly smile
- a sound
- an aroma
- the same background music to trigger the memory
- a touch
- a gesture
- a message left on the desk
- a note to be found later
- a sign taped to a chair, the diary or locker
- cue cards.

Providing structure means arranging the conditions in the classroom to give every student the best chance to function well. Poorly organised kids depend on prompts about when tasks need to be tackled, what comes next and the belongings required. Start by setting up places where things belong and play with ideas to encourage students to do things the same way, at the same time, every day:

- encourage students to arrive at school at the same time each day;

- hats always go on the hook or in a box;

- school bags in the locker or on the assigned hook;

- school diaries placed in the diary box;

- homework placed in the homework box;

- notes or communication from parents placed in the mailbox;

- check the white board to find out the morning lessons and what materials are required;

- school books on the desk ready to start the day;

- as students enter the classroom in the morning have them reach for their notebooks and solve the 'QQF' – a question, a quote, and a fact – displayed on the board;

- a sign to illustrate how to keep a neat desk;

- pencil case and ruler on the desk;

- complete the lunch order;

- empty lunch boxes returned to the bag after eating;

- a verbal or visual reminder about what is required to take to specialist subjects;

- time for homework to be recorded in the school diary at the end of the lesson or day;

- time for the books and materials required for homework to be gathered up and placed in the bag;

- replace the novel or reader with a new one;

- activity materials returned to the appropriate activity box;

- time at the end of the lesson or day to place the diary in the schoolbag packed and zip it up.

Ideas to manage time, task and belongings

Many kids beyond those formally identified with a difficulty, disability, disorder or deficit find schoolwork requiring independent research extraordinarily challenging; they face uncertainty about how to begin, where to begin and what to use, they're unsure where to find the information, become confused about prioritising what's important and can feel overwhelmed by the process. In the end, the task can become so daunting that they'd rather let it slip by than tackle it.

There are strategies to support all kids who show procrastination, poor planning and time management difficulties with larger, long-term project-based work:

- Always provide a task sheet with the topic and assessment criteria clearly stated.

- Design the task sheet so it's concise and uncluttered. A task sheet ensures students have the opportunity to read and re-read instructions. It also helps parents to understand the task, rather than having to rely on unreliable student recall.

- Offer a list of specific websites and texts students can consult. The provision of specific websites is much better than allowing students to become lost surfing the net as they try to 'google' information.

- Create a progress checklist: a check of what needs to be done helps to keep students on track.

- Give those one or two students who put things off a jump-start by organising yourself, an older student, another teacher, a school support officer or a tutor to spend two or three sessions with them early on.

- Provide the student with opportunities to talk through how they intend to tackle the task: create mind maps, word webs, drawings, dot points and sketches. It's worth exploring the computer programs Inspiration and Kidspiration (www.inspiration.com). These allow learners to flexibly organise their ideas on the computer screen. They help students to collect and sequence ideas for assignments or provide a means to keep track of what is happening in each chapter of the novel they have read. Later, this information can be converted to a word document or a PowerPoint™ presentation. By talking through the logical order of what needs to be done enhances motivation and the chances of success (Buzan 2003).

- Together keep an eye on the time. Check in frequently by creating review times. During these times review what has been done and work on solutions to avoid the difficulties you instinctively know will arise. At each of these times break down the remaining tasks into smaller, more easily managed pieces so the student really knows what to do.

- Every individual learns best when the task presented is meaningful to them. This helps to secure their engagement. Sometimes tasks become more meaningful by shortening, modifying and making them more manageable.

- Maintain a routine. Incorporate the activity into every day, until the task is done. Remember, the success of these kids is very dependent on poised adult management.

- Encourage the student to record what they have done on a 'progress checklist' as this will help them arrive at the end point at the same time as their peers. Take a look at the chunking form provided at the end of the book. It may deliver instant help!

- Home help is vital, so develop ideas and opportunities for parents to know what is happening and how to best support their child.

- Once students reach middle primary it's time to teach them how to use 'AutoSummarize' effectively (www.microsoft.com). This easy to use technology can identify the key points in electronically downloaded articles and reports. Although the summarising is not perfect it is easy to use and highlights the key points from each piece of reading. It is well worth a look at because it is very useful.

- Be patient. It takes longer for the kids who are the focus of this book to gain independent research-based skills. They rely on plenty of opportunity to watch, listen, discuss and participate ways to read, research, chunk and present information. Supportive structures do help students to conquer planning and stay in control of managing time.

- Finally, there is a crucial component worth coaching parents about. No matter what the age of the child, if they choose not to participate in constructive plans to support their time and task management, parents need to withdraw from becoming caught up in the typical last minute emotionalism over assignments that are due in the next day. Give parents permission to decline such demands. Remind parents who regularly help out at the eleventh hour that the message they give to their son or daughter is, 'Why should you take seriously any of the planning ideas we've put in place? After all, I will, at the last moment, always rescue you.'

Reduce books, folders and possessions

This is a lead set by shrewd educators. Instead of leaving poorly organised students with an unwieldy batch of exercise books their teachers pare them to a minimum. Then, they colour-code the covers and arrange for two subjects to be worked in each book: one subject beginning at the front and the other starting from the back. The combination of having fewer books to sort through and knowing the red covered book is for maths, quick maths and graphs makes keeping track of their books so much easier.

Work in progress folder

Rather than risking task sheets and bits of paper getting lost at home, around the classroom, or worse, somewhere in between, encourage all of your students to use a brightly coloured plastic folder to keep assignments that are 'in progress' in. Once the assignment is done and handed in, the folder is cleared ready for a new task. It's a very straightforward system that allows work to be located in one spot.

School bags

It is challenging for disorganised students to keep all manner of things ordered, and keeping school bags organised is doubly hard. The ideal approach is to not allow schoolbag chaos to become an issue of consequence. Instead, make an arrangement with the student's parents that once a week they'll go through the bag with their child. Promote the idea that the student takes the leading role as they sort through their bag and the parent takes more a reminding and supportive function. Remind them that they will be amazed by what they discover in their child's bag: notes, newsletters, library books, lunch bags, toys, collector cards and foods that have scrunched their way to the bottom of the bag. So many students say what a great feeling it is to begin the new week knowing exactly what is in their bag! Finally, if you think this approach is only suitable for young children, you couldn't be more wrong. This is an approach I consistently use with motivated, but disorganised students in the upper years of high school. Carried out with respect, it works beautifully!

Drawers and lockers

If we know our poorly organised students can't control the growth of mess then it is up to us to tactfully manage this with them. A good idea is to set up an arrangement with your student that you, their parent or a school support officer will stay back in the classroom with them one afternoon each fortnight to go through their locker or drawer with them. So many students will tell you just how much they really hate their lockers being in a mess, but don't know how to tackle the problem or maintain it independently.

Case study

Clarkey's locker

It was too hard for thirteen-year-old Clarkey to keep his locker tidy and organised. As much as he wished for this, and try as he might, by the end of a week or so his locker was a confusion of crumpled notes and papers, overdue library books, pencils, texta colours, expired food and bits and pieces brought from home. This made finding things between lessons near impossible and in part was the cause for his frequent lateness to classes. In response, his kind home group teacher set up an arrangement so that at the end of each fortnight Clarkey would empty everything from his locker into his school bag to take home. Clarkey and his father would clean through the belongings over the weekend so everything was sorted and ready to be returned to the locker first thing on Monday morning. Clarkey loved the idea because it worked!

The pencil case

Ensure each student owns and regularly uses a pencil case. A great idea is to keep a small laminated checklist inside the pencil case so there is no mistake about what needs to be in it. By the way, this is especially applicable for those students who continually collect up odds and ends to store in their pencil case. This adds to pencil case confusion. Each fortnight remind parents to reorganise and restock the pencil case with the basic requirements.

Ideas to improve memory

Note-taking

These techniques do not come easily to students with distractible traits or to those with learning difficulties. Start by explicitly teaching students how to highlight notes and create notes. Try providing lesson notes to students and expect them to highlight the central points during the lesson. Encourage kids to draw pictures or make a simple comic strip to record key ideas. This works as well for a chapter in science as it does for recording what happened in each chapter of the novel. Sometimes photocopying the notes of another student and asking the student with the learning difficulty to highlight the key points is useful.

Teach test-taking skills

Use low-key tests as an ordinary teaching vehicle to assist students to learn more effectively (Elliot and Thurlow 2006). Assess manageable portions of information continuously. This is such a help for students with poor concentration and those who suffer from anxiety. Some students become deeply convinced that the purpose of testing is to expose their learning weaknesses.

Teach memory helping techniques

Memory weaknesses are common within this group of students, so teach ideas to underpin memory. Make a game out of the things that need to be remembered. Employ some of those basic junior primary games to help remembering. Secondary students love them because they work! Remembering tricks like acronyms, mnemonics, flash cards, rhymes, silly ditties, drawing pictures to scaffold ideas and concepts are sensible, sustainable supports.

The piggyback technique

Piggybacking is an appealing strategy to put together something a student tends to forget with something that is part of their everyday routine. Piggybacking can work for lots of things, both at home and school. It's the very reason most of us leave our car keys hanging from the lock on the back door. Piggyback combinations are endless!

Case study

Sam's school diary and Neighbours

In complete desperation Mandy delivered the ultimate piggyback challenge to her twelve-year-old son, Sam. He was passionate about watching *Neighbours* every week night and was far less passionate about bringing his school diary home or accurately recording his homework tasks. Sam was willing enough to do homework, but without the homework being recorded his poor listening and memory often let him down. When watching *Neighbours* became directly linked to Mandy having to see Sam's school diary filled in each night, the age old diary problem was a problem no longer!

Prompts

Prompts enhance the performance of students. Just as they serve us, they assist kids to remember, plan, feel organised, return to task, finish off tasks and maintain momentum. Everyone has a preference, and part of the craft of teaching is to discover which mode works best to optimise the memory, organisation and persistence for the students we teach. Some do better when they can see what they need to do (visual prompts) because the listening load is too heavy to carry and overwhelms them. Others respond more effectively to the spoken word (auditory prompting). Prompts can be delivered so they appeal to the tactile, fragrant, auditory and visual senses. The best suggestion is to regularly employ a combination of prompts and this section is designed to stimulate a few ideas.

Tactile prompting

This requires minimal effort and can be as simple as a touch on the arm or placing a soft foam ball in the student's hand to deliver the message to persevere a little longer. This silent action immediately opens a link for the student to override their habitual style to procrastinate, drift off or forget. A prearranged tactile prompt is effective because it inconspicuously redirects a student's attention without the loss of their dignity.

Fragrant prompts

Fragrant reminders are not widely used. Perhaps it's because they're less convenient and may pose a health and safety issue. Nevertheless, a number of teachers believe the aroma from an essential oil is helpful (try www.aromaweb.com). Rosemary and lime are frequently recommended to enhance concentration, cedarwood and frankincense are used as relaxing agents and anger is said to be tamed by bergamot, jasmine and neroli. Some believe that by asking a student to rub an oil essence onto the back of their hands when quiet and concentration are needed, students are better able to persevere. Others vow that burning an oil burner during classes that require sustained concentration delivers an improvement in student performance. Such improvements are most likely linked to a phenomenon called time–place cueing. That is, by doing the same thing, in the same way, at virtually the same time each day a series of potent but subtle messages about how things need to be is drip fed into a student's memory.

Visual prompts

A visual prompt is any visual option to support a student's understanding about what to do, when to do it and how to do it. These ideas usually include: schedules, timetables, stamps, charts, sticky notes with reminders, an email or text message, pictures, PowerPoint™ presentation, lists, dot point instructions, checklists, calendars, the same silly smile, notes, signs, messages, cue cards and even a string tied to a finger (Savner and Smith–Myles 2000). For additional information on the building of visual strategies browse through the section called, 'visual strategies' in Chapter 6.

Case study

'*A visual strategy can be the difference between success and failure for some.*'

'I recall working with a dyslexic nine-year-old and we were tackling sequencing and story building skills. What happened in our session highlighted the importance of visual scaffolding for these kids. I was checking to see if he had a grasp of the temporal concepts we use in our everyday language and when writing narratives, specifically the words 'before' and 'after'. When I asked what day comes before Tuesday or what day comes after Thursday he just couldn't do it. However, when the days of the week were written down in a calendar format the same task was easy for him to do. This experience highlights that a visual strategy can be the difference between success and failure for some kids. Just because a student doesn't seem to understand doesn't necessarily mean they don't understand. What made the difference was that he had a visual reference to work from.'

Marney Yates, Speech Pathologist and Director of TALK

The class timetable

Just as contemporary educators discuss, develop and display class rules to build a caring and cohesive group, a well developed class timetable delivers similar benefits. A large class timetable displayed so it is visible to everyone in the classroom is a great starter and takes on efficacy when students know that their teacher consistently follows it and reviews it when changes need to be made. All students are reassured by knowing what to expect.

Morning lessons and materials required

As students begin to enter the classroom first thing in the morning many teachers already have the morning lessons and materials required written on the whiteboard. In this way students can see how the morning will unfold and know the things they need.

Class-monitor systems

Some develop extensive class–monitor systems and rotate them regularly so students are thoroughly connected to the systems and to one another. This is crucial to help kids feel as though they are a part of things.

Personalised mini daily timetables

Find worksheet on page 208

Having a student pick up their personalised mini daily timetable from the teacher's desk each morning can be both organisationally beneficial and emotionally stabilising for some. In the case of students identified with Asperger syndrome, they often have a strong need to know what is going to happen so they can prepare for it. When they can't work out what is going on they can easily become anxious, disconnected and unsettled.

Homework and homework timetables

On the surface homework seems a perfectly simple idea, and for quite a few it is. Kids who eagerly embrace it please their parents and teachers as they commit to this unique learning process. They find homework stimulating, relevant and useful. For these students homework enhances learning and connects the family to school life. Yet, the reality for the students who are the focus of this book, those battling learning difficulties, immaturity, concentration problems, impulsiveness, mood swings or chaotic home lives, is that regular homework practice is tricky to achieve. These kids rely on our insight and resourcefulness to reduce and modify tasks to make homework manageable and meaningful for them (Bryan *et al.* 2001). For a few others, however, the problems surrounding homework are far more serious. Their poor connection to homework is just the tip of the iceberg. Sometimes the best decision for these kids and their families, is to do away with homework altogether, for a while or forever.

Great teachers can nourish the endeavour of students and parents to get the homework conundrum right. A good starting point is to help students to make their own homework timetables. Organise for the class to fill in a blank 'after school timetable'. Ask students to record each of their regular weekly activities: must watch television programmes, dance lessons, scouts, karate, time to play computer games and so on. In this way they quickly see that little time is expected for homework compared to the total amount of leisure time they have. Suggest they select the best time for homework for each day and draw up a neat, colour-coded timetable. Recommend they place it in a prominent position so that the planned homework time has value.

Find worksheet on page 209

There is also value in presenting the 'homework essentials, for students' list below to students of all ages. These provide a wonderful catalyst for realistic discussions and the development of shared practical understandings. Without this sort of dialogue around homework we shouldn't be shocked when kids become expert at avoiding and sabotaging it.

Homework essentials, for students

- Find a spot that works. Best places are bedrooms, the kitchen, the dining room table, or the study. Try working in the same spot at the same time so it becomes your routine.

- Working in front of the television doesn't work when it comes to thinking your way through a maths problem, learning spelling or writing. Although, if you have a picture or map to draw, colouring in or cutting out and gluing, then it is fine to do this in front of television (always do the thinking parts first).

- Make a daily timetable and display it on the wall. Try to start your homework early. Get it out of the way! A routine helps to keep a balance between fun and homework.

- If you don't do your homework then expect your teacher to get you to do it at a time that is not so good for you the next day.

- Your homework does not have to be perfect. It just needs to be done.

- If you like using your computer, and it helps, talk to your teacher and parents about using it more often.

- When you do not understand a question, ask for help. Listen. Then, insist mum or dad moves away. Never let them do your homework for you because teachers soon work that out.

- If you often don't know what to do for homework, or come home with the wrong books, ask your teacher to set up homework reminders to help you. Most teachers are happy to help out.

- It shouldn't matter whether you like homework or not. Think of it as a way to practice doing something someone else wants you to do. This way of thinking is truly a skill.

- Figure out how you work best. Some go to their homework spot and stay focused until they are finished. That's great if you can. Others need to take a short break between each part. Some need a snack and wind down time after school. Others do it straightaway. Experiment and find out what works for you!

- *Never* let mum or dad turn your homework into, 'now, lets teach you how to do this,' unless you want it to happen. If they think there is something they should teach you, tell them to arrange it at a different time and make sure they use the same methods and words to teach as your teacher does.

- Sometimes homework looks as though it's going to be hard. Your first thought might be to not do it. Instead, say to yourself, 'First, I'll read the instructions'. 'I'll do one thing at a time'. Start by thinking out loud and talking to yourself. It will help you to make your way through each task.

- When you finish your homework put it into your bag. Then go and enjoy yourself!

Planners

Find worksheets on pages 210–11

The idea of constructing a planner onto a whiteboard and making a point of adding and deleting things as they crop up with the class is a popular idea. This practice immerses students into knowing what's coming up, and when they forget, they can look at it! Alternatively, use the largest wall calendar you can find and hang it up for all to see. Have students participate as you record due dates of their assignments, up and coming school excursions, events and so on. As plans change, discuss the changes with students and make alterations. As this becomes routine your students will begin to see the value of this visually striking and very practical visual tool.

School diary

The school diary has the potential to be an uplifting planning and communication tool, but the reality is there's more to it than simply issuing the diary and expecting a win. When your instincts shout that the diary will not work for a particular student become inventive and create alternative reminding and remembering systems:

- faxing
- emailing
- personal organisers
- USBs
- iPods
- mailing work
- texting

- telephoning
- a dictaphone carried between home and school
- leaving messages on answering machines
- placing photos of the homework onto the student's mobile phone.

Another idea is to use a diary buddy. Schedule an accomplished student to help fill out a less organised classmate's diary each afternoon. Train the buddy to maintain the same method each day: filling in the diary, clearing the desk, returning used items, gathering belongings needed for homework and placing them into their school bags. Try the system for a term using several diary buddies, so they do not wear out. Then allow the student who has been helped to become a diary buddy to someone else.

Grab their attention!

When it's time to explain something or give an instruction, and you think the information is vital, hold up a brightly coloured object as you speak. Alternatively, slip on something visually striking – a hat, a coat, a jacket, plastic glasses, a plastic nose, a scarf or a glove! Use the same thing every time. Despite how you may look to others, this is a powerful visual prompt to remind students that now is the moment to look, listen and remember. Teachers who use this to perfection don't overplay it and rarely repeat the instruction once it is given. Otherwise, there is no incentive for a student to listen when it really matters.

Case study

'It's on the sandwich board'

You might like to emulate Frank's approach. It's novel and works! To get the attention of his senior high school students he walks into class with vital information written on his red sandwich board. As he places the red sandwich board on his desk his students scramble to read the information written in bold, black text. Frank does not utter a sound and students in his classes know that not to read it and fail to remember it is at their own peril. Frank doesn't overplay it, but when it comes out it always contains a single important message:

'Maths test is Thursday. Review Chapter 4. I like the look of pages 223 and 225.'

'Friday 15th March is the day to have subject selections handed to me. Mark it in your diary. If you have any problem I need to know tomorrow.'

'Everyone is complaining about quadratic equations. I don't blame you. I'm available after school today, Wednesday and Thursday in room 10 to help you. See you there. Bring sweets!'

The look

A look is worth a thousand words. The messages received from facial expressions convey a wonderful silent language. Teach kids how to read your face and interpret your critical expressions. Alternatively, if they feel unsure about what to do, teach them to use a signal to alert you that they need help. Develop simple cues together; a wink, a scratch of the head or touching your nose sends a message to help modify behaviour. Work on the cues together so they operate both ways. The bonus is that it will strengthen your bond too. Rehearse it to a point where you can simply look at a particular student, use the cue and they know what you mean and what to do (Rogers 2003).

Highlighters can help

A highlighter can make a world of difference to a student's remembering, understanding and organisation. A good start is to teach young children to scan text and highlight key words and phrases. Obvious places to begin are highlighting the information in school newsletters, proofreading work and prioritising research information. Using a highlighter also offers the chance for kids to sort through information while using their busy fingers. Eventually, your student's senior secondary teachers will appreciate this early input. They often lament over their students' inability to efficiently highlight relevant text.

Progress charts

Find worksheets on pages 212–13

Make a simple chart that shows the number of individual parts that make up the entire task. Encourage students to colour, stamp or place a sticker on each part of the chart as they complete each sub-task. This really supports perseverance. Another innovative idea is to hand a number of cards that match the number of sub-tasks involved in the activity. Each card might contain a subheading and a brief explanation. As the student completes a sub-task they place the matching card in a box. When all cards are in the box the task is done!

Lists and checklists

Find worksheet on page 214

Most of us panic when we're suddenly caught without our list. Whether it's for shopping or for work our list reminds us what needs to be done and encourages us to prioritise. Yet, we often forget to teach and strengthen this ordinary, effective remembering strategy. The best idea is to keep the list in the same place and make sure it can be easily accessed. Arrange for students to keep their list on their desk or hanging on the side of their desk so they can add to it, delete things they have completed and live with it as a part of their daily routine. Oh, don't forget to attach a pencil to the list! Checklists are also valuable because they can be set up to contain word or picture prompts that can sequence the task into smaller steps. They don't take long to make on the computer, or alternatively, they can be bought from stationers and newsagencies. As for lists, a checklist is best attached where it is most likely to capture the student's attention and trigger their memory. Also remember, kids benefit when they see their teacher working from their list or checklist on the board!

Auditory prompts

Auditory prompts include anything from a friendly whisper of encouragement to openly shouting, 'Oi! Drop it. It bites!' The style educators most frequently rely on in the classroom is auditory prompting. That is, using our voices all day to give instructions and deliver requests, directions, orders, reminders and reprimands. While calling out instructions may seem efficient to us, it is obvious that many students simply switch us off as they become teacher-deaf. For many of the tough kids, the spoken instruction is precisely what they miss. As they mishear, miss out or forget, even a relatively simple task looks too taxing right from the very beginning. Never overlook the value of whispering or miming an instruction, or saying one puzzling word or phrase that makes students turn to you and wait for more to be said. Try anything that changes the predictable auditory prompt into something new and unexpected!

Say it and write it

As much as you can, back up verbal instructions with written prompts. One way to do this is to record brief dot points on the board for students to refer back to later. Alternatively, draw a simple illustration or a silly stick figure to highlight the essence of the information or to emphasise what needs to happen next. Listening memory difficulty is an infuriating problem and can undermine a child's self-confidence. So often it leaves kids feeling as though they must rely on others.

Pair instructions

Develop a habit where you consistently state instructions in pairs to certain students. Before you know it these students will automatically expect to remember two items every time you ask something of them. For instance, 'Grab the book from my desk and put it in my mail box in the staffroom' or 'Go to the G7 class next door and bring back the newspapers for art'. There is always scope to build this approach out. At the next level instructions can be grouped into three, say, 'I want you to remember three things. One, clear up your desk! Two, put your homework in your schoolbag! Three, return to me carrying your lunchbox!'

Repeat it

State the instruction and have the student repeat it.

'What?'

When a student calls out, 'What did you say I had to do?' try replying with, 'Tell me what you need to do?' It sounds odd, but this curious response encourages the learner to rethink and remember independently. It is a valuable strategy to help students to reach a little more deeply into their listening memory.

A keyword prompt

Develop 'keywords'. For example, when a situation becomes emotional and tension starts to build, use a predetermined keyword such as 'break-time' or 'walk' to indicate time out is needed. This gives everyone time to regain their composure.

Pre-teach

Pre-teaching or giving information a day or so before it is required, improves a student's capacity to understand and perform when they need to use it. This may be about what's going to happen on the following day, and by giving them the advantage of processing new information overnight they are likely to deal with the upcoming events more easily.

Conclusion: what can a busy teacher do to help kids with learning difficulties?

Offer reassurance

Students are reassured when they know their teacher understands the difficulty they face. One of the best ways to do this is by maintaining an optimistic dialogue (Pavey 2007). Openly discuss the sorts of special provisions, modifications and curriculum adjustments available and quickly get the most helpful in place (Bender 2007; Byrnes 2008). Set up a practical, respectful option for the student to use when busy subject teachers or relieving teachers forget their needs. A popular idea for both primary and secondary students is the development of a student access card. The access card can be fastened into the back of the student's diary with the special provisions highlighted so it is easy for all teachers to see. For students identified with Asperger syndrome, learning difficulties or AD/HD the access card is likely to state at least several of the options below:

- exemption from reading aloud in class;

- student to receive handouts instead of copying notes from the board;

- supervision of diary entries for homework;

- follow up of homework the next day;

- this student has a modified homework programme;

- a 5-minute break from class is allowed each lesson when requested;

- extra time in tests and exams;

- a 5-minute break during tests or exams for every half an hour when requested;

- use of computer in lessons and tests;

- use of calculator in lessons and tests (Bouck and Bouck 2008);

- use of hand held spell checker in lessons and tests;

- assistance with organisational strategies when planning an assignment;

- work to be marked without penalty in relation to spelling and grammar;

- 'study buddies' have been organised in each class to support the student;

- provision of a reader in tests;

- provision of a scribe in tests;

- provision of a scribe and a reader in tests;

- permission to be given if the student wishes to leave the classroom and go to the special education centre.

Let kids see that you and the school can keep them connected

- Investigate how their difficulty is recognised by the Government and their education system.

- Invite guest speakers into school from appropriate organisations to highlight to students how their difficulties are compensated for. It is heartening for students to know that they are not the first in the world to experience the difficulty and that people really do know how to help them succeed (Purkis 2006).

- Students with confounding issues benefit from having a Negotiated Education Plan, an Individualised Educational Programme or some form of recognition. Once this recognition is applied, either formally or informally, it allows all staff to understand and cater more appropriately for the student's needs and reduces the risk of inept conclusions being made by busy teachers or subject focused teachers.

- Every so often read a book, or an inspirational excerpt, to students written by someone with Asperger syndrome or some sort of learning difficulty (Jackson 2002; Green 2008). Occasionally invite a motivational guest speaker to school who has made it despite the challenge of their difficulty.

- Unite students with learning difficulties. This can be as easy as making the learning centre welcoming for students. At one school, the Adaptive Education Centre is the place to be! It offers hot chocolate in winter, cool drinks in summer and the opportunity for casual conversations where students can plan assignments, have drafts reviewed, debrief and offload their worries.

- Take understandings to a new level and organise an advisory group of students to have input into the school's special provision policy. As you well know, all manner of issues crop up in schools that an advisory group can deal with. Two recent issues taken to an advisory group included a Year 10 maths teacher who explained to his modified maths class that none of them could achieve an 'A' because that would be unfair to the students in regular maths classes! Then there was Kat, a Year 4 student, with a serious learning difficulty. Her teacher insisted that all students fastened the spelling contract into their exercise book each week. Poor Kat spent all of her time flipping pages because she could only ever remember two or three letters in a word at a time. The process was torturous. To give her relief the school support officer photocopied her spelling contract so Kat could keep the extra one nearby to look at to save on flipping pages. The upshot was that Kat and the school support officer were reprimanded by the teacher. The teacher's mistaken explanation was, 'How would Kat's memory ever improve if she was offered the additional sheet?'

Go multi-sensory

These kids, more so than most, tend to be better at receiving and processing information when it is provided in as many modalities as possible – seeing, touching, hearing and doing – rather than just listening. Most know that when kids are engaged in hands-on activities the quality of their learning increases. Gradually educators are beginning to appreciate the significance of individual learning styles and that it is legitimate to draw on a diverse range of products to support learning styles: surveys, debates, jingles, concept maps, simulations, lyrics, experiments, dances, conferences, slide shows, class meetings, newsletters, story maps, charades, collages, designs, sociograms, interviews, raps, personal journals, DVDs, opinion polls, lists, calligraphy, recipes, audio tapes, illustrations, etc.

Rely on visual supports

Students with learning difficulty regularly struggle with the auditory processing load, and because of this develop a heightened visual awareness. The visual detail can be processed with far greater accuracy because it is longer lasting and can be accessed for longer. Verbal instructions or information is so much more transient.

Organise together

As we develop routines and participate in a student's organisation we place them in a position of learning readiness. As comprehensively explored in this chapter the use of constructive talk, diaries, planners, schedules, rosters, routines and the colour coding of books for different subject areas can help. Work with the student to discover their preferences.

Set realistic goals

These kids always need a goal to aim for! The setting of a small, achievable goal, with or without incentives, supports them to see their improvement rather than living with an attitude that it's all too hard and overwhelming. As they see progress towards the goal they are far more likely to feel that they want to achieve because they are achieving (Le Messurier 2004).

Boost confidence

A few years ago a wonderful educator, Loretta Giorcelli, raised an emotionally healthy concept termed 'Islands of Competence' (Giorcelli 2000). Her idea was for teachers to design various forums for students to showcase their interests, talents, accomplishments, ideas and dreams to the class. In this way, students had the chance to present themselves so others could see and hear what they were skilled or interested in. The upshot of course is connecting deeper appreciations between students. Mediums for kids to showcase themselves abound and may include: a short film, a slide show, a photographic display, a poster, a news report, a cartoon set, art or craft, dance, a brochure or newsletter, music, song, role-play, a personal time line or the opportunity to teach a skill to a younger group of students. Without this sort of recognition Giorcelli felt it was too easy for kids with learning difficulties to feel lost in continents where they felt incompetent.

Use a reading programme

Kids with reading difficulties require a reading approach that is explicitly designed to meet their learning needs and the earlier the intervention takes place the better (Bender and Larkin 2003; Boyle 2008). Any reading programme will not do. Edward Kame'enui, Professor of Education at the University of Oregon and the first Commissioner of the National Centre for Special Education Research, promotes *5 Big Ideas in Beginning Reading* as guiding principles (www.reading.uoregon.edu/big/ideas/):

1 *Phonemic Awareness.* The ability to hear and manipulate sounds in words (Gillon 2005).

2 *Alphabetic Principle.* The ability to associate sounds with letters and use these sounds to form words (James and Kerr 2004).

3 *Fluency with Text.* The effortless, automatic ability to read words in connected text (Cohen and Cowen 2008).

4 *Vocabulary.* The ability to understand and use words to acquire and convey meaning (Lubliner 2005).

5 *Comprehension.* The complex cognitive process involving the intentional interaction between reader and text to convey meaning (Carlisle 2002).

Research indicates that proficiency in each of the *5 Big Ideas in Beginning Reading* are good predictors of success in learning to read (www.nationalreadingpanel.org). As well, never overlook the advice and support available from passionate and experienced personnel within your system who work in the reading difficulties area. In many cases they are a source of knowledge, resources and inspiration.

Finally, as a means to supplement a planned approach there are many free educational websites that teach and consolidate essential literacy and numeracy skills. They are interactive and fun. Explore:

• Chateau Meddybemps, www.meddybemps.com/funandgames.html
  Suitable for preschool children through to lower primary aged students; reading, writing and maths

- BBC School for Phonics and Letter-Blend Activities, www.bbc.co.uk/schools/wordsandpictures/index.shtml
  Suitable for preschool and junior primary aged students; spelling and reading

- FunBrain.com for reading, maths games and puzzles, www.funbrain.com
  Suitable for preschool children through to lower secondary aged students; reading, maths and spelling

- Starfall.com for letter sounds and reading activities, www.starfall.com
  Suitable for preschool kids; reading

- National Library of Virtual Manipulatives, http://nlvm.usu.edu/en/nav/vlibrary.html
  Maths activities for all ages and all abilities

- Arcademic Skill Builders for educational maths and word games, www.arcademicskillbuilders.com
  Suitable for junior primary kids through to students in middle primary years; reading, spelling and maths

- SoftSchools.com for maths, handwriting, phonics and language activities, www.softschools.com/games/games.jsp
  Suitable for junior primary kids through to students in middle primary years; maths, writing, spelling and language

- Mathematics Resources by Topic and Number for number facts, quizzes and times tables, www.teachers.ash.org.au/mikemath/resources/number.html
  Suitable for middle primary through to middle secondary students; maths

- PrimaryGames.com for language and maths games and puzzles, www.primarygames.com
  Suitable for preschoolers through to middle primary aged students; spelling, writing and maths

- Prongo.com for maths and language games and puzzles, www.prongo.com/games/ages9–12.html
  Suitable for preschoolers through to upper primary students; maths and reading

- KidBrainGames.com for educational word and maths games, http://kidbraingames.com/
  Suitable for preschoolers through to upper primary students; maths, reading and spelling

- Gamequarium for interactive maths games, www.gamequarium.com/math.htm
  Suitable for junior primary through to upper primary students; maths

- APlusMath.com for developing maths skills, www.aplusmath.com/Games/index.html
  Suitable for junior primary through to upper primary students; maths

- Gamequarium for interactive maths and language games, www.gamequarium.com/index2.htm
  Suitable for preschoolers through to upper primary students; reading, spelling and maths

- The Learning Box for mathematics and problem solving activities, www.learningbox.com
  Suitable for preschool level through to upper primary students; maths

- Mathletics for mathematic activities, www.mathletics.com.au
  Maths for all ages

- Spellodrome for developing spelling awareness and vocabulary, www.spellodrome.com.au
  Spelling for all ages

Take advantage of assistive technology

One of the most important measures of success for students at school is to maintain pace with their peers in the mastery of literacy and numeracy skills. However, the kids who make up the learning difficulty group demonstrate persistent delay in their skill acquisition. Some will, in due course, achieve functional skills and others will experience unrelenting difficulties evermore. Avoid the pitfall of thinking assistive technology should be postponed until the student learns the basic skills of handwriting, spelling, grammar or reading first. These kids learn differently, and no matter how competently you teach many will never cope with these rudimentary skills. They need legitimate opportunities to take short cuts to reduce the frustrations of intermittent memory weaknesses for spelling rules, grammatical conventions and basic number facts. Why make a student agonise over their memory difficulty when they could use an inexpensive device to take the pressure off recalling a spelling or number pattern? Not only does this practical approach allow kids to access their higher level thinking skills more easily, but helps to buoy their motivation as successful learners.

Mobile phones

More and more students carry mobile phones. This technology is here to stay. Its sophistication continues to expand. Teach kids how to take advantage of the organising systems built into their phone. These include calculators, reminder notes that appear when the alarm sounds, a built-in alarm clock, a stopwatch, a camera, a video and a countdown timer. It is a bonus for all students to know how to use these systems because their mobiles rarely leave their sides. One of the fourteen-year-old students I work alongside recently received permission from his principal to use his mobile phone to take photos of the homework instructions written on the board at the end of lessons. He experiences serious spelling and handwriting difficulties and this approach has been invaluable. Once he arrives home, he places the image on his computer and can see the task.

Organisers

Small hand-held organisers are fabulous for everyone, with or without organisational issues. There is now an expansive range. At the top end are the pocket PCs and Personal Desktop Assistants. These offer amazing functions (try www.hp.com). However, those at the less expensive end are easy to use and worthwhile. They can be set to 'beep' as reminders flash on screen and display what needs to be done. Homework can be typed in, notes, reminders, tasks and phone numbers. If you run Apple Macintosh computers teach students how to make 'stickies'. These are easily made messages that appear on the screen once the computer boots up. Stickies can be used to remind, to explain, to give instructions, or record phone numbers or web sites that have to be remembered. Similarly, Microsoft Office Outlook can be used as a wonderful little memory jogger having the capacity to set up lists, schedules, time lines for assignments and reminders.

The computer

For some students the mastering of basic word-processing skills provides the edge to maintain order and find a little more success (Cullen and Richards 2008). Presentation looks so much better, and word processors help to check spelling, grammar, save work and store it in neatly arranged folders. This is so much better than physically handling and risking losing pieces of paper. Most children are ready to start on this in the early primary school years.

Computer competency checklist (suitable for most middle primary students):

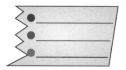

- Boot up the computer
- Touch type
- Create and begin writing a document
- Undo mistakes
- Change font, size and colour of print
- Use the spelling check
- Use the grammar check
- Use the thesaurus
- Check the word count
- Cut and paste
- Cut and paste text and pictures from a website into a document
- Use 'auto-summarize'
- Access drawing documents
- Save and retrieve the same document
- Save as

- Save onto a USB/flash drive

- Retrieve from a USB/flash drive

- Copy onto CD

- Create and label folders for storing files

- Access and send emails.

Most schools are usually well stocked with a selection of touch typing programmes to support the development of keyboarding skills. As well there is an ever increasing number of quality websites offering free online touch typing tuition (start by trying www.bbc.co.uk/schools/typing/ and www.columbia.k12.mo.us/mce/keyboarding/keyboarding.htm). Children are almost never too young to begin to explore the keyboard and learn to type, but there does come a time when they become too old and too resistant to learn. So, seize the moment!

Reading

New technologies have completely revolutionised how information can be gathered from print. Text displayed on the screen can now be read out loud so that instead of a student constantly tripping over their reading problem, they can access their higher-level thinking skills. Try a Google search for *Microsoft Reader* (freeware) and e-Books and you will find many free electronic books to download ready to be listened to. In addition, *Microsoft Reader* offers a digital voice recorder so students can record their thoughts and responses as an alternative to having to respond in text.

The *ClassMate Reader* is a newly released audio book player. It is about the size of a Playstation controller and reads text from its screen out loud with a naturally sounding voice. As it reads it highlights the text. It also has a number of other useful options (classmatereader.com). Alternatively, *Natural Voice Reader* (www.natural readers.com) can read text on the internet, in emails, in MS word and in many other applications, and it is free. The website www.nextup.com offers the product *TextAloud* at a small cost. It reads out loud any PDF or MS word file in rich male or female voices. Similarly, the Nuance Corporation has developed amazing software called *Realspeak* that converts text into high quality speech in both male and female voices. With the computer reading to the student, electronic literacy has the capacity to turn a non-reader into an eager learner (www.promo.net/pg).

Help with written work

Software called *textHELP Read and Write Gold* (www.texthelp.com) is a word-processing program intended to be used alongside Microsoft Word. This program can read out words as they are typed, read back text, check spelling and can automatically correct frequently made errors. Its capacity to read back the text on screen enables the user to listen to what they have written making it invaluable for editing and proofreading work. Similar word processing and prediction programs are: *Text Ease 2000, Text Help, Clicker 4, Penfriend, ClickNType, Co:Writer 4000* and

Kurzwell (www.dyslexic.com for more information). It is also worth exploring the innovative literacy software tool called WYNN (www.quantumtechnology.com.au). Available in two versions, *WYNN Wizard* will scan printed pages, word processing documents, PDF files, text files and the internet and convert them into electronic text to be read aloud. The text is highlighted as it is spoken.

Let the computer write it

That's right! New generation software, *Dragon NaturallySpeaking*, can convert what is being said into print that instantly appears on the screen. The future is here and the price is now very affordable. *Dragon NaturallySpeaking* for Windows is valuable for students who have handwriting problems, spelling difficulties, cannot type or just don't like typing. It allows them to say exactly what they are thinking and get an immediate written result. Recently it has also become available as a lab pack with a site licence available to schools. Training the program doesn't take long, although younger students (middle primary age) require a planned training programme. Usually, students see an improvement in the speed and accuracy of voice recognition within a few days, and find it inspiring. Sixteen-year-old Rhodri, identified with dyslexia and dyspraxia, recorded his experience with *Dragon NaturallySpeaking* for the Westminster eForum held in April 2007. It is enlightening to watch his video at www.youtube.com/watch?v=lXHawlHLmtI.

Social skills

It is a good idea to closely monitor how these kids are developing and maintaining friendships. The nature of learning difficulty does not confine itself to reading, writing, spelling and grammar alone. Its complex impact can influence how an individual perceives the world and interacts with peers. Social difficulties may be the result of expressive or receptive language problems that cause kids and teens to misread and misunderstand social interactions. In addition, years of humiliation about learning does not set the perfect footing for reciprocal friendships. There are ways to support quality social interactions, and a number of these are explored in Chapter 6, 'Ideas to enrich social and emotional connections'.

Help them love their disability

Perhaps this sounds fanciful, but it's a much better option than leaving students wishing they were dead because the emotional burden of their disability is too much to carry. If they cannot love their disability or difficulty, then at least ease them towards accepting it. After all, it will always exist.

A simple thing to do is to investigate a few of the amazing individuals from the past and present identified with learning difficulty. Guide kids to discover their rich, wonderful lives and the contributions they have made. Many of their autobiographies and biographies are inspirational. Look at the problems they faced, how they got around them and why they became successful. Explore, for example, how dyslexia affects people. Explain that the organisation of the brain that produces the dyslexic difficulty is also thought to account for unique artistic, personal, musical, dramatic, athletic abilities and mechanical gifts. Highlight that most individuals identified with a learning difficulty (and many other issues) say they would never trade away their difficulty because they would be incomplete without it. Raise the idea that their different way of thinking and processing the world may be the very thing to create their own rich niche to succeed in life.

Thirteen-year-old Brett provided an emotionally healthy snapshot of how to compartmentalise problems. I remember asking him how he felt about his significant learning difficulty. He reached for a black jumbo-sized texta and a blank sheet of paper. Then he proceeded to place a dozen bold black dots randomly over the page. He explained that each dot represented something good and not so good about himself. He explained that a particular dot, as he circled it, concerned his downhill racing and he lived for it. Another dot indicated the value he placed on his friendships, another was about his connection to his family and he continued until he reached the last dot. As he circled it, he explained this one was his learning difficulty and it was just one part of his life. As kids begin to understand the link between their strengths and challenges they are in a much better place to learn and to tackle life's inevitable challenges.

Find worksheet on page 215

Worksheets

Refer to p. 190 for useful websites and further reading.

Creating the best start for challenging kids
Inside tough kids with oppositional styled behaviours

The control of student behaviour has always been a major component of an educator's skill repertoire. Today, as teachers face increasing numbers of students with challenging emotions and behaviour, there is a clear expectation on them to expand the quality of how they go about managing students (Appelbaum 2008).

Every so often a teacher will find themselves having to deal with the behaviours of one or two students who battle for attention and power. When challenged they'll become defiant or loud, and occasionally vindictive and intimidating. Oppositional styled behaviours, from even just one student, can be a perilous time. Such encounters place a teacher's reactions under the closest scrutiny of the class, and depending on their responses, either an atmosphere of care, strength and fairness is stirred, or the class can suddenly set itself against a teacher it perceives as mean and unjust. The tone of the classroom can quickly unravel and the confidence of students to learn and participate in a warm interactive class environment falls apart.

Taking on the challenge to find success with oppositional styled students is the focus of this chapter and it starts by acknowledging several key points. First, the best 'disaster recipe' occurs when a teacher displays the same reactive and inflexible traits as these kids. Educators who order students about, who deliver quick ultimatums where students feel backed into a corner invite kids to say and do things that they would not dream of saying or doing in the normal course of events. These kids are truly reliant on intelligent, poised educators who can speak quietly or privately to them when reprimanding, who give time for responses and can cleverly sidestep until the heat of the moment subsides.

Second is the significance of developing and maintaining class cohesion and unity. Teachers who do this well are regularly found sitting in a circle with class members where everyone has the chance to talk about what has happened, how they feel and how things can be made better. These are the teachers who build a sense of community by using words as 'we', 'us' and 'ours'. Through helpful discussions teacher and class are able to negotiate expectations and rules that inherently bring structure, predictability and emotional comfort. They ask students, no matter their age:

'What rules do you think will help our class?'

'What rules should be negotiable?'

'What sorts of understandings are best being non-negotiable?'

'When rules are broken must we always punish?'

'How can we work problems out?'

'Is this the best solution?'

In truth, it is not any one single rule that tips the balance, but the act of everyone in the group participating, discussing and owning decisions that makes the difference.

Third, without a plan, some helpful collegiate support and an understanding of what drives you to react the way you do to student misbehaviour, you've lost before you've started. The oppositional behaviours of a few of these kids can easily destroy the belief you have in yourself as a teacher, destroy your classroom tone and wreck the confidence students and parents should have in your ability to provide a safe, productive classroom environment (Axup and Gersch 2008).

What lies beneath behaviour?

Behaviour always happens for a reason and observation is a good way to understand what may be driving it. Researching the ABCs of behaviour has the potential to provide a valuable piece of the puzzle that busy teachers can easily overlook (Holverstott 2005). Start by working through the questions below.

Find worksheet on page 217

Antecedents

*   To begin with, when does the difficult behaviour start?

*   What sets the behaviour off?

*   Who is around at the time?

*   Do you think the environment is safe for this student?

*   Speculate on the likely triggers for this behaviour.

*   Has it to do with: working in groups, interactions at play time, social miscuing, sadness, tiredness, homework, anxiousness, avoidance, excitability, inflexibility, poor planning or language difficulties?

*   Where does the problem behaviour usually happen?

*   Does it happen at the same time most days?

*   Is the behaviour the result of too high an expectation or too little structure?

*   Might the problem behaviour be the result of emotional overload? If, typically, by lunchtime there is always a blow-up it is likely that the student's coping abilities are running on empty. At this point an unstructured environment is too overwhelming.

Behaviour

- Record exactly what the behaviour is.

- How frequent is it?

- Is it becoming more or less frequent?

- What does the student say?

- What does the student do?

- What does the student want?

- How severe is it really?

- How much of this behaviour really matters? Is it behaviour worth tackling? Why?

- Do you think the behaviour is a result of the student's level of physical, emotional, social or intellectual development?

- Might a clever change to routine or a creative 'circuit-breaker' minimise the problem?

Consequences

- What usually happens following this behaviour?

- What do they do?

- What does the student say?

- How long does it take for their anger to subside?

- Is their calm down time improving or worsening?

- Are they usually prepared to discuss it?

- Do they understand the impact it has on others?

- Do they always blame others?

- What is their response when they listen to the thoughts and feelings of others who were affected?

- Do they show remorse?

- What do you say or do?

- Are your responses largely punitive, educative or relational? Is there a balance?

Next, ask a trusted colleague to observe the student and you at the classically challenging times. Ask them to consider the same set of questions. Compare their responses with yours. This provides a catalyst for discussion, deeper understandings and the generation of new ideas. It may be, for example, that the learning environment you have created for the student does not work in their favour. It may be too interactive, too stimulating and offer too many choices. Play with the idea whether the student would benefit by being placed in a less confronting environment at critical times. The concept of Positive Behavioural Support (PBS) principles is always worth visiting (Conroy *et al.* 2005). PBS emerged in the 1980s and continues to gather momentum. It focuses on reducing the challenging behaviours of students through assessing their behaviours and redesigning the environment to improve their functioning. Results from the clinical research are very clear. When PBS is appropriately and consistently applied students always experience academic, social and emotional improvements (Hendley 2007).

Designing an improvement plan

Once the ABCs of behaviour have been thought through it's time to get the student on board. A great way to do this is to construct an improvement plan as a valuable agent of change. It doesn't matter what you call the plan. Name it by whatever term best suits your situation or system: a learning plan, a behaviour plan, a way to change plan or a success plan. In essence, it is an explicit tool aimed at providing improved structure, more powerful reinforcers and higher levels of accountability. It is ideal for kids who need more than praise and usual social reinforcers.

Improving student behaviour begins by developing an emotional connection with them. However, finding an emotional connection is often ignored by some because they feel jaded by the difficulties the student has displayed. Their response is to tighten the rules and create more stringent rules: time-outs, detentions, exclusions and suspensions. This may work for a few, but quite a few others become defiant to the disciplinary upgrade. When this happens the optimistic influences that may have guided a student towards making a few positive changes virtually evaporate.

A thoughtful starting point is to talk to the student about what is happening. Explain what you want. A simple question like, 'What can I do to help?' can dissolve barriers and trigger new beginnings. Listen to them. Actively discuss what might work to meet your needs and theirs. This sort of conversation has the scope to get teacher and student on the same side of the fence.

Introduce the improvement plan optimistically. Present it to the student as a way to shake off an old behaviour that is not working for them by replacing it with one that will help them to reach a new goal. Two improvement plan worksheets are offered at the end of the book: 'Success plan – go for the cup!' and 'My new way to do it'. Take a look at them. Discuss the idea of positive and negative reinforcers. Positive reinforcers are best seen as an investment to fire-up the student's desire to do better, and negative reinforcers strengthen their responsibility to maintain personal accountability.

Find worksheets on pages 216 and 218

Positive reinforcers

A positive reinforcer is a bonus of some kind received by the student that follows a pleasing behaviour. Positive reinforcement is of course best applied immediately following a desired behaviour. As a rule, a social reinforcer such as a smile, a wink, an uplifting comment, a silly face, a nudge, or an 'I dare you!' with a laugh is enough to reward, motivate and enthuse. The students who we are particularly interested in often need more tempting reinforcers. Praise alone is not enough. These kids benefit from repeated social and concrete reinforcement as a way to strengthen required behaviours.

Ideally, get the student to participate in choosing the reinforcers that will be on offer. They do not have to be expensive, but need to be meaningful to the student so their desire to do better is captured. More often than not, parents are prepared to support the plan by providing reinforcers selected by the student.

Popular positive reinforcers

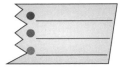

- extra time on the computer
- Lego, Lego technic and Bionicles
- canteen vouchers
- puzzles
- boardgames
- a toy
- a snack
- free time in the library
- free time using the computer
- collector cards
- collectable cars
- music CDs
- a DVD
- a gift voucher
- selecting something from the lucky-dip box
- tokens such as fake money, points, stars, stickers or tickets that may later be exchanged for a predetermined item.

Although open to question this form of encouragement, built out and well managed over time, can lead to improved internal motivation, which of course, is the ultimate goal (Cameron and Pierce 1994, 1998; Fabes *et al.* 1989; Lepper *et al.* 1996; Maag 2001; Pfiffner *et al.* 1985; Rockwell 2007; Weiner 1998; Wiersma 1992).

Negative reinforcers

Negative reinforcement occurs when an undesirable behaviour displayed by a student is followed up by an appropriate negative response.

Popular negative reinforcers

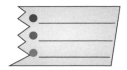

- the temporary loss of a privilege;
- missing out on something anticipated;
- reduction of free time or play time;
- accepting a consequence from the person or group who have been harmed;
- moving to a less desirable place in the classroom or spending time in another classroom;
- time out, quiet time or rethink time;

- internal or external school suspension;

- reflective discussion on an action with someone (the principal, deputy principal, school counsellor or the class);

- verbally apologising;

- writing an apology;

- taking on additional jobs or tasks (community service).

Negative reinforcers are used to reduce unacceptable behaviour because most agree that when they are carried out suitably and consistently the student's undesirable behaviour usually diminishes. However, unlike positive reinforcement, use negative reinforcers cautiously. Do not overplay them.

Define the new behaviour and how it will attract positive reinforcers

- Decide on one or two behaviours that are not working for the student and are worth changing together.

- Discuss them and redefine each in positive terms.

It is always best to place the spotlight on strengthening the new positive behaviour. Evidence demonstrates that direct attempts to stamp out unwanted behaviours are far less successful than structuring an increase in the frequency of the more desirable behaviours (Barkley 2006). As an example, two undesirable behaviours frequently displayed by ten-year-old Luke are that he constantly calls out in class discussion and distracts others while they are working.

Redefining the behaviour with a positive spin might see Luke being guided to create these statements:

- 'I need to put my hand up and wait to be asked.'

- 'When I have something to say I will always put my hand up without calling out.'

- 'Before I put my hand up I will count that four people have had a turn first.'

- 'Instead of interrupting others in quiet work time I can take one of my tokens and fasten it to the page I am working on.' Two or three tokens are available to Luke in selected lessons. When used in this way they tally up to provide a positive reinforcer. A token may not be used if the teacher has had to provide the prompt for Luke to stop talking first.

Be very specific about the new behaviour and how it is to be targeted. The student needs to be clear about how they need to look, act and sound (Marron 2002). Think, 'Is the expectation I have developed reasonable for this student's age, maturity, personality, capacity and so on?'

Filling out the improvement plan

Write the newly defined positive behaviour into the improvement plan. The higher the student's involvement at this stage the more likely you are to tap into their internal sense of pride and this, more than anything, will help carry the new behaviour forward. Specify exactly how often and how much of this new positive behaviour is required to achieve the positive reinforcer and reach the final goal.

Next, encourage the student to select a negative reinforcer and record it onto the improvement plan. Try to choose reinforcers they will seek to avoid as this increases their personal accountability. Explain that the negative reinforcers will only be used when their old behaviour gets in the way of their new thinking. Agree when and how the negative reinforcer will be used. A valuable idea is to decide on a 'secret signal' between you and the student as a quick reminder to them to stay with the new positive behaviour. Students identified with ADHD are naturally impulsive and are less inclined to be able to see too far ahead. Our planning has to do this for them. Discuss and role-play how the student might show their frustration without threatening their chances of success. Work out a safe place or a safe person they can retreat to if they are feeling overwhelmed, put out or angry. If, however, they choose to ignore the signal and allow their unthinking behaviour to take over, then the predetermined negative reinforcer becomes the consequence.

To make the plan official ask the student to sign off on it. The addition of your signature reminds them that you want to inspire a successful change.

Select a place to keep the plan.

An idea is to take several photographs of the student performing the new target behaviour. Once printed, the photographs can be attached to the improvement plan as a reminder of the new behaviour being strengthened.

Sometimes using an improvement plan in combination with a tracking chart such as 'blast off!', 'go and fly your kite!', 'you can count on Winston's segments!', 'staying on track with my dragon tracking chart' and 'staying on track with my duck tracking chart' at the end of the book is an influential visual reminder for kids to stay on track.

Find worksheets on pages 219–23

Place the improvement plan and the tracking chart where they can be seen as often as needed. Each lesson, each morning, every afternoon or at the end of each day encourage the student to add a sticker, a colour or whatever has been agreed. Most kids prefer a reasonable degree of privacy and confidentiality when using this process, and this is more so as they become older. Always discuss with the student just how public or private is comfortable for them.

Different students respond best to different systems

Younger children, especially those who are busy, impulsive and forgetful, respond best to immediate feedback and positive reinforcers for using their new thinking. This helps to keep the new goal fresh in their mind. A consistent drip-feed that nurtures small changes seems best, rather than 'if you're good all week, you can have a reward'. Older children are able to respond to more complicated token-styled systems that have longer delays built in between behaviour and reinforcement.

Case study

An improvement plan with a difference

Eleven-year-old Joe was the youngest of three kids. He was sensitive, intelligent and showed good application when doing something he was interested in at school. He loved the garden, and sometimes he chose to work in it at lunchtime. He also adored football. His mum and dad had separated a few months ago and things were very bitter between them. After the split Joe had to live with his mum, his thirteen-year-old sister and sixteen-year-old brother, yet he'd always been dad's boy. He had wanted to spend time with his father, but dad took the dramatic step of cutting himself off from his children. Recently, both Joe and his brother's birthday passed without any contact from their father. At home mum and the kids were often in conflict. Mostly it was verbal and the language was usually hurtful or hateful. Mum was barely coping and as a consequence the kids had a free reign on television, video games, food and the Internet, and much of what they chose was inappropriate.

Joe had always displayed mild oppositional behaviours in class and in the playground, but once dad left his oppositional behaviours skyrocketed. When things went wrong for Joe he would refuse or ignore what he was asked to do. He would walk off with eyes fixed to the ground swearing for all to hear. Often his language was sexually inclined and directed at uninvolved, unsuspecting girls. All sorts of things were tried to curtail his negative, antisocial behaviours. For example, a 'behaviour contract' had been set up with Joe. The goals were for him to cooperate and work to the best of his ability, and use any one of three 'emotional circuit breakers' when he felt things were going wrong. Marginal gains were made, but his emotionally charged behaviour still frequently occurred. His play times and extracurricular activities were removed at times, and sometimes his behaviours attracted an internal suspension or an exclusion from school.

Recently, Joe started to see Kay, the year level coordinator, to help build his self-awareness and improve his responses, particularly at times when he felt overwhelmed. Kay hit on a remarkable strategy worth sharing: a positive reinforcement plan with a real difference! Joe, with Kay's help, decided to ask for sponsorship support from school staff and selected parents for each day he was able to 'stay cool'. Kay helped Joe to make up a sponsorship form and wrote up the information that the sponsors needed to know. Joe took great pride in approaching adults to sponsor him. Joe and Kay decided that the proceeds would go to the Ronald MacDonald Foundation. The programme ran for four weeks and in that time Joe had only two days when he lost it, couldn't be cool and resorted to swearing. Subsequently, he received no sponsorship for the Ronald MacDonald Foundation on each of the days. This positive reinforcement plan resulted in a huge turn around for Joe's seemingly interminable behaviours. It took the focus away from the negativity of his behaviour that took his emotion and behaviour to heights we could have only dreamt of.

Perhaps Joe felt as though he had very little control over his life, let alone trying to grapple with feelings of abandonment. Perhaps the idea of presenting the money he has raised to the Ronald MacDonald Foundation gave him a sense of something he could control. It's hard to know. It's hard to imagine what any of us would do in Joe's situation.

Case study

Gardening and school maintenance as a positive reinforcement plan

In one of the primary schools I work at, the Chaplain places a few hours aside each week to work individually with half a dozen of the older boys on gardening or school maintenance projects. These boys find schoolwork difficult and easily become disengaged. Each has a reputation around negative and disruptive behaviours in the classroom, but adore the two 40-minute sessions they can have with him each week. While engaged in the various projects he chats with them and occasionally will raise an idea to help them sort through an issue. This very simple format has helped to build relationship and self-esteem, and given the boys a chance to do something positive that is noticed by peers and the school community. Each of the boys knows that their time with the Chaplain is dependent on respectful attitudes in the classroom, although no one overplays this.

Case study

Collector cards as positive reinforcement

Here's a motivational idea. Eleven-year-old Nick, who was highly impulsive, loved to collect football collector cards. At the beginning of each week his mother supplied the teacher with a new pack. The pack was available to Nick at the end of the week and receiving them from his teacher was the only way he could get his hands on these precious cards! Nick's teacher cleverly used the football cards to help Nick make better choices. When Nick looked as though he needed reminding his teacher discretely placed a small green token in Nick's hand, nothing was said, but Nick knew this meant it was time to stop, think and change from what he was doing. Subsequently, if Nick chose not to respond a red token was placed in his hand. Receiving a red token meant that Nick would lose one card from the pack at the end of the week, but once again no words were exchanged. Nick didn't lose too many cards over the six months and those he lost each week were gathered together so he could achieve them as a new pack later.

What is earned cannot be taken away

Anything a student has worked for and earned remains theirs. When the student's old unthinking behaviour gets in the way of the new positive behaviour, despite a reminder or two, the prearranged negative reinforcer is attracted. When this happens, as it will, do not interpret the plan or the student failing. Your job is to create the opportunity for a restart without the connotation of failure or loss of dignity. Use the hiccup as an insightful moment to learn from. At this point it will simply take the student longer to reach their goal.

Train to proficiency

Once the programme starts, use the plan every lesson or every day over the agreed period. Talk about it, talk it up and review progress. Praise the student's effort and perseverance as well as success.

Once the plan expires, the next step is to extend the standard required to earn a positive reinforcer. This is referred to as building the programme out. Never hesitate to change the appearance of the improvement plan to add interest, and gradually aim to replace concrete rewards with social reinforcers. As the student begins to adopt the new behaviour more regularly you may consider targeting a new behaviour that could do with some fine tuning. Finally, a common pitfall is to keep on working at behaviour too long after the goal has been achieved. Remember, this approach is not about achieving perfection, it is about normalising behaviours.

Inside oppositional defiant disorder

Occasionally the struggle to connect with a student and find optimistic ways forward is far, far more challenging. A few of our students meet the criteria, or would meet it if they had the opportunity to gain identification, for oppositional defiant disorder (ODD). These students have a strong reactive need to control, to have their own way and will use socially exploitive, emotionally explosive or totally annoying ways to get what they want. Typically they temper tantrum, argue, bend and defy the rules of adults. They blame and annoy others, get annoyed by others, then pay them back and deny any responsibility. Remarkably, these young individuals appear to tolerate the negativity they attract, and seem to thrive on the conflict, anger and condemnation of others. Yet in between the torrid times when their emotional coping skills are not being put to the test these kids can be warm, compassionate and a joy to be with.

Case study

'I'm the boss, not you!'

When thirteen-year-old Rebecca hears a sudden or outright 'no' or feels as though she has been treated unfairly she turns the matter into a war that she must win. She becomes unrelenting in her quest to get her way. It matters little to her whether the battle rages in the privacy of her own home or whether it's in the public arena in front of peers in the classroom. Typically, she'll say,

'No!'
'You can't stop me!'
'You can't make me.'
'I can and I will.'
'You don't matter.'
'I'm the boss, not you!'
'I don't care.'
'I don't care what you think.'
'Wait till you're not looking.'

Case study

Rebecca's 'Golden Snitch' improvement plan

Rebecca's plan for success was inspired by her love for Harry Potter. Rebecca, her class teacher, the assistant principal and her parents struck the improvement plan together. The plan was later discussed with staff members who had contact with Rebecca. Each was given a copy.

The Quaffles

Rebecca can always earn a Quaffle per lesson, and for each break and lunch period when she shows the following behaviours:

- is prepared to listen;
- follows instructions;
- works constructively;
- tries to complete tasks;
- speaks and treats other respectfully.

The Golden Snitches

When Rebecca has earned three Quaffles she automatically qualifies for a Golden Snitch. Gaining two Golden Snitches means she can celebrate her success by having an immediate 10-minute reward time. However, the option exists for her to save four Golden Snitches because with four Snitches in hand Rebecca is able to enjoy a 20-minute success time at the end of the day. She may choose to celebrate with a friend or enjoy it alone. Reward times include time using the computer, playing with Lego/Bionicles, continuing a jigsaw puzzle, drawing, reading her book, scrap booking, reading and so on.

The following is also written into Rebecca's success plan and was written with Rebecca steering the process.

Rebecca knows her early warning signs that lead to anger.
She knows that:

- her arms go tense and sometimes she clenches her fists;
- her shoulders become raised and her body feels tight;
- her arms fold across her chest;
- her voice becomes raised;
- her head says argue and win!

Things that make Rebecca angry are when someone:

- is mean to her (teachers or students);
- steals her ideas;
- tells her that she can't do something that she's been expecting to do.

Agreed action for staff to follow when things are starting to go wrong

- Say, 'Are you working towards a Quaffle, Rebecca?' This reminder replaces statements such as 'calm down', 'don't be silly' or 'If you continue to behave like this you will lose a Quaffle!' These statements inflame Rebecca's annoyance.

- If Rebecca isn't able to modify her behaviour staff will ask her to do something else that will help her feel happier. In her case this means reading her novel for 10 minutes, going to her buddy class or finding her designated safe teacher for 10 minutes.

- Once Rebecca feels more settled she is expected to return to class.

- If Rebecca refuses to follow the steps above, or returns to class and stays angry and disruptive, then the principal, deputy principal, school chaplain or school counsellor will be asked to take her to a quiet place to help her find a better way forward.

- If she chooses not to participate in this, or returns to class and is disruptive again, one of her parents or a nominated relative or family friend will collect her from school and take her home. As strange as it may seem Rebecca enjoys being at school and going home is not something she wants. At home Rebecca is expected to complete school work that has been pre-packaged in an envelope to replace the work she has missed out on at school.

- Re-entry the next day is contingent on this work being done. The next day is always seen as an opportunity for everyone to make a new and optimistic start.

Behaviours that attract the reminder, 'Are you working towards a Quaffle, Rebecca?'

- When she is finding it hard to follow an instruction.
- When she starts to argue (teachers have been taught how to de-escalate her argumentative way).
- When she refuses to have a go at the task or refuses to participate in a discussion to modify it.
- When she begins to treat others disrespectfully.
- When she is becoming disruptive.

Behaviours that attract an automatic go home with no warning

- Hitting, punching, slapping, pulling hair, pinching, kicking, pushing and spitting.
- Continually touching to annoy others.
- Running away from teachers.
- Damaging school property or the belongings of others.
- Using disrespectful language towards teachers and students.

Three go homes result in a one day internal suspension.

She must prove to the adult, or the group, that they are wrong or unfair and will go to extraordinary lengths to do so, even if it means retreating under her desk and making incessant baby noises – blah, blah, blah, blah or goo, goo, goo, goo – to thoroughly annoy and disrupt.

Besides being identified with ODD Rebecca also has a diagnosis of ADHD. ODD is a condition frequently associated with ADHD and being identified with both makes a world of difference. Children and adolescents with ADHD alone do things without thinking. Basically, they are impulsive. The addition of oppositional defiance disorder takes Rebecca's responses, especially when she feels she's been treated unjustly, to new dimensions! The precise causes of ODD are not known yet. Researchers suggest that oppositional behaviours appear more frequently when there is either too much or too little available structure. When rules and expectations are too rigid, too demanding and too punitive, oppositional behaviours seem to escalate. Conversely, structures that are flimsy, loose and inconsistent also promote difficulties. It appears that the best recipe to reduce the volatile emotion around ODD, is a style that aims to balance appropriate and consistent structures with low emotional responses, care and quality dialogue. A style much easier written than practised in the classroom!

Rebecca's parents say that as a toddler she was far more pedantic and demanding than her younger sister. She was tough work from the beginning! These days she can still be expert at dividing her parent's opinions and authority. She cleverly exploits their natural differences. Their emotional resilience and relationship is always at risk because it is always being tested. They often disagree on how best to handle her tricky behaviours. Yet, they know that airing their disputes in front of Rebecca limit their chances of success. At times Dad accuses Mum of allowing Rebecca to press her buttons and spending too much time either justifying or arguing with her. Mum accuses Dad of coming down too hard with too little warning. Parenting Rebecca is certainly not easy. Indeed, dealing with a child or teen with ODD (and ADHD) is one of the most stressful situations parents face.

In Rebecca's case school is less problematic and less emotionally charged. This is because her teachers have built some very obvious structures and expectations for her to work within that she sees as essentially fair. What's more, the staff's consistency, predictability and low emotional response appears to assist her steadiness. When things go wrong the first step is to use the improvement plan Rebecca helped to create. The improvement plan plainly states the positive behaviours the school wishes to see from Rebecca and how using these will attract good things. It also details how they will respond to Rebecca's unacceptable negative behaviours if she chooses to use them at school.

Essentials to support oppositional styled kids

Teachers who have experienced the volatile emotions that live with oppositional behaviours quickly learn a few essentials that really help. These same principles apply to both children and adolescents.

Relationship

Managing the emotion and behaviour of kids with oppositional behaviours is hard. The best starting point is to show that you like them (Glen and Nelson 1989). And, if this is difficult, work hard to find a thing or two about them that you can like! Actively showing care towards them is essential because these kids have inbuilt radar that tells them when a teacher doesn't like them, and making up lost ground can be very, very tough. Find moments to exchange a laugh with them. Tell them you care. Actually ask, 'What can I do to help?' Kids often know what will work best for them and draw strength from a teacher's perseverance. Remember, when things go wrong, as they most certainly will from time to time, do your best to show emotional dependability and steadiness. There's no mistake about it, these kids are reliant on poised adults at school – perfect role models. They are dependent on adults, who want to engage them and can treat them with respect, especially when redirection is required. Their connectedness, desire to learn and emotional steadiness will remain keenly connected to the quality of their teacher's input. Continuing reassuring communication is doubly important for kids with oppositional behaviours because, given the amount of conflict that bubbles away in their life, it is easy for them to feel unloved or unwanted by their parents and teachers. If we allow them to stay in this place for too long they bunker down, become hardened to the needs of others and erratically lash out as a means of self-protection.

Think fast

As soon as you find yourself in conflict with an oppositional student know that you've got to make a good decision fast. If you cannot or do not, the behaviours of these kids will quickly skyrocket out of control. Very quickly decide whether this is really worth pursuing. Decide on what is reasonable as an outcome that the student and you can live with. Think, how can I achieve this without raising their emotion past the point of no return? And, always have 'Plan B' in the back of your mind in case you make the wrong call!

Every now and then, a situation can be successfully diffused by merely changing the subject, distracting the student and not 'buying in'. Precisely the same tactics we use more naturally with much younger children. This is the moment to mention several questions teachers should never ask kids who are flexing their oppositional behaviour in front of other students. They are:

'What did you say? Repeat that!'

'You're on step three now. What do you think of that?'

'Why did you do that?'

'Tell me what that was all about?'

These questions, especially when accompanied by strong teacher emotion and finger beckoning, invite students to protect their dignity and to do this they will launch a forceful, desperate verbal reprisal superseding anything you anticipated.

Wraparound: a team intervention

Build a team who can reliably support one another because it is too much to ask the class teacher of the student to deal with this alone. As a rule teams are comprised of the student's parent or parents, school leadership, key teachers, a child psychologist or psychiatrist and perhaps interagency personnel. Getting the team together for regular review meetings always reaps benefits simply because they get everyone talking. The spirit is to review what's happening, what's working and what's not. It presents a forum to discuss, make changes and plan. Outcomes from meetings do not have to be perfect solutions, but ideas that are workable and progressive often make a world of difference. It can be uplifting for students to meet with their team from time to time (Eber *et al.* 2008). For students to see and hear each team member caring, participating and wanting the very best for them can be therapeutic. As they meet with the team they are also reminded that what they have to say is very important. Teams that do best also value the idea of team maintenance. In other words, everyone within the team takes care of one another because they openly acknowledge this is genuinely hard work. This translates to:

- Teaching parents how to take time out. How to find a babysitter, get out and maintain their relationship.

- Allowing teachers and parents the opportunity to complain about the complexities they face.

- Responding constructively and with sensitivity when a team member is having trouble coping with a student's behaviours.

Bad patches

Every so often kids with oppositional defiant disorder tend to hit a bad patch. This is just the way it is. Sometimes a trigger can be found, but often it seems impossible for anyone to work out why what's happening is happening. At this point it is best to stick with the sensible, grounded ideas the team has already developed. Try not to lose confidence or become derailed. This is the time to trust in one another and trust the thought and effort you have developed to manage this erratic condition.

Dispel poor reputation

Part of taking a proactive role for these kids and their parents concerns what we quietly do behind the scenes. It is surprising how often a young person's poor choices from the past combined with mindless, unforgiving gossip seals their fate in a school community. When appropriate, work to promote the facts and insert new information with a positive spin on the grapevine. Actively dispel damaging mythology that impedes the spirit of progress and transformation.

Keep talking with parents

By actively participating with and supporting parents we help to underpin the quality of our own professional practice. Gently feed parents information from newspapers, journals, magazines, websites, YouTube and television programmes that is likely to be helpful. Encourage parents to link with other parents or staff members who may have a child with similar difficulties and deal with it really well. Place parents in touch with organisations and professionals who can educate, be supportive and offer practical interventions. As the student's emotions are better managed at home you are likely to reap advantages as well.

A personal reflection: student misbehaviour and you

Dealing with student misbehaviour and the gamut of emotion that accompanies it is stressful for teachers. In fact, student misbehaviour is one of the biggest factors influencing teacher stress and burnout (Maag 2008). Educators who do best learn to live by the Four Goals of Misbehaviour, an effective tool to help understand behaviour (Dreikurs and Soltz 1989). The Four Goals of Misbehaviour were coined by psychiatrist, Rudolf Dreikurs who was inspired by Alfred Adler's work (Adler 1929). Dreikurs suggests that children usually misbehave for one of four reasons. Typically there is a struggle for attention, power, revenge or a display of inadequacy. A valuable way to understand which of the four misbehaviours you might be facing is to identify exactly how you are feeling. When you feel annoyed, and the student doesn't seem to respond to your care or direction, they probably want attention. When you feel threatened or defied, the student probably wants power. When you feel hurt or scared they probably want revenge and when you feel you have tried everything without success the student's objective is probably to show their inadequacy (Dreikurs *et al.* 1998).

Adler and Dreikurs appreciated that mutual respect between adults and children was invaluable in teaching children the true depth of respect, and how to apply it. They thought that most problems around misbehaviour were the result of poor relationship where encouragement had diminished or disappeared. Both believed that improvements in a child's behaviour had to be linked to a deliberate strengthening in the relationship with the adult. Dreikurs also acknowledged that as the balance of power in society and schools moved away from the traditional power over children to a freer, more democratic structure, the relationship between adults and children was tested. In essence, they promoted a common sense, practical approach to help educators respond to student misbehaviour more effectively, and there are two central points embodied in their work. The first is that educators who do best when confronted with student misbehaviour are those who choose to shift their focus from feeling as though they must defeat the child's misbehaviour in order to win. A better way to proceed is to respond in ways that are likely to convince the child to abandon their misbehaviour. The second point is that none of us can really squash or defeat a child's misbehaviour. Constantly directing our energy and power at the child's misbehaviour will not turn the child or adolescent into a likeable, responsible or happy person. The solution lies in looking beneath the behaviour to find what may be driving it and what can be addressed (Dreikurs and Soltz 1989).

To successfully live and work by the Four Goals of Misbehaviour the idea is to stop, just for a moment, and reflect on what is actually happening inside you. This is the moment to examine the feelings that will likely drive your initial response to the problem behaviour.

- Recognise the feelings. What are they?
- How intense are they?
- Why is this student's behaviour influencing your emotion so deeply?
- Is it wise to allow these feelings to drive your response?
- What is it you really want to achieve?
- Will this emotion contribute or diminish a truly constructive solution?
- What is it this student really wants?

When a teacher can steer him or herself away from overreacting to a student's misbehaviour, their level of emotional upset decreases, and this in turn provides them with increased levels of emotional control to make much better decisions (Maag 2008). As we become more aware of the emotion aroused in us by student misbehaviour we are likely to find that the best way to respond is to do virtually the opposite to what the initial flush of feelings suggest. Otherwise it is too easy to instinctively react and overreact to poor student behaviours in emotionally demanding ways that are unhelpful.

Effectively applying the Four Goals of Misbehaviour takes thought and practice. It asks educators to review how they respond and think about student misbehaviour (Dinkmeyer and Dreikurs 2000). They challenge educators to reconstruct their thinking, because for a long time we have been caught up within a format of *behaviour management* that duped us into thinking how we responded to student misbehaviour was less important than the rules embedded in the *school's behaviour management policy*. The Four Goals of Misbehaviour also bring us closer to the motivations behind poor student behaviour. So often what they do is an awfully clumsy attempt to fit in, find purpose, keep dignity or feel a sense of belonging. What they do may be disobedient and disruptive, but for some it is a style that has progressively emerged because somehow they believe it works for them (Nelson 1987).

Attempting to live by the Four Goals of Misbehaviour is well worth the effort because they offer truly therapeutic and educative understandings. As soon as we enter the arena of examining feelings, our own and our students, we begin to manage differently and more successfully. More than this, we activate a process of emotional growth within ourselves.

Responses around the Four Goals of Misbehaviour

1 Students who seek attention

Student thinks . . .

'I matter most when everyone is busy with me.'

'Keep looking at me. Keep talking to me. It's my turn!'

'The busier I make you and others with me the more I matter.'

Teacher thinks . . .

'This kid is driving me mad!'

'You want to keep me busy with you, but I've got 29 others!'

'Back off. Give someone else a go.'

'You are not being fair.'

Teacher feels . . .

Annoyed

Irritated

Fed up

Acting on these feelings the teacher will . . .

Reprimand

Get angry

Use sarcasm

Confront

Punish

When the teacher does this the student thinks . . .

'Yes! It's all about me again!'

'I really do matter.'

'She's sent me out of the classroom. Look I'm the only one standing here. I really do know how to get the teacher's attention!'

Best approach . . .

- Discuss what you want with the student. Share with them that it is harder for some kids to wait and understand the needs of others. Reassure them you can help and want to help.

- Develop a positive plan that involves the student receiving recognition from you, the class, the principal or a parent as more appropriate behaviours are achieved.

- Work on catching the positive behaviours: catching kids doing well and commenting on it is the best way to get the behaviours we want.

- When things go wrong and the student will not respond to a predetermined reminder, use a straight forward consequence that you have previously discussed together.

- Respond pleasantly and deliberately build out your response frequency. A little clever, tactical ignoring can go a long way!

- A very practical approach is to develop the 'helping hand' initiative used with Luke earlier in this chapter (see p. 109). Hand the attention-demanding student several 'helping hand' tokens at the beginning of the lesson. The idea is that each time they want you they must put their hand up. As you respond they hand one of the tokens over to you. Once all the tokens have been handed over the understanding is that you are not available to them for the rest of the lesson. Tokens that have been saved by the student can be added together to provide a more powerful positive reinforcer.

2 Students who seek power

Student thinks . . .

'I matter when I'm in charge.'

'I have to be the boss.'

'This is my classroom. Everything must work around me.'

'I have many ways to show my power and importance.'

Teacher thinks . . .

'Why, you little . . .'

'You have no right to push like this. I'm the one who went to university and studied for years. I deserve to be in control.'

'It's my classroom, my workplace and I have the system to back me up.'

Teacher feels . . .

Threatened

Vulnerable

Humiliated because their authority is publicly challenged

Defeated

Acting on these feelings the teacher will . . .

Threaten, ridicule, shout, humiliate and punish to grab back power.

Give in, and then randomly seize opportunities to reassert their claim to power.

When the teacher does this the student thinks . . .

'Let the games begin! Bring out your best weapons. They'll be no match for mine.'

'I really am the boss. Just look how hard you're working to keep up with me.'

'It's my classroom and you are mine!'

And the power struggle intensifies.

Best approach . . .

- A good start is to accept that this is not easy. Enlist support from colleagues, leadership and parents.

- Appreciate that power seekers become power drunk. They love to battle. It is in their habit and they have little idea how much they are reliant on perceptive adults to defuse situations for them.

- Try to remove yourself from becoming part of their power struggle. After all, there is no point in challenging a teacher who remains emotionally steady and highly logical.

- Talk with the student about what you want. Acknowledge that this may be hard for them, but you want to help.

- Do more of the unexpected. Take the wind out of his or her sails by doing the opposite to what they think you'll do. Humour, without sarcasm, can be wonderfully therapeutic for everyone. And, many a situation can be rescued by simply changing the subject, just like we do with four-year-olds.

- Look for opportunities to encourage cooperative behaviours and find good moments together.

- Agree with the student, say, 'You're right I can't make you do something you don't want to do.' Tell them that when things go wrong you will listen and always attempt to find a way forward. However, if they choose not to participate, and continue to disrupt, your only choice will be to use the straightforward consequence that you have negotiated together.

- This is most certainly the time to maintain strong class unity. You need the group to be with you and understand what you are doing. Create opportunities through class discussions concerning fairness, responsibility and expectations.

- Be practical and tactical. Think hard about the behaviours really worth tackling. A sensible rule of thumb is to allow most of the student's low-level annoying behaviours to slip by and only pick up on the ones that honestly matter. In other words, choose your battles wisely and learn the art of avoiding and side-stepping. Learn to be an adaptable chameleon!

- Avoid defending your position, opinion or instruction. Unfortunately, as soon as you do, the oppositional student feels they have gained power and the situation becomes poised to escalate. Instead, respond with comments like:
  - 'If you want to stay change the subject.'
  - 'If you want to stay stop complaining.'
  - 'I like you way too much to argue about this.'
  - 'This is the way it stays.'
  - 'Regardless, this is how it is going to be.'

Using these phrases sparingly, but repetitively with confidence usually helps to gently de-escalate a situation. In addition you may choose to remove yourself from their space and walk away, and if they follow, keep walking.

3 Students who seek revenge

Student thinks . . .

'You should have never done that to me.'

'I'll get you back.'

'I'll show you how it feels.'

'You weren't fair, now suffer the payback.'

Teacher thinks . . .

'How dare you do that!'

'Things will never be the same between us again.'

'I'll give you a punishment to even up things.'

'I've had enough of you.'

Teacher feels . . .

Hurt

Disappointed

Scared

Enraged

Fed up and wants no more to do with the student

Acting on these feelings the teacher will . . .

Tighten up the flexibility usually afforded to the student.

Impose a hefty punishment to rebalance the scales of justice.

Rely on disciplinary support from superiors.

Remain emotionally distant from the student.

When the teacher does this the student thinks . . .

'You want a war? I'll give it to you!'

'You're not worth anything. You're pathetic.'

'I've got some new rules for you too.'

'You hurt me, and then I'll hurt others.'

Best approach . . .

- As you would expect, an over-reliance on reprisal or payback has severe limitations with these kids.

- Try to find some sort of ground to build or rebuild the relationship, even if it is slow.

- Keep working at building trust, cooperation and loyalty.

- Avoid retaliation at all costs.

- It can be restorative to focus on the student's strengths. For example, create situations where the student can use their strengths or interests to help others.

- Find opportunities where the student can participate, feel good about what they are doing and succeed. As an example, Liam, who was eleven years old, could not participate at school as part of a basketball side. He would find fault, wildly criticise and get even with others when things didn't go his way. However, as soon as Liam became the umpire a new constructive and conciliatory persona emerged.

- Promote the understanding that no one fails when things go wrong. The times when things go badly are fabulous opportunities to learn! Help them see that without trying and possibly failing, they will never find their true potential.

- Once again, preserve class cohesion. Run group discussions on ways to highlight the good things about students in the class. Have fun with class and take advantage of the team building and energising activities in Chapter 7 to lift the spirit of the class.

- Consequences for these kids require careful planning. They are rarely as straightforward as you might hope. A suspension away from school for a day or two where the student revels in playing computer games at home is not appropriate. Neither is having the student sit out from a string of their favourite lessons, watching on, seething and feeling humiliated in front of their peers. Often, the best consequence is to negotiate with the student a way to repair whatever their act of revenge damaged or hurt. However, don't embark on this while your emotions, or theirs, are running high. Sometimes it's wise to bring in a mediator to help steer this such as the school counsellor, principal or a clever colleague.

- Teachers who do well with this behaviour are those who know how to help the student return to the class group without feeling an awful loss of dignity or sensing their return is resented.

4 Students who display inadequacy

Student thinks . . .

'I'm helpless. My teacher can do it for me.'

'I can't. I might get it wrong.'

'I won't. I don't want to fail.'

'I never have. I never can. I never will.'

Teacher thinks . . .

'I've tried everything.'

'I don't know what to do.'

'It's useless!'

'This is beyond me!'

Teacher feels . . .

Discouraged

Pessimistic

Thwarted

Desperate

Acting on these feelings the teacher will . . .

Feel demoralised

Blame the student

Blame inadequate structures within the school

Blame the student's mother, father or past teachers

Give up and fuel the student's reputation that their difficulty is intractable

When the teacher does this the student thinks . . .

'You have to keep helping me. I've always needed help.'

'You know I worry, you can't let me become depressed.'

'If you can't help me then no one can.'

'So, you're giving up on me too. I thought you would.'

Best approach . . .

- Sometimes these kids have endured distressing experiences that have caused them to feel deeply hurt, humiliated and discouraged. Others appear to have had a blissful life and there is no accounting for their helplessness. Whether their displays of inadequacies are real or imagined, all of these kids wear a badge of honour that says, 'I can't do this myself. You can't expect me to.'

- Show patience. Be a skilful model and believe in the value of seed planting.

- Use optimistic talk, genuine encouragement and never give up.

- Set a few achievable goals together, chase them and celebrate!

- Develop an encouragement plan that involves the student (and others in your class) formally receiving recognition from you, the class, the principal, the school or their parent to recognise achievements.

- It can be uplifting to focus on the student's strengths. Construct opportunities where these kids can find success. Acknowledge the positives, but refrain from overdramatic or insincere praise. All kids can identify it immediately and most hate it. Become expert at encouraging what the student has done (process focused praise), rather than praising the student himself or herself.

- Avoid criticism, although if you have developed a trusting relationship, balanced constructive feedback is helpful.

- Share the load and involve others (peers, parents, teachers, professionals and so on) who are able to offer something to this student along the way.

- Gently assist the student to appreciate more about themselves, so that they might be able to appreciate their functioning in a broader, more positive context.

- Develop the understanding that things often go wrong. So much of life is all about regrouping from the unexpected. These kids need a contingency plan – they need to know what to do when things change, unfold in an unexpected direction or go wrong. They benefit from pre-rehearsed options. This may be as simple as working out how they can signal for assistance in class to gain clarification.

Conclusion: strength through composure

The intent of this chapter is to confirm that managing the challenging emotions and errant behaviours of students with oppositional behaviours is genuinely difficult. These taxing behaviours can quickly wipe out a teacher's self belief, devastate the tone of their classroom and wreck the confidence students and parents have in their ability to provide a safe, productive learning environment.

Teachers who do best are those who display strength through composure, even when under duress. A few are able to do this quite naturally. Most of us however, have to learn how to do this. Our perspective is always enhanced when we consciously monitor our reactions against where we sit in the Social Control Window and take Dreikurs' Four Goals of Misbehaviour into regular account. Astute educators also draw on community. They actively build class unity as a means to navigate more steadily through these difficult times. Similarly, they look for collegiate support and will build a team who can reliably support one another because it is too much to ask one educator to deal with this alone. Getting the team together for regular meetings is productive simply because they get everyone together – talking, thinking and caring.

While the understandings and approaches presented will not cure oppositional defiant disorder, they will when used consistently dampen the problematic behaviours. Surrounded by planned and emotionally steady management at school and at home, many children with oppositional behaviours improve and a surprising number eventually outgrow their difficulties.

Worksheets

14   ABCs of behaviour
15   Success plan – go for the cup!
16   My new way to do it
17   Blast off!
18   Go and fly your kite!
19   You can count on Winston's segments!
20   Staying on track with my dragon tracking chart
21   Staying on track with my duck tracking chart

Refer to p. 191 for useful websites and further reading.

Ideas to enrich social and emotional connections
Inside tough kids with Asperger syndrome

Dylan, like many of my clients, has Asperger syndrome. This chapter is inspired by the deep admiration I have for the courage he shows. Can you imagine having to interact in a socially and emotionally rich world, yet consistently finding it difficult to interpret your own feelings and understand the feelings of others? This is what confronts Dylan and others with Asperger syndrome as they do their best to find happiness and success every day.

I can't really tell you when I got it or how Asperger syndrome feels because it's the way I am. If I had to say one thing about it I'd say it's confusing, but I couldn't have told you that when I was younger. No one can see Asperger syndrome and that's part of the problem. In some ways I'm the same as anyone else, but in other ways I know it makes me different. In class when the teacher writes page 57 on the board everyone else seems to know what to do. For me it's not obvious. Once I stop worrying and work it out everyone else has almost finished and that's so annoying. I suppose I've had to learn another language, your language. The language I do understand is computers. They don't fight me, they're not mean to me, they do exactly what I tell them to do and they are organised the way my brain is. They are almost like a best friend to people with Asperger syndrome and that's why I like them so much.

(Dylan, 14 years)

Overview: Asperger syndrome

The Austrian paediatrician Hans Asperger first described children with autistic personality disorder in 1944 (Asperger, cited in Frith 2001). He suggested that the disorder was part of a continuum of abilities that merge into the 'normal range'. Much later, in 1981, British psychiatrist Lorna Wing proposed the term Asperger syndrome (AS) as recognition of a group of children who had autism, but were able to make good progress with early diagnosis and intervention (Wing 1981). Through her work and the work of Christopher Gillberg, Peter Szatmari and a number of notable others, the criteria for a diagnosis of AS was published in the tenth edition of the World Health Organisation's *International Classification of Diseases* in 1993 (Szatmari 2004). In the following year, the American Psychiatric Association published Asperger's disorder in the fourth edition of the *Diagnostic and Statistical Manual of Mental Disorders* (DSM-1V, American Psychiatric Association 1994). Suddenly, the AS puzzle made sense and ideas surrounding its nature, identification, intervention and management became accessible to practitioners. Most recently Tony Attwood's contribution has helped to clarify many of the mysteries and mis-understandings that have surrounded AS (Attwood 1998). His work has transformed this complex neurological condition into healthy understandings for allied health practitioners, school administrators, teachers, parents and the community (Attwood 2007). The depth of Attwood's work cannot be overstated: it has been healing, revitalising and life saving for many with AS. Our communities also owe a debt of gratitude to the wonderfully influential individuals diagnosed with AS such as Temple Grandin, John Edler Robison, Liane Holliday Willey and Luke Jackson to mention a few who have invited us into their world so we may better understand how they interpret it. They have taken us so much closer to understanding the person who has AS, rather than clinically knowing more about a syndrome on a spectrum.

It surprises many to find that autism spectrum disorder (ASD) is not a single diagnostic category, rather it is a collection of traits that fluctuate widely across a broad spectrum. ASD is viewed as a pervasive developmental disorder. It is pervasive, because it impedes an individual's social and communication skills along with presentation of repetitive patterns of interest and activity that do not match what we expect from a person at that particular level of development. ASD is considered a developmental issue because the difficulties are apparent early in life, and in varying degrees, affect the course of the individual's development. ASD groups together both autism and AS. While individuals on the spectrum have similar core processing impairments, it is the differences in the severity of the patterns of behaviour that distinguishes between the two. It is also thought that the level of an individual's intellectual functioning is a vital determining factor in their ability to learn to navigate around the core impairments. AS appears to run in families. It is thought that the brain-based differences are biological in origin and that we may be close to identifying the genetic transmission (Cerderlund and Gillberg 2004). Professor Simon Baron-Cohen has referred to Asperger syndrome as 'the extreme male brain theory' (Baron-Cohen 2004). His preliminary investigations appear to support a hypothesis that autism spectrum disorder may be the result of an extreme male brain profile. Namely, poorer abilities to empathize and elevated abilities to concentrate on specific interests and find patterns within systems. In 1999 he organised the collection of 235 samples of amniocentesis fluid and had them tested for foetal testosterone levels. As these children reached eighteen months those with higher levels of testosterone had appreciably poorer eye contact. Later, at eight years of age these same children had higher autistic traits. The thinking is that this little hormone in elevated levels may have a vast effect on brain development. This researcher is now embarking on what he calls a definitive study into this with 90,000 children in Denmark (*The World of Asperger's* 2008).

Recently released figures from the Australian Prevalence study into autism commissioned by the Australian Autism Advisory Board tell us that 1:160 Australian children aged between six and twelve years are likely to have ASD (MacDermott *et al.* 2007). This translates to about one student in every fifth class, and the numbers are growing. According to this study eight males are diagnosed with Asperger syndrome for each female identified.

A wise starting point to understand the differences in how people with autism and AS perceive, react and interpret the world differently is to glimpse at the neuro-imaging research. There is now growing neuro-anatomical evidence that the amygdala, responsible for regulating emotions, may explain the reason why kids with AS appear to be in a hyper-vigilant state constantly scanning the social horizon for the next emotional or physical threat, being pessimistic, anxious and ever ready to overreact (Adolphs *et al.* 2001). Similarly, recent studies have shown that individuals with AS almost certainly suffer from face blindness or prosopagnosia. As a consequence they process facial information in bit parts that can lead to inaccuracies as they attempt to 'read' others (Barton *et al.* 2004). New neurological research also helps to explain why people with AS find it difficult to identify and describe states of feeling. It takes us closer to understanding why many kids and teens regularly ask how others are feeling as a guide to how *they* are doing and feeling; 'Mum, you love me, don't you?' or 'She was alright about that, wasn't she?' or 'We have had a good day, haven't we?' The result is that AS renders a disabling impact on one's ability to interpret the world of people, and how they fit into it (Berthoz and Hill 2005).

There are of course some classic behavioural features associated with AS. The unusual language mannerisms often catch our attention first. Typically these kids present with a flat, expressionless voice described as monotone. Sometimes there is the hint of an accent that sounds vaguely American. Their speech style can be pedantic and repetitive, especially when they want to get a point across or feel excited about a topic. Their word choice is precise and they will quickly pick you up in conversation when you use an adjective they would not have used. These kids are not conversationalists! They'd much rather hold a one-sided conversation that remains on their topic of their interest, whether the listener is interested or otherwise. While speaking they are likely to be too loud or too soft, or stand too far away or too close, as judging social–physical proximity is elusive. Accompanying the socio/spatial difficulties is poor eye contact. Mostly, parents say they have spent a lifetime reminding their son or daughter to 'look people in the eye' when they speak. After a while most kids with AS get it, but it takes a lot of hard work. Another classic feature is the obvious deficits in theory of the mind. Theory of the mind is an ability most of us take for granted; it is the ability of an individual to understand what another is thinking or to 'read' what they might be thinking and feeling. These kids usually have little idea.

Many of these kids are socially withdrawn. They are more comfortable mixing with older or much younger social groups appreciating the safer, more predictable contact. Some long for friendships, but because they have suffered unfortunate incidents from peers they learn to stay aloof as a means of protection. Quite a few, however, have little ability or desire to form friendships and will tell you that they are happy enough to be alone and would prefer it that way. Most know that they don't read social cues or pick up on the gestures of others very well. As a result, when something goes astray they'll overreact, or worse still, they'll under-react when a big reaction is called for. Subsequently, they hear others say they lack care and empathy. The impact of their substantial social dysfunction can take the form of anxiety, isolation and depression. A study by Hedley and Young in 2003 found a high incidence of depressive symptoms in Asperger youth, and identified a strong relationship between feeling different, being socially isolated and suffering from depression.

In day-to-day school life these kids are seen as clumsy and poorly coordinated. Some hold an odd posture and walk with an awkward gait. It is a stiff-legged walk with arm movements that don't quite synchronise that draws attention. When they become excited or troubled they'll run on the spot, run in circles, twirl or flap their hands. Teachers often note their poor sporting ability, but will insist students maintain a sport at school. This is a curse for many students, especially the boys, who attend boy's schools steeped in strong traditions around competitive sport. They know they don't move well and find it hard to anticipate how the game works. They look and feel out of place, finding themselves in yet another situation where they are different.

Teachers worry over their limited, untidy written communication. Their hand-writing is spidery, difficult to read and quite often in upper case. When questioned they'll tell you that if it's good enough for the keyboard to have upper case letters on it then it's good enough for them to use upper case. For many, their drawings look immature and match their scant, untidy book work. For others, their drawings are odd, but infinitely detailed. Their extremely meticulous drawing of guns shooting lines of bullets that destroy the person with blood and flesh exploding everywhere is a distinct style. Fear not – they are no more likely to grow up a crazed killer than the supposedly well adjusted kid sitting next to them!

Classically, these kids are extraordinarily inflexible. They hate surprises and find change hard to cope with. They have a strong need for routine and order because intuitively they know their functioning is so much better when they feel in control. Parents learn to compensate for their child's rigidity at home, but every parent has stories about their child's peculiar need for control: magazines that must be stacked in a certain way on a certain table, cars that have to be lined up in a precise order, toys that must be grouped according to size, shape, cost, material or colour, collector cards that must be stacked their way in their bedroom before lights out, exclusive foods, toast that must have the right spread at the right thickness and cut in the same way every time, and how as a baby they would only feed from the breast if held in a particular way. Given their deep inflexible traits it should not surprise you to find that these kids are highly vulnerable to sensory overload: too much or too little noise, heat, humidity, smell, taste, colour, activity, physical contact and so on. Sudden distressed behaviours can rapidly spiral from their under- or oversensitive sensory input system. Their mothers and fathers relay stories about their remarkable over sensitivities and the big reactions they can bring. Obsessional or ritualistic behaviours are a part of the cluster of inflexible traits too. These kids develop remarkable and intense passion for particular interests: dates, timetables, buses, trains, planes, electrical circuits, computers, computer games, weapons, street directories, stickers, collector cards, drawing, *Warhammer* and accurately remembering slabs of lines from books and movies are common. For the most part obsessions are harmless and as one wanes a new one emerges. Sometimes the preoccupation of cultivating a quirky obsession results in a highly refined splinter skill or talent.

These inflexible and obsessional traits are more easily accommodated for at home, but the complexly layered and highly social environment of school presents great challenges for these kids. As an example, a teacher may call out to the class, 'Hurry up! Pick up your feet!' The student with AS is likely to reach down and physically pick up her feet as she walks. Or, the teacher may shoot a hurried glance at the student with AS who has just finished their work saying, 'Stick it on my desk'. When the teacher returns to their desk the student has actually stuck the work to the desk! These kids take things very literally, so nicknames, idioms and double meanings either confuse or are completely lost on them. Social comprehension regularly proves difficult. While they may not understand ordinary jokes, irony or metaphors, so often these children and teens show a brilliant offbeat humour similar to Monty Python or Mr Bean. On a similar note, an interesting characteristic of students with AS is that they may read accurately, but demonstrate reduced reading comprehension in combination with significant difficulties when it comes to 'reading between the lines' and making inferences from text.

Finally, don't be deceived. Individuals with AS certainly share a set of highly distinctive traits, but their individuality is as unique as yours and mine. It is unwise to assume too much about AS. After all, you would never think, 'Yes, I know all about Tibetans or Nigerians' having taught one or two Tibetans or Nigerians.

Eventually, with understanding, practical family support, a responsive school environment, bursts of formal social-skills training and exposure to safe, accepting social groups, most kids with AS learn to intellectualise how to fit in and feel more connected (Dodd 2005). Never underestimate the importance of great role models and honest communication for these kids (Prizant 2008). We all benefit from someone to look up to, someone who has paved the way before us. Sometimes there is an adult in the family who also has AS, and despite this they have made their way successfully in the world. Recognising this can be wonderfully affirming and can help to steer children and teens in healthy directions.

Guiding principles to create emotionally sustaining opportunities

In this chapter you will find an assortment of ideas that teachers, school support officers, school counsellors and psychologists can use to build socially and emotionally nourishing opportunities for all kids who experience communication delays and differences. The primary focus, of course, is for students identified with Asperger syndrome. For them, not being able to flexibly interpret the social world triggers emotion and behaviour that is tricky to manage.

Realistically, how much scope is there for us to raise the happiness and emotional connectivity of children at school? The short answer is that providing we have the will, educators can contrive countless opportunities to generate optimistic relationships and situations for young people (Lord and McGee 2001). Our collective wisdom and care is potent! Yes, it may be more challenging to influence transformations in children with core processing differences, and it is probably more testing to influence constructive change as they become older, but we are a significant group who understand the kinds of structures and messages these kids need to receive (Ilot 2005).

Raising acceptance and happiness

Belonging

To feel valued kids have to know they are included and accepted by the group (Sicile-Kira 2008). Baumeister's study described the effects of rejection on an individual's IQ and ability to reason analytically and the results were astonishing! Participants who believed that they had not been chosen to work with the group, compared to those who thought they had been chosen, were shown to have an increase in impulsivity, an increase in aggression, an IQ drop of 25 per cent and a 30 per cent plunge in analytical reasoning. The study concluded that sadness, isolation and rejection interferes with an individual's self-control and can lead to emotional and behavioural difficulties (Baumeister 2002). It is conclusive – disconnection and rejection does interfere with a person's self-control and can lead to behavioural difficulties. So no matter what year level you work with, arrange:

- Time for joke-telling sessions. It's good medicine and lifts everyone's spirits.

- Time for the exchange of real life embarrassing moments. We all have them and they're such good fun to tell and listen to. These little life snippets also help class members to appreciate a little more about one another.

- Success nominations. Once a week, ask the class to nominate someone (self-nomination is acceptable) who has made progress in a particular area. Invite others to share their thoughts about the improvement. Impromptu heartfelt acknowledgment by peers is a powerful emotional connector.

- To present awards, certificates, house points or medals to students to acknowledge their effort, improvement and academic achievement. As trivial as this may seem, such consistency does play a role in maintaining student connections to school.

A good idea to highlight the beauty of differences is to send home graphs asking parents to fill in when their child first sat up independently, started to walk, first talked, when their first tooth arrived, when they lost their first tooth, first slept in 'big bed', rode a bike, learned to swim and so on. Constructing a simple graph is a strong visual means to illustrate diversity. Graphs are wonderful visual reminders that some learn earlier than others, some learn more smoothly, some are hungry learners and others do it differently. The healthy message is that being different is okay; what matters most is being in a place where conditions favour acceptance, belonging, learning and transformation.

Find worksheet on page 224

Direct, positive feedback

For the kids we have in mind in this chapter direct, positive feedback is priceless. As we catch a buoyant attitude, an optimistic behaviour or a piece of work that's heading in the right direction, the act of commenting on it lets kids know they are on the right track and reinforces its continuation. Our positive feedback alerts them that what they are doing is what we want (Gardner *et al.* 2003). This really counts given their difficulties in reading and interpreting the social world. As mentioned earlier in Chapter 3, 'Inspiration to improve concentration and task completion', this can be taken a step further by inventing simple non-verbal cues such as a wink or a scratch of the head that sends the message to them that they are doing well (Rogers 2003). The up side is that it will strengthen your relationship as well.

Case study

'That's normal?'

Helen is my friend. She's a committed, enthusiastic upper primary teacher who really enjoys her students. I know through indirect sources that the kids in her class say she's firm, fair and fun. As a friend, I see her fun-loving spirit as her most beautiful asset. Several years ago she had Danny in her class and Danny had Asperger syndrome. Danny tended to drift into doing what he wanted, when he wanted, rather than what Helen wanted or what was desirable. Helen and her class gave Danny the freedom to unhook from the group or from tasks from time to time because they understood it was his way of coping. One afternoon while students were immersed in their personal project work Helen found Danny wandering about on his hands and knees under his desk. Quietly she dropped onto the floor and crawled towards Danny. She met him under his desk.

As she pulled up, head to head in front of him, Danny asked, 'What are you doing Ms Habel?'

Helen replied, 'I'm doing the same as you.'

'Oh, I'm doing that. That's not right,' Danny responded.

'I know,' replied Helen, 'I want both of us to be right for a while.'

Immediately, Danny stood up, moved back to his seat and got on with his task. Helen did the same. What Helen did, with true affection, was to help Danny actually see his behaviour in the social context required. Gradually, she taught Danny to measure whether what he was doing was appropriate by asking himself three easy questions:

- What am I doing?
- Is it the same as everyone else?
- Am I engaged in the task being asked of me?

The need for heroes and role models

Dylan, who wrote the introduction to this chapter, recently mentioned he felt lost after hearing Bill Gates had officially retired from the Microsoft Corporation. You see, Bill Gates had long been his hero. Dylan had grown up learning all about his amazing accomplishments, his wealth, his awesome generosity and the idea that Bill Gates had achieved all of this having distinct traits of Asperger syndrome. Dylan had long held a simple but powerful thought: if Bill could make it, so could he. It is therapeutic and motivational for kids to discover other people who have had Asperger syndrome (or any difference, difficulty, disorder or disability) and have made their way successfully into the world. Do what you can to help students find heroes. A good start is to google appropriate websites using famous people with Asperger syndrome/autistic traits/ADHD/learning difficulties/dyslexia/epilepsy/cerebral palsy and so on.

Mentorship

With hindsight, many adults are able to reflect on the gift they received through mentorship when they were young. They will tell you how a little encouragement from a significant person made a difference to them. For some, mentorship broadened social connections, triggered confidence and helped with learning at school. For a few, the gentle nourishing nature of the mentoring relationship was life saving. Their mentor may have been a teacher, an older student, a school counsellor or principal. Occasionally, mentoring takes place outside school through a friend, a neighbour or a relative, but what appears common is that the mentee felt their mentor liked them, believed in them and wanted to help them discover more about themselves.

Within schools, untapped resources exist for ongoing mentoring. A popular approach allows the student to check in with their mentor each week to talk, review and organise for what is upcoming. As a student develops a relationship with their mentor they discover ways to improve routines, develop strategies to build friendships, deal with conflict and find avenues to lift organisational and academic skills.

Through conversation, mentors are able to mirror back events and ask the hard questions:

- Why do you think that happened?

- Did your fast feelings get in the way?

- Was there another way you could have handled it?

- What may have happened if you had done it another way?

- What gives you the right to keep doing this when others . . .?

- Let's work on one way to handle this better next time.

As a consequence of mentorship a student's world can become more predictable, allowing them to feel and function far more steadily. Mentoring has provided many children and adolescents with the impetus to find greater success.

Build a team

A support team to maintain the buoyant spirit of children and adolescents is an emotionally healthy initiative. The approach is to work with the student to identify individuals they may gather back-up and inspiration from to maintain their happiness and perseverance. As we know, many of the kids we are familiar with wrestle with all manner of feelings. They can fluctuate from attacks of depression, to crippling anxiousness, through to grief. First, encourage students to consider their needs and suggest who they want on their team. This is the right moment to raise your thoughts as well because it's vital that those selected are reliable, approachable and will deliver whatever is asked. The team may include an assortment of individuals: mother, father, tutor, teacher, counsellor, Chaplain, a relative or friend – anyone at all. Next, assign a role to each of the team members. This is a therapeutic strategy for students of all ages because it provides a strong visual message that they are cared for.

Find worksheet on page 225

Unify attitudes

A popular idea gathering momentum is to organise a meeting with all parents of the class at the beginning of the year to explain the problematic emotions and behaviours of one or two students. This opportunity is always stabilising for all involved. Nothing is more powerful than parents listening to another parent, and hearing the emotion in their voice as they explain why their child has been identified with AS, ADHD or ODD, and what this really means. Such meetings pave the way for better understandings and cohesion between students and parents.

A mood diary

Assisting students to maintain a mood diary or journal is a good way to help everyone keep track of how things are really travelling for them. As you are well aware, quite a number of these kids are on emotional roller coasters and journaling feelings can be a cathartic activity. Suggest that students journal the good and not so good things that happen to crop up. Devise a simple 'happiness continuum' so they can rate their day. Keeping a journal helps reinforce that although they may have faced difficulties during their week, there have also been some enjoyable moments. This helps to capitalise on the fact that there has been a balance and life really is full of ups and downs for everyone.

Easing anxiety and stress

Be mindful. Kids with Asperger syndrome have slower processing speeds, especially when under duress. They need time to answer your questions.

> 'Did you kill the dog?' he asked.
> I said, 'I did not kill the dog.'
> 'Is this your fork?' he asked.
> I said, 'No.'
> 'You seem very upset about this,' he said.
> He was asking too many questions and he was asking them too quickly. They were stacking up in my head like loaves in the factory where Uncle Terry works. The factory is a bakery and he operates the slicing machines. And sometimes the slicer is not working fast enough but the bread keeps coming and there is a blockage. I sometimes think of my mind as a machine, but not always a bread-slicing machine. It makes it easier to explain to other people what is going on inside it . . .
> The policeman said, 'I am going to ask you once again.'
> I rolled back on to the lawn and pressed my forehead to the ground again and made the noise that Father calls groaning. . . .The policeman took hold of my arm and lifted me onto my feet. I didn't like him touching me like this.
> And this is when I hit him.
>
> (Haddon 2003, p. 8)

Surrounded by the action of school it is easy to forget the slower response speeds and the edge of anxiety these kids live with. Expecting quick answers, succinct replies or clear explanations following a difficulty or incident is a dependable recipe for a disastrous outcome.

Similarly, when the worksheet or writing task feels too confronting, their sensory system rockets into overload and they do not cope well. As their stress hits the danger zone even a relatively simple task takes on a frightening dimension for them, looking bigger and far more complicated than it is. Once these students move into this zone their ability to make a rational decision evaporates. Rational thoughts are replaced by: 'This is too hard.' 'This is stupid.' 'I can't think.' 'I can't.' 'I won't.' 'You can't make me.' Sometimes severely reduced written output is a debilitating problem. The pattern is that these kids are often able to talk through their ideas, but transferring what is in their head onto paper is a monumental challenge. They may or may not struggle with basic spelling or grammatical skills, but as they try to formulate thoughts onto paper their perfectionist tendencies get in the way. Their words don't seem to be right, the handwriting gets messy and it all takes too long and feels wrong. There are a number of ideas to support written output of these kids in the section titled 'Ideas to stretch written output', in Chapter 3 (see p. 68).

Without clever interventions or circuit breakers, what occurs are the classic patterns of behaviour that deliver escape and comfort: hand wringing, hand flapping, pacing, twirling, hiding under the desk, head in the work tray, animal noises, refusal, defiance and even aggression. When issues remain unresolved in the eyes of these kids they begin to refuse to go to school. Their emotional withdrawal from school occurs quickly because their motivation to attend is not intrinsically strong. Suddenly the unresolved anxiety takes on a life of its own. At this point outrageous behaviours may escalate in the hope it will earn them a suspension so they can remain safely at home and immerse themselves in activities that bring peace and solace.

Every so often we may not be able to identify the trigger for the anxiety or stress, but we do need to know a few instrumental steps to help lower it:

- When the student is calm, discuss the problem.

- Deliberately say you can help them to fix it and that you want to.

- Let them see you engaged and listening. They need to see your empathy and authority, and trust it.

- To reduce over-stimulation find a way to reduce the number of activities presented in the work.

- Consciously place fewer activities on each page and offer just one page at a time.

- Structure instructions for tasks and the tasks themselves into manageable, bite-sized pieces.

- As their oversensitivity reduces, gradually increase the quantity of work.

- Always manipulate a 'fresh start' for the student each week. This helps to avoid them feeling as though they are falling behind and feeling overwhelmed by having too much to catch up on. In this circumstance, less work translates to more ongoing work.

- Arrange a place the student can withdraw to when feeling anxious that offers comfort. Later in the chapter how to go about developing break cards and safe retreats is explored (see p. 153). In essence, a break card allows a student to take a break from the classroom when feeling stressed or anxious. The student does not need to say anything, all they need to do is present their break card, leave the classroom and go to a previously designated safe place or safe person. Safe havens are emotionally restorative because they provide time for kids to process what is happening.

- The use of break cards requires rehearsal everyday for a week or two while emotions are not elevated.

- One way to reduce anxiety is to pre-teach the key issues to be tackled in the up and coming lesson. This helps to expedite processing and provides the student with a sense of certainty about what will happen and what will be expected. Arrange for a suitable peer, a school support officer or another staff member to go through what will be presented in the lesson. Some students take comfort in having their own notebook where they can record what they will need to do and refer to it later. Another idea is to break the task into distinct components so the student can tick off each component as they complete it.

- Finally, teach these kids how to cheat! Many of them are as honest as the day is long and it would never occur to them to watch how another student is tackling the task. Legitimise this as a valuable way to find out what to do.

There is no doubt that some of these suggestions do create extra work for teachers in the short term, but longer term benefits for the student, other students, the classroom learning environment and the teacher far outweigh a little extra planning.

Visual strategies

A visual strategy is any visual means to support a student's understanding about what to do, when to do it and how to do it: schedules, timetables, stamps, charts, sticky notes with reminders, an email or text message, pictures, PowerPoint™ presentations, lists, dot point instructions, checklists, calendars, the same silly smile, notes, signs, messages, cue cards and even a string tied to a finger (Savner and Smith-Myles 2000). The only limitation to visual options is our imagination! They are invaluable for all, but because they are especially useful for the kids this chapter is built around I have decided to raise their profile again. For a broad selection of ideas and handy worksheets turn back to Chapter 4, 'Strategies to help organisation and memory' (pp. 78–103).

Well-crafted visual strategies provide kids with a permanent and personalised way to improve social/emotional competencies, as well as being brilliant little anxiety lifesavers as they give reassurance about how to improve a desired behaviour, habit or routine. They offer a consistent way for kids to find greater independence. Students can carry their visual helpers with them from one learning situation to another in the forms of business cards, key tags, wallets or attached to lanyards. This makes them very effective to support students with transition. As you would expect, older students prefer their visual strategies to be more discreet, so reducing them down to business-card size and laminating them works well.

Ideally, the introduction of a visual strategy is best executed when a student is feeling calm and when their receptive language is optimal. Make it a gradual process so the student is not overloaded by too many ideas at once. A good starting point is to identify a skill to be learned, and then together develop an idea that they feel responsive to. Persist with what you construct because some students take longer to see the advantage being delivered. Once the student shows improvement or success with self-management do not assume they no longer need the visual structure. Kids usually reduce their need for it in their own time.

Finally, the product 'Boardmaker' is one of a number of useful software packages to customise visual prompts. The pictures are simple and can be used in conjunction with photos to make personalised boards. Take a look at the website for online support, www.mayer-johnson.com.

Strengthening social skills

Formal social skills programmes

A formal social skills training programme at school where students are explicitly taught how to solve social problems and behave in prosocial ways benefits everyone. Such instruction is vital for all kids who suffer from social blindness. Social skills programmes teach kids how to establish and maintain friendships as well as how to handle teasing, aggression and peer rejection. So often, explicit coaching is required to draw attention to the rules of friendship.

Kids and teens often refer to the rules of friendship below as 'recipes' for success. They know it is one thing to meet new people and get it right, but takes quite another set of skills to maintain friendships. Even if the rules of friendship provide little more than a basic instrumental guide to hang new behaviours on, their place is invaluable.

Rules for keeping friends

- Be nice and always show you care.

- Include them and share.

- Talk, and remember to stop and listen as well.

- Ask them questions about how they feel, what they like to do and their interests.

- Find out what they like and don't like.

- Sometimes do things together outside of school.

- Allow them to play or be with other people too.

- Tell them that you are their friend.

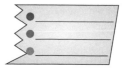

- Give them feedback. Say what it is you like about them and what you enjoy doing with them.

- Notice how they look. Observe their feelings:
  - ask, 'What's wrong?'
  - ask, 'Are you okay?'
  - ask, 'How can I help?'

- Think before you speak because uncaring comments put others off.

- Remember, friendship is not perfect. Friendships change and this is normal.

Rules for making friends

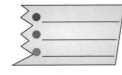

- Be brave, walk up and introduce yourself.

- Always smile!

- Say your name, face them and make eye contact.

- Ask them about themselves.

- Listen to their answers.

- Talk about the things you have in common.

- Be yourself. Try not to brag or be too cool.

- Sound and look kind.

- Making a good impression means thinking about what you say.

The internationally recognised STOP THINK DO programme is my preference. It links feelings to behaviour and develops a way to insert thinking between feeling and reacting before the uncontrolled reaction turns into a behaviour they'll later regret. This programme develops self-control and communication skills at STOP, problem-solving skills at THINK and behavioural skills at DO (Petersen and Le Messurier 2006). Best outcomes are achieved with the continuing support of significant others: parents, teachers and peers, for maintenance and transfer of skills. The research suggests that when children are relating well and behaving in friendly ways learning outcomes improve (Petersen and Adderley 2002). Other well regarded programmes that teach children and adolescents to understand more about themselves, about social life and how to increase their resilience and friendship building skills include:

- STOP THINK DO – www.stopthinkdo.com

- Friends For Life – www.friendsinfo.net

- Resourceful Adolescent Program – www.rap.qut.edu.au

- Cool Kids Program – www.psy.mq.edu.au

- Bounce Back – www.bounceback.com.au

- Rock and Water Program – www.rockandwaterprogram.com
- Friendly Schools and Families – www.friendlyschools.com.au
- Program Achieve – www.youcandoiteducation.com
- Seasons for Growth – www.seasonsforgrowth.co.uk
- Tools of the Mind – www.mscd.edu/extendedcampus/toolsofthemind/

Social skills programmes offer a reliable framework for students to successfully deal with confusing and stressful situations. Always have a social skills programme running in the classroom! Continuing daily input where students are given the right prompts, the right language and cueing at their point of performance is where the best gains are made.

Informal social skills practice

Despite educators wanting the best for students, the socially rigorous environment of school is not always the best place for all kids to find friendship. This applies especially to students identified with Asperger syndrome who can suffer dreadful isolation, hurtful taunts and sophisticated bouts of bullying. For some, the best chance they have to develop real social connections will take place outside of school where they are able to connect with others through a common interest. Now and again, their interests lead them to meet people who will influence their career pathway. With this in mind, think about gathering up the contacts of clubs, associations, groups and organisations that might offer the chance for kids to improve their interests, confidence and esteem. There are a myriad of groups within the local community worth exploring. Never underestimate their potential benefits.

Social stories

Kids with Asperger syndrome have difficulties understanding social interaction, find it puzzling to know what they should do and how others may be feeling. In 1991 Carol Gray developed the design of 'social stories' for students with ASD to help explain the social world and teach them what to do (Gray 2000). More recently, social stories have also been successfully used with younger and older individuals who experience broad-based social and communication delays and differences.

Social stories are used to help students learn new routines, how to tackle tasks, how to respond to various situations and how interpret the feelings of others. They strengthen the social functioning of kids because they give the rules and guide the making of appropriate choices (Baker 2001, 2006). Studies with school-aged children on the autistic spectrum show social stories work because they explicitly teach the culture: how social common sense works (Reynhout and Carter 2008).

As a rule, there are two types of social story. First, there are stories that explain what to do and how to do it in specific situations (Tullemans *et al.* 2005). They address the important skills such as how to line up for class, sit on the floor, be a friend, work in a group or with the music teacher, deal with not coming first, share pencils, pack up, and how to happily share favourite play equipment with others. As an example, nine-year-old Sean loved dinosaurs, but did not show the same passion for getting to school on time. Not surprisingly, his social story was about what he needed to do to get ready, leave the house by 8am and arrive at school to meet his teacher with a smile by 8.30am each morning. His social story included himself as the main character and his brother, mother, father and teacher. Sean and his teacher decided to use dinosaur pictures for each character in the story. Sean delighted in asking each person which dinosaur they would like to be. However, he'd reserved the velociraptor as it was his favourite. After they had talked about the best ways for Sean to be successful in the morning they wrote the story together. He and his teacher combined images of dinosaur bodies with real head shots of everyone in the story. Amazing what can be done with a digital camera and a little imagination!

The second type of social story is one that explains the thoughts and expectations of others. It tells clearly and simply how the student's choices or behaviour make others feel (Howley and Arnold 2005). In Sean's case, a subsequent social story was made to show how each of the dino-characters in the first story felt when he made good and bad choices in the morning. An emphasis was placed on the happy feelings and congratulatory actions of others when he made good choices, but the social story also provided scope for Sean to understand the feelings and responses of others when he made a poor choice.

The conventional way to build a social story has been to develop a small book with the student (Gray and White 2002). However, other options include writing a script and using it to develop a short film or a slide show.

Finally, it is ideal to introduce social stories using a calm, bright approach where the student has the best chance to learn from the social story before experiencing it. The story can be read to the student daily at first, to the class group, or may be copied and sent home to be read as a bedtime story. As the student begins to use the skills presented in the social story, the story can be gradually faded by reviewing it once a week, then once a month. In the meantime a new social story can be developed.

Playful ideas to strengthen social and emotional muscle

Reading voice, body and face

Stretching the social awareness of students starts at asking them to interpret the voice, body and face of others (Barekat 2006). Train kids to appreciate that how an individual presents their voice, body and face gives volumes of information to others about them. The way we sit, stand, use our voice and bring eye contact and facial expressions into play sends powerful messages to others. Knowing simple facts such as maintaining eye contact suggests confidence and interest, or sitting up and leaning slightly forward while listening is seen as being interested, works in one's favour when communicating. On the other hand, mumbling, avoiding eye contact and looking at the floor expresses uncertainty, and folding arms gives the impression of defensiveness and disinterest. Unthoughtful body language can set individuals up as victims for failure and rejection.

One idea to stretch these skills is to pull together some large images of people interacting together with close-ups of their faces. Alternatively, watch part of a movie or a clip where people are interacting with the sound switched off. Discuss what's happening and what the people might be saying and feeling. Ask, 'How do you know?' Most often the kids with Asperger syndrome will pick up on what is happening but will not easily read the emotions on the people's faces. They enjoy and need this practice to tease out and expand on what is happening emotionally. Also try role-playing body language, facial expressions and voice tone seen in others. Act out disgruntled faces, surprised bodies, quizzical faces, embarrassed faces, sad bodies and so on. Ask students to read the voice, body and face of others and describe what they might be feeling. Get them to make the same face.

Watching behaviour

Try an emphasis on watching the behaviours of others. A perfect place to start is to choose an appropriate movie or sitcom. Discuss:

- why certain characters were funny, loved, odd, disliked, or unhappy;

- who their favourite character was and why;

- who their least favourite character was and why;

- who was the victim and how could you tell?

- who was at fault and how could you tell?

- how did each person feel?

- what cues helped you to make this judgement?

- how would you have made things better?

Observing behaviour and emotion in this way guides kids to see that relationships are complex, and there is much more to them than anticipating a right or wrong, a fair or unfair outcome. The value of watching the behaviour of others was illustrated by a nine-year-old girl who asked the kids in her socials skills group, 'Why did that girl have rain in her eyes?' after watching a film vignette. The opportunity for young people with Asperger syndrome to gain better insights into social situations comes from consistent teaching and discussion. A wonderful discussion point around anger is to watch the highly frustrated and aggressive Basil Fawlty in *Fawlty Towers*. This makes for rich discussion. Basil's bad temper in combination with having to be right and wanting the last say causes him so much trouble.

Play detective

Arrange for the student to secretly observe how another child interacts with others. Start by asking the question, 'Who do you think gets along with most kids really well?' Sometimes the student with Asperger syndrome will choose who you would. Sometimes this question reveals they have less idea than you had realised. Don't despair. At least you have a starting point and it fits with current evidence that one of the greatest difficulties for kids with Asperger syndrome is to mimic behaviour (Attwood 2007). The consequence of this failure is serious because imitation is a most powerful learning tool. It's through imitation that a child learns to mouth its first words and master the non-verbal body language of body posture and facial expression.

This is the time to identify the better models in class, and to connect them to the kids who model great relationships. Together, agree on a particular student. Then, ask them to start observing and collect data on how this student interacts with others. Develop a few categories to compile notes within: what do they say? What phrases do they use? What are the popular topics or conversations? What do they look like when they listen? What is their voice like when they speak with friends? Are they good at conversation? Are they good at turn taking? Why do you think they get along so well? Do they say nice things to others? What do you think others like about them? Highlight the notion that this person has the sort of qualities others like (Gutstein 2001). Suggest that these are worth developing because they are qualities that lead to acceptance and belonging.

Literal versus illusive

So many kids and adults with Asperger syndrome think too rigidly to get their head around metaphors. Use them as a wonderful springboard into the fluidity of the social world. Discuss the not so obvious meanings behind proverbs, myths, fables and clichés, and be amazed by the quality of conversation and learning that follows:

- A bird in the hand is worth two in the bush.

- A chain is no stronger than its weakest link.

- A friend in need is a friend indeed.

- A rolling stone gathers no moss.

- Absence makes the heart grow fonder.

- Actions speak louder than words.

- All good things must come to an end.

- All that glitters is not gold.

- All work and no play makes Jack a dull boy.

- An apple a day keeps the doctor away.

- Beauty is only skin-deep.

- Better the devil you know than the devil you don't.

- Birds of a feather flock together.

- Blood is thicker than water.

- Do unto others as you would like them to do unto you.

- Don't cut off your nose to spite your face.

- Dying of thirst.

- Easier said than done.

- Every dog has his day.

- Experience is the greatest teacher.

- Fake it until you make it!

- Fools rush in where angels fear to tread.

- Give credit when credit is due.

- Has the cat got your tongue?

- He who hesitates is lost.

- He's a sheep in wolf's clothing.

- Honesty is the best policy.

- I laughed my head off.

- If a job's worth doing, it's worth doing well.

- Ignorance is bliss.

- It is best to be on the safe side.

- It is no use crying over spilt milk.

For easy access to more of these, try www.phrases.org.uk/meanings/

Compliments

Most of us give too few, but the delightful response a compliment brings reminds us how valuable they really are. Examine what a compliment is, how to deliver them well, how to receive them and what their true value is in day to day interaction. Set compliment homework for your students. Ask them to give a compliment to one or two people of their choice over the next day or so. Brainstorm appropriate things they could say and rehearse the best way of doing it. Follow up to find out how it went and build on new ways to do this. Let them know that delivering well placed compliments is reassuring to every relationship. Optimistic feedback is one sure way to positively influence the behaviour of others towards them.

Saying sorry

The word 'sorry' is a repair mechanism that can rescue so many situations. Yet, it can be difficult for many to say. Have fun with students' role-playing situations where sorry would be helpful. Try sorry with a smile, a gesture, a wink, a handshake, a rub on someone's arm or a hug. Brainstorm an assortment of words and actions that mean the same as sorry rather than saying it. Help kids to understand that saying sorry isn't necessarily an admission of wrongdoing; more to the point, it is a gesture to ease resentment and assist the relationship to heal.

Empathy

Purposefully teach kids how to show compassion and sympathy to others. The ability to respond with care and ask the right questions at the right time using the right tone of voice is a prized tool in one's social repertoire. This set of skills rates highly on the list for maintaining successful relationships. At the end of the day, if someone is able to give the right look, use the right words and behave empathically then they pass the test with flying colours.

Obsessions and collections

The obsessional nature of some kids can be a real hindrance in developing or sustaining relationships with others. Most find having to listen to the obsessions of others a real turn-off. Explain from the earliest of times that talking about their obsession may give them comfort or a sense of authority, but going on and on explaining infinite details about something that doesn't rate on the 'socially popular' radar is damaging to relationships. It is wise to address this awkward behaviour early as we owe it to these kids to explain the social landscape on this matter. An idea is to make a rule together: never talk about your obsession or collection at school. Actually nominate people who are safe to discuss the obsession or collection with, and even then, put a time limit on it and put understandings in place that discern between a conversation and a monologue. Most obsessions are relatively healthy and rather than trying to stamp them out steer them in productive directions. Who knows, their evolving obsession may lead them to be a collector of great repute in the future!

The smart advantage

Those who learn to stay calm when things go wrong give themselves the advantage of thinking more clearly and making better choices. It's the smart advantage! When someone says something that's annoying, hurtful or threatening think of new ways to address the problem: smile, shrug, walk away, tell a joke, ignore, run, roll your eyes, duck for cover, be quiet, say you agree, say sorry or become invisible and blend into the background. Teach them to creatively press the 'delete key' in their mind or to shrink those they are having trouble with into little babies with smelly nappies. In this way they can say, 'it doesn't matter'. Teach that just because someone looks as though they are being mean or thoughtless, it isn't a cue to get even, get back at them or have the last say. Develop the saying, 'When I stay calm I can use my intelligence and find the best options'. All kids need to know that when they stay calm they give their brain the best chance to send powerful help messages to deal with problems. When they do this they exude confidence and poise, and this will have a positive influence on how others see them.

Write yourself onto a list

Every so often, construct lists to use as comparisons. Together, make a list that reveals who in class has the most difficult or the best behaviours, who is the nicest to the teacher, who does the least or most work, who has the easiest or angriest behaviours and who is the most or least organised. Ask, 'Where do you rank yourself on the list?' 'Is that where you want to be?' 'What can you do to change this?' Every so often review and update the lists. This approach offers insight, stretches awareness and allows new goals to be set.

PowerPoint™

Many students with Asperger syndrome have quite sophisticated ICT skills. They will happily spend hours developing short movies, animations and slide shows. One idea is to encourage them to develop a PowerPoint™ presentation on one of the following subjects: the art of conversation, how to make friends, how to keep friends, the secret of reading emotions from faces, or an explanation of Asperger syndrome. Usually, the student requires little more than an explanation of the criterion, a handful of books and websites and they are away! Quite often it is helpful if the student sees the exercise as a medium to teach others. This takes the spotlight away from their deficits and allows their talents to shine.

Teach how to think flexibly

The natural style for these kids is to think their way and only their way. Once these kids engage in a task of their choice they become single-minded, even obsessed. They will keep at it even if the rest of the world begins to crumble around them. This inflexible style of thinking reduces their capacity to stop a task on command and smoothly move to a new task. Yet, a student's capacity to freely switch from one task to another is heavily relied on by teachers. We depend on students being responsive, flexible and adaptable.

Associate Professor Robyn Young from Flinders University, South Australia, highlights that in order to teach these kids to be more flexible we should deliberately and intelligently 'rock their boat' more frequently (Young 2009). Resistance to change is a big issue, so do what you can to 'tolerance build'. In other words, contrive thoughtful ways to make things different, such as moving kids to different seats, getting them to work with a different buddy or teacher, getting them to help out with different tasks and take on new responsibilities. While this requires preparation and structuring, this must be a goal. A useful idea to stretch thinking flexibility is to present a random object to these kids while in the company of others, and ask them to describe different ways in which it might be played with or used. Take a humble set of chopsticks for example. How many different purposes could they be used for? Let them see and hear the others brainstorming a diversity of ideas. The approach here is to progressively switch their single-track thinking to a more adaptable style; when kids think more flexibly they can change set patterns of behaviour more easily.

As Robyn Young observes, the impact of neglecting to teach a child to become more flexible is having an 18-year-old yelling out 'Last drinks!' at 8.52 pm each night and expecting mum or dad to hand deliver it. Perhaps that may have been cute when the child was 4-years-old, but at this point the family has become more 'autistic', rather than their child becoming more flexible.

Review, review, review and celebrate wins!

Constantly review progress and celebrate gains. Reinforce that there are always bumps and curve balls in life. That's the one sure thing about it! All of this needs to be carried out in the context of engineering these kids to see how the good kids click together and of opening connections so they can interact with them and find a degree of acceptance.

Transitional strategies

A consistently challenging trait for students identified with Asperger syndrome is their difficulty to cope with change. We know from experience that preparing all students in advance for changes to routine, for unstructured time and for brand new occasions is helpful. Students identified with Asperger syndrome have a strong need to know what is going to happen and need to prepare for it so they can deal with it comfortably. When they can't work out what is going on they are more likely to become anxious and reactive. Here are a few ideas to prepare kids for transition.

Six months before starting at the new school

Arrange to take your student to the secondary school they will start at next year. Briefly introduce them to several key personnel and be sure to pick up a school diary. Then, for the remainder of the year allow them to use the secondary school diary every day so they become expert at using it.

Several months before starting at the new school

A pre-emptive strategy is to organise for two, three, four or five transition visits to assist the student to familiarise themselves with the new school situation before they begin. During each visit be sure to physically move about the school with the student to visit their new locker, student services, the uniform shop, the toilets, the canteen, the resource centre/library, the special education room and so on. Expert educators use their digital cameras and capture the student with their home group teacher in their new classroom, at the canteen with the manager, in their art class with the art teacher, with their special education teacher and principal. A thoughtful idea is to include a group photograph of students (Christian names included) who will be in the new class or home group. Making a head start to learn the names of students in the class is wise; without this, September will arrive and the students with Asperger syndrome are lucky if they know the names of three class members. The next step is to place the photographs, the weekly timetable, pages from the school diary, school rules and helpful information into a transition book for the student to take home and refer to. Ideally, the transition book or a PowerPoint™ slide show is best gradually built up with the student during each visit so they understand every page or every slide. Many schools designate one person to coordinate all major transitions. It is a reliable means to deliver consistency within the process.

Preparation for new events

Starting back at school after a short break, listening to a guest speaker, attending assembly or going on an excursion or a camp is often challenging. These kids are natural worriers, and because they remain switched to a hyper alert state, an uncertainty can throw them into complete disarray. Use the rehearsal technique to help kids process information. In other words, pre-plan by rehearsing how the event is likely to unfold. Write a script together and ask the student's parent to run through it with them too. Pinpoint and discuss the times that may prove most challenging, develop an option or two to best cope with this and then role-play it. Rehearsing helps students of all ages to intellectualise the feelings likely to arise, which in turn supports their composure when the time comes. Another option is to provide a 'go to' person in the rehearsal stage. When the plan is not working the student knows they can go to this person for respite, relief or comfort.

Day-to-day transitions

All kids are steadied by developing regular organisational patterns and routines they can fit in to. The best starting point is to have a class timetable clearly displayed in the classroom, and actually follow it. As students enter the classroom in the morning it is reassuring for them to see the lessons and the materials required written on the whiteboard. In this way they know how the morning will unfold and what they need to organise. Similarly, a personalised mini daily timetable, similar to the one displayed in the worksheets for Chapter 4 (see p. 208), that can be collected by the student on arrival provides both an organisational and emotional advantage.

When the class teacher is to be away from school try to give the student advanced notice, and if advanced notice is not possible develop a regular compensatory routine. A good idea is to designate a staff member, well liked by the student, to let them know that their teacher is away. The staff member introduces them personally to the relieving teacher and explains what needs to be explained and that the student has a 'break card' they can use. In this way the student is reassured that their needs are understood and will be met.

As a final point, some of the simplest things can cause turmoil for these kids: lining up for class, walking across the playground with the class, entering the classroom after lunch, or entering the class of another teacher. To avoid these spills of emotion find creative ways to limit the time the child spends in such situations. For example, instead of getting them to line up, arrange for the student to collect you from the staff room, or arrange a buddy who understands to walk with them when moving between classes. There's always a creative solution.

The trouble with choice and ambiguity

Students with Asperger syndrome, and those with similar traits, respond best to specific choices and fewer of them. Vague instructions and too many choices are confounding. Their difficulty to infer, united with an anxious nature, compels them to worry. Time and again they will tell you that they over-think and worry about making the wrong choice. The best way to proceed is to tell these kids exactly what you want them to do, not what they shouldn't do. Phrase instructions and directions positively as, 'Tom, here in art lesson today you will share the paints with everyone'. The indefinite contrast would be to say, 'Tom, selfish students keep the paints to themselves and we don't want that do we?'

Abstract or generalised thinking is a stumbling block for these kids. As Dylan mentioned at the outset of the chapter, 'In class when the teacher writes page 57 on the board everyone else knows what to do, but for me it's not obvious. Once I stop worrying and work it out everyone else has almost finished and that's annoying.' Dylan needs to know exactly what to do on page 57, whether the exercise is to be completed in that lesson or whether it is for homework as well. He also needs to know what to do when he's unsure. Similarly, Rhett's Year 10 economics teacher asked him, along with each member of the class, to create an imaginative place that successfully operated by using a simple barter system based on the their natural resources and lifestyle. Most of the class revelled in the freedom of choices, but Rhett was besieged by them. To find success he needed precise guidelines, structures and criteria to work within. Otherwise he and many others dealing with Asperger syndrome are too easily derailed.

Homework

Students by and large fall into three categories when it comes to homework: they either like it, comply or reject it. Quite a few students identified with Asperger syndrome (and some without) take their loathing for homework to dizzy heights! Typically they'll say: 'I spend all day at school doing what I'm told to do. No way am I doing homework! My time is my time outside of school. No one has the right to make me do schoolwork at home.' Other, gentler souls may feel the same way, but attempt it.

> School is rush, push, rush. It's so many people, so much noise, and assignment after assignment. The day never ends. When I get home I feel as though I've spent all day chewing my way out of a train wreck. I can't do homework. Mum and I fight and I do some. Then I do the same thing all over again the next day. That's my life.
> (Charlie, 15 years, identified with Asperger syndrome)

Their objection to homework may be driven by utter exhaustion. By the time they arrive home the pressures of holding it together all day long, let alone their academic difficulties, have taken an exacting toll. Parents learn that by forcing homework, a fight is never more than a heartbeat away. Students with social, emotional and learning difficulties do it so much tougher than those without. Their struggle demands that we consciously prioritise what is most important and that our expectations remain very realistic. There are battles over homework that should not be fought. In some instances, students benefit by homework being dramatically modified or regularly completed at school. For a few, the best solution is to do away with homework altogether.

An alternate lunchtime

Many of the kids who run into trouble at lunchtime do so because the playground is too unstructured, too exhilarating and too stressful. They can't control their overactivity, can't quickly interpret the social/emotional cues of others or become besieged by the chaotic play time interaction.

Some present as too loud, too boisterous, too explosive or too unpredictable. The playgound frenzy excites them and takes their overactivity to uncontrollable heights, which reminds peers why they don't like them. Others live on the outside of social groups because they are too young and inept emotionally. They are just not ready to independently interact with kids their own age. Their immaturity and social clumsiness sets them apart, and it is not unusual for them to become targets in this turbulent environment. To survive the rigours, they spend the time sitting on a bench reading a book. Sadly, this instinctive survival behaviour draws further attention to their social awkwardness, often from the students looking to push buttons and create stimulation for themselves.

Many schools are trialing new ways to accommodate the kids who cannot cope with the freedoms and perils that accompany lunchtime play. By and large they are doing this by creating structured environments that are safe, support kids to find friends and develop friendship skills in a constructive guided format. Even though the possibilities are endless, here is a brief selection of ideas to inspire:

- Perhaps the simplest idea is for the student to be collected by a parent, a relative, a friend or a caregiver and taken home for lunch, or part of it, several days each week. This quiet time offers them respite and a chance to regroup frazzled emotions.

- Another option is to ensure the library or resource centre is welcoming at lunchtime for those special few to retreat to.

- Sometimes just making sure that the building blocks, the Lego, a board game, a pack of cards or the computer is available for a student and their friend for the last 15 to 20 minutes of lunch is restorative. One innovative principal rostered a student (with troubling playground behaviour) and a friend to water the indoor plants throughout the school several times a week in the last 15 minutes of lunch. The student noticed after a term or so that the number of plants needing watering was increasing. And, so they were. The principal and her staff had seen the benefits, and each had contributed a pot plant to be watered!

- As a trial, one of the schools I regularly work with placed an extra teacher in the playground each lunchtime. While on duty they either played games with students or wandered about talking positively with students handing out awards and canteen vouchers when they spotted great behaviours. The outcome was astonishing, primarily because teachers placed an emphasis on targeting the students who traditionally had difficulties in the school playground.

- A popular idea is to organise a part of the playground so it is regularly supervised by a staff member and set up to provide students with a safer, less confronting environment. This quieter space is then promoted as the place students can go when they are feeling uncomfortable or overwhelmed: no matter what, there is always someone there for them. Managed with some sports equipment and a structured activity or two students can move in and out at will. Besides enjoying the recuperative affect the safe space offers, students also like the steadiness of having an adult on hand. In one school an old bicycle shed was converted into a toy-car racing track. There is little more than a staff member, lengths of timber and old crates that students configure into racing tracks, and for them it's the place to be! Students are invited by teachers based on their age, social style and likelihood of connecting with the others.

- Regular lunchtime interest groups for students have long been of assistance. The kids who live on the fringe of social groups in the playground are often the first to take advantage of the clubs: science, environment, plants and propagation, cooking, rock and mineral, chess, drama, darts, model trains, photography, gardening, charity, car, choir, karate, *Warhammer*, music and band to mention a few. The structure found within clubs is comforting for them.

- Peer mediation is a realistic way to solve the inevitable conflicts that arise between students during break or at lunchtime (Cremin 2007). Many kids view whatever happens in life as black and white, and when there's a problem, they either lash out or withdraw to fix it. Peer mediation hinges on the idea that conflicts can always be solved by talking, listening and negotiating. It drip feeds the skills required to handle conflict in relationships, and in the process develops the important social and emotional skills in all children. In most schools older students are asked to take on this vital leadership role. Those who wish to become a peer mediator are involved in a formal training programme. They learn how to effectively mediate by:

  - using conflict resolution skills to create win/win situations from conflict;
  - showing poise, common sense and leadership;
  - developing reflective listening, clarifying and speaking skills;
  - learning the skill to present a fair argument;
  - strengthening a culture of resolution rather than one of blame and punishment.

  During play times students seek a mediator for help. The trained peer mediator will guide students to be fair with each other and think of solutions that will work for both. While peer mediation is an excellent vehicle for older students to offer community service to their school, it is also useful to involve students known to have their own social and conflict resolution difficulties. The very act of supporting others and following the principles of the programme helps to reinforce their own thinking and maintains connections to others. Having well-trained peer mediators on hand in the playground can be a better option than Ms Smith, the teacher's assistant, out in the playground shadowing the student identified with Asperger syndrome just in case something goes wrong. As one boy recently grumbled, 'I can't wait to get to high school. Ms Smith won't be there stalking me at lunchtime anymore.'

- Student radio stations in primary and secondary schools are increasing in popularity. The station is broadcast throughout the school in the morning, at break, lunchtime and after school each day. Would it surprise you to learn that the students with the golden radio voices are not always the popular kids, but can be the kids who don't do well in the playground? More specifically, they are students identified with Asperger syndrome.

- Café de School was the name emblazoned across the door and over the windows of an empty classroom. The room had been imaginatively set up and decorated as a café. Half a dozen café tables, each with a bright umbrella through them, and chairs oozed the atmosphere of a genuine café. This was the place students of all ages came to talk, to flick through magazines, to play a card or board game with a friend, or to play their hand-held computer games. As you would expect there were cups and jugs of water set up on the bench. This room worked! It was low maintenance for staff and attracted a particular style of student who appreciated the environment.

- The zone is an inventive social development programme for junior primary and primary aged students. It offers a nurturing space to promote friendly interactions, the strengthening of social skills and good fun between students. Open every lunchtime, the zone is a supervised inside and outside area providing activities such as hand tennis, woodwork, beading, origami and paper construction, music, knitting, board games, cards, puzzles, indoor bowls, air hockey, books, magazines and comics.

Under the watchful eye of a staff member, older student volunteers and students who have 'graduated' from the zone become zone mentors to support new students and learn new ways to interact. As you'd predict, the older students enjoy helping the younger and less able build new skills, but the process also consolidates the improvements 'the graduates' have made to their social functioning. The zone is also a popular place for staff to drop by and build connections with students.

An integral part of this highly successful concept has been to inform parents and get them to see value in their child's participation. Initially parents are contacted and the zone is explained as a constructive environment for kids who experience play and relationship troubles in the playground. Attending the zone is not compulsory, but parents are asked to stimulate their child's motivation about accepting the impending invitation.

Later an invitation for the student to join the zone is mailed home. It also contains their entry tag on a school lanyard. Each time the student attends for half a lunch period or more their zone tag is hole-punched. This is a loyalty system, and once five holes have been punched into the tag they are eligible to collect a reward from the school canteen. Some days the zone students are encouraged to bring a friend. These days are always popular!

Restoration: down time and break cards

Safe havens

For kids who are prone to sensory overload, a place to escape from the pressures of the classroom or playground is restorative. A place they feel comfortable, an adult they feel safe with and where they have a voice to tell how they are feeling or what went wrong is the ideal therapeutic mix. Many students need time to process what has happened, to regroup their emotions and plan. The kids with Asperger syndrome are part of a group who have to work their guest mode very hard at school so they can function as well as they do. Forcing them to stay in guest mode for too long takes its toll. In fact, parents will commonly explain that their child regularly has an 'off day' where they appear more autistic and cope nowhere near as well.

Creating an emotionally renewing island of solitude takes very deliberate planning within the dynamic school environment. Places developed as a safe refuge include purpose-built corners, or a sensory area, in the classroom filled with a few calming activities and switch toys. Switch toys are objects and toys that are appealing either visually, or from a tactile or auditory perspective. Students quickly latch on to favourites to soothe their anxiety or anger: watching goo-timers, listening to a favourite story with headphones on, playing with magic and magnetic boards or holding a soft teddy bear or squishy ball and rolling it over their face is comforting (Smith-Myles and Tapscott-Cook 2000). One effective way to create a sensory de-stress area is to permanently erect a small tent in the classroom. It works a treat if you have the space.

The reality though is that it is difficult for most teachers to build a separate place in their crowded classroom that invites kids to de-stress. The most practical idea is for the student to leave the room and visit the school counsellor, or go to a friendly teacher's classroom or spend some quiet time with the school support officer. Students can access the retreat by using their break card or go as part of a regular arrangement to wind down and rebalance. Usually, the friendliest Asperger destination is the resource centre or school library. Why, you may ask? Think about it. Libraries are quiet, structured, ordered, offer an abundant supply of knowledge, are filled with computers and gentle, helpful staff. A perfect place for emotional recuperation!

Never rule out the notion giving the student a day or two off when stress build-up is obvious. This adaptation of down time does of course need to be cleverly managed in consultation with parents.

Break cards

Find worksheet on page 226

'I can't be good all the time,' eleven-year-old Christian grumbled, 'I need to get away from them (the class) and their noise. They make me go mad.' And, so they did until Christian designed his own break card, wrote the terms of use on it with his teacher and started to use it.

Making his own, personalising it and wearing it his around his neck on a lanyard added to his security (Miller 2008). Break cards can also sit on the teacher's or student's desk. As the student makes their break card some clever teachers make one as well. They explain to the student they will draw on their card when they feel the student should take a break. Wisely, let the student know that sometimes we see the need for them to take a break before they do. It is best to work out a discreet way to do this. Students with Asperger syndrome do not gain the same sort of pleasure from highly interactive activities and events as most do. This may forever be an issue and you may have to accept their partial participation. A break card helps make it legitimate for a student to remove themselves from a stressful situation that is likely to lead into breakdown or conflict. There isn't a fixed rule about how to use them, but the design is that a student usually has several break cards opportunities they are able to draw on each day. Students are encouraged to use them wisely and not pull them out to avoid a challenging task. In times of emotional crisis or when a student really needs a break they present the card and go to the assigned person or safe haven. Developing appealing ways for students to help keep their dignity intact and regroup their emotions is a gift we can offer.

Conclusion: influencing change requires planning, commitment and teamwork

The intention of this chapter was threefold. Its first objective was to increase the capacity of educators to understand Asperger syndrome because identification of the condition is well and truly on the rise, and is challenging for school systems and teachers. We also know that a sound knowledge and explicit early intervention gets these kids off to a much better start (Janzen 2003).

Second, I wanted the chapter to offer a sense about how students with Asperger syndrome function and feel. The differences in how they function compared to other children have got to be embraced if we are to do any good. Neurologically they are wired differently and this accounts for differences in their perceptions, reactions and interpretations about the world. As mentioned earlier in the chapter, the ideal approach is to engage with these kids because as we learn about them we give them the chance to learn about us and our intentions. It is one thing for an educator to learn more and more about the condition and quite another to understand a student's functioning at a truly personal level. These kids are absolutely reliant on poised adults at school – they make perfect role models. They are dependent on those who want to engage them, want to understand, who can set up opportunities for them to find emotional engagement and appreciate not to construe the inevitable set-backs personally.

Finally, the chapter has presented a broad selection of playful and practical designs with the aim of emotionally nourishing all young people who are challenged by the social and emotional domains of life. A big part of maximising their success lies within the implementation of socially and emotionally supportive strategies, but this is hard work because influencing constructive change requires planning, endless commitment and a strongly teamed approach. Don't be fooled – progress is slow and takes a lot more than another new programme, the miracle of technology or the promise of additional funding. While each of these may add some value, it's more about the will each of us has to make a difference that will be most successful.

Worksheets

Refer to p. 191 for useful websites and further reading.

CHAPTER 7

Designs to lift moods
The inside knowledge on how to refresh tough kids

An hour of play is worth a lifetime of conversation.

Plato

Never forget the value of mood lifts! They offer precious moments to unify, refresh, build enthusiasm and lift the spirits of kids and adults. Mood lifts, change-ups or energisers are a set of versatile activities with the capacity to alter the emotional climate of the classroom or tone of the group. They can be drawn on as icebreakers and team-building exercises to help build class cohesiveness at the beginning of the year, or are a sparkling remedy when the attention or the mood of the group starts to wane. As well, they are perfect to repair the emotional fallout in class following an unpleasant incident, and can be drawn on as the student later returns to class following the ugliness. As the student returns to a classroom that feels lighter, welcoming and a good place to be they are more likely to feel included, rather than perceiving resentment because they have returned.

So when the going gets tough or when there seems to be one too many tough kids in the classroom think about using a restorative energiser! Sadly, these playful connecting moments are often the first casualty in tough times as our spontaneous reaction is to search for more stringent control techniques.

Popular ideas are as easy as speaking faster or slower, louder or more softly, changing your style of presentation, using an odd voice or an accent, tell a long-winded terrible joke, invite jokes from others, give students a minute to solve a brainteaser, continue your trivia quiz and then get back to the lesson. Consider a mood lift as anything a teacher does to introduce fun or amusement into the day. The good medicine of laughter reduces tension and rediscovers happiness. As we laugh, the muscles in our face, neck, chest and diaphragm all work hard enjoying themselves. In this sense, laughing is often compared to a mild internal physical workout. When we stop laughing, these muscles relax and we feel more relaxed.

If you're not a spontaneous person, then programme your mood lifts so it looks like you are! The best advice is to develop a collection of favourites that you know work and gradually expand your repertoire by trialing a few of the ideas presented in this chapter. The two best sources for energisers and mood lifts are from the kids themselves, or alternatively, go to your computer and google 'class energizers', 'class icebreakers' or 'class team building activities'. You will be amazed by the creative ideas on offer from both sources.

Mood lift and energising possibilities for kids and teens are limitless! Just adapt them to suit your group. Here are a few of my favourites, and feel free to add your own flavour or adaptations.

Mood lifts and energisers

Walk and talk

This is so simple and will always improve the cohesiveness of the group. I find it handy with older groups of students. When you think the time is right, take your students from the class for a slow 5- to 10-minute walk around the sports pitch or school building. As they walk they will of course talk. You'll be surprised by its calming influence. A bonus is that it also provides the chance for you to chat casually with students. A number of teachers use this technique immediately after lunch as it helps to steady students before re-entering the classroom.

Chinese whispers

This is an old favourite and always draws a laugh. Sit everyone in a circle. Whisper a phrase or a sentence into the ear of a student. The phrase should be more complex for older students. This first student then whispers the phrase to the next, and in turn, the whisper travels from person to person right around the circle. The last person to receive the message announces what they heard. Rarely is it the same phrase or sentence that began the journey.

The sleeping pirate

All students, except the sleeping pirate, sit in a circle on the floor. The sleeping pirate is blindfolded and sits cross-legged in the middle of the circle guarding a large bunch of keys that are on the floor nearby. A student is silently nominated to creep up and take the keys away from the pirate. The student tries to return to their place in the circle and place the keys on the floor behind their back without the pirate hearing anything at all. The sleeping pirate listens intently, but says nothing. Next, the sleeping pirate is asked to remove their blindfold and have three attempts to find the raider. If the raider is successful, they become the pirate in the next round.

Detective

Like many of these activities, 'detective' involves looking, listening and remembering. Tell your students to cover their eyes and listen carefully. If you like, to ensure they cannot see, ask them to bend over and place their heads in their laps as well. Describe three general features of a student in the group. You might say, 'This person (without naming them) has black hair, is quite tall and is wearing blue tracksuit bottoms'. At this point everyone keeps their eyes closed. When they think they know who the mystery person is they put their hand up ready to be asked. If the group begins to struggle throw in an additional clue. An interesting addition to this game is to include clues about what this person likes, does, is known for or should be known for. This is an engaging way for students to receive feedback about how others see them and to find out more about one another. Finally, if you think this game is just for lower primary students you couldn't be more wrong. Seventeen-year-olds just love it!

Alphabet list game

First, create a scenario such as 'Today we are all going to the zoo and we will see aardvarks'. The next person follows on saying, 'Today we are all going to the zoo and we will see aardvarks and baboons'. The next might say, 'Today we are all going to the zoo and we will see aardvarks, baboons and cats'.

As you can see, each student builds an animal onto the list following alphabetical order. It is important to have each new player repeat all the items on the list, and then add their new item. If they forget an item or get the order wrong they are out. Alternatively, you may choose to play the game without having winners and losers, and allow the group to assist anyone who needs help. Continue until everyone has had a turn.

Other examples of the alphabet list game are:

- 'Today we are all going camping and need to take. . .'
- 'Today we are all going to the supermarket and need to buy. . .'
- 'Today we are all going to Mars and need to take . . .'

Kim's game

This perfectly simple memory game has provided great entertainment for years! On a tray, place six to a dozen small items such as a pencil, watch, book, shoe, an apple, toy car and so on. As students get older increase the number of items on the tray. Cover with a cloth. Next, sit everyone in a circle. Place the tray in the middle of the circle and remove the cloth for 1 minute. At this point students try to remember the objects on the tray. When 1 minute has lapsed replace the cloth. Ask students to record the items on a small piece of paper, but keep what they write hidden. In turn, each student attempts to name one object they believe was on the tray. The first person to fail to name an item, repeat it or name something not on the tray is out. The idea of course is to stay in the game.

Can you guess?

Sit the group in a circle on the floor and ask them to face away from you and close their eyes for a few moments. While they do this place a small item onto the floor in the middle of the group and cover it with a thick towel. Select a person to slide their hands under the towel and feel the object. Ask them to take three guesses as to what the object might be. If they are unsuccessful they finish their turn and choose someone new. When someone finally guesses correctly you might allow them to keep the item!

Silent ball

This works for any age group. It's a quick game that rejuvenates. Have students stand somewhere in the classroom. Engage eye contact with a student and throw a beanbag or a soft ball at the student's chest. Once the student has caught the ball they engage eye contact with someone new and throw it directly to them. When a student misses the catch they are out of the game. They return to their seat and return the ball to the previous thrower. The last two or three students standing win the round.

Wink murder

Choose a detective from the group and ask them to leave the room for a few moments. The group needs to be very quiet. Next, choose a murderer from the group. The detective returns and stands in the middle of the circle. The murderer secretly winks at members of the group. This unfolds fairly slowly and as group members receive the wink from the murderer they fall to the ground and die. And, it's fine for the person dying to be dramatic. The detective's task is to find the winking murderer before too many class members are killed off.

Bobsledding

Before introducing this game to your group, try finding several images or a video clip of bobsledding – it will nicely set the scene. This is a team game, so try to make the teams even. Aim at 4 to 6 players in a team. Each team sits in a line, one person behind the other. Next, each team member wraps their legs around the waist of the person in front of them and squeezes firmly. To create a finishing line place a piece of masking tape on the floor about 5 metres from the start position. On 'go', teams can only use their hands on the floor to slide their way to the end. If a team breaks apart, they must go back to the start together before they continue. The first team with every member over the finish line wins! Kids love slightly extended versions of this so they can have points and experience a grand final play-off. Points can also be accumulated when bobsledding occurs over an extended period of time.

Happy faces

Discuss with the class a particular behaviour you want to see more of in the next 10 minutes: better cooperation, having a go, looking tuned in, giving great positive feedback, the most beautiful smile, the best compliment, the quickest or most creative answer. Explain that each time you see a great attempt you'll stamp their happy face card with a happy face stamp. At the end of the nominated time collect up the cards

Find worksheet on page 227

ready to bring them back out in several days. As a card becomes full the student achieves a small reward predetermined by yourself and the group. It's a simple approach and can be varied to suit any circumstance and all age groups.

Raffle tickets

Instead of happy face stamps, give away raffle tickets that can be collected by students and 'cashed in' later for prizes. This really is a way to motivate students. And, when executed with finesse it works beautifully with much older students too! Negotiate how many tickets students will need to earn particular rewards and display this on a large chart or menu in class.

Pass the parcel

Here is another classic guaranteed to be enjoyed, but this time it is with a slight twist! Wrap a small toy, a piece of stationery, a sweet, a bar of chocolate or an inexpensive gift in about ten layers of paper. If you pride yourself on presentation then use gift paper as your last layer. The twist is to write a message on each layer, such as: hop on one foot sixteen times, sing a short song, tell a joke, tell someone you don't know well something you like about them, etc. The group may be seated at their desks or in a circle and as the music is played the parcel is passed from student to student. When the music stops, the person holding the parcel removes one layer of wrapping and follows the instruction written on the next layer of paper. Repeat until the last layer of wrapping has been removed.

That person wins the present.

Musical chairs

For this old favourite place four chairs side by side, and then arrange four more with their backs touching each of the first four. Have the rest of the group watch because what is about to unfold is fabulous fun to watch. Start with a group of nine students. Students walk around the chairs while music is playing or the class sings. When the music or singing is suddenly stopped each student must immediately sit down on a free chair, the player left standing is out. Take away one chair each time and repeat until there are two players and one chair left. Of course, the one to sit down first wins!

Port and starboard

This memory-come-listening game is ideally played on a basketball court. On command, using the list below, students must quickly perform the appropriate actions. Give students a while to warm up and remember the commands, then start removing the slowest players to respond until only one, two or three are left. Commands include:

- 'Port' – run to one side of the area
- 'Starboard' – run to the other side

- 'Captain's coming aboard' – stand to attention, perfectly still and maintain a salute

- 'Submarines' – lie on the floor as stiff as a board

- 'Hoist the mainsail' – run vigorously on the spot (like climbing the rigging)

- 'Mess deck' – sit cross-legged on the floor (looking as though they are gobbling their lunch)

- 'Davey Jones' – lie on tummy or back with feet kicking wildly in the air – anything so their feet are not on the floor

- 'Up periscope' – stand up straight and hold both hands to eyes as if looking through binoculars.

Stuck in the mud

Stuck in the mud is best played outside or where there is plenty of room to run. One person is 'it'. 'It' must run round wildly touching as many people as they can. When they have touched someone, that person has to stop, stand with their legs wide apart and their arms outstretched. There, they must wait until a free player crawls through their legs. At this moment they are released and are also free to run and keep away from 'it'. Once they have been caught three times they retire from the game and sit out. The game ends when everyone left is standing still. Kids of all ages love stuck in the mud!

Mr and Mrs Wright

Have everyone stand and then read the story below aloud to the group. When you say 'right' everyone takes a step to the right. When you say 'left' everyone takes a step to the left.

The story begins . . .

This is a story about Mr and Mrs WRIGHT. One evening they were baking cookies.

Mrs WRIGHT called from the kitchen, 'Oh, no, there is no flour LEFT! You will need to go out to the store RIGHT away.'

'I can't believe you forgot to check the pantry,' grumbled Mr WRIGHT. 'You never get anything RIGHT!'

'Don't be difficult, dear,' replied Mrs WRIGHT. 'You could have LEFT by now and been on your way. It will only take 20 minutes if you come RIGHT back.

'Go to the Post Office up on the main road, and turn LEFT at the stop sign. Then go past the fruit shop we usually go to, and turn RIGHT, and there it will be on your LEFT,' declared Mrs WRIGHT as her husband LEFT the house.

Mr WRIGHT found the store and asked the shop assistant where he could find the flour. The shop assistant pointed and said, 'Go to aisle four and turn LEFT. The flour and sugar will be on your LEFT.'

Mr WRIGHT made his purchase and walked RIGHT out the door. He turned LEFT, but he couldn't remember where he had LEFT his car.

Suddenly he remembered that he had driven Mrs WRIGHT's car and that his car was in the driveway at home RIGHT where he had LEFT it. He finally found the RIGHT car and put his things RIGHT inside.

Eventually, a weary Mr WRIGHT found his way home.

Mrs WRIGHT had been waiting impatiently. 'I thought you would be RIGHT back,' she said. 'I LEFT all the cookie ingredients on the kitchen counter, and the cats got into the milk. You'll just have to go RIGHT out again.'

Mr WRIGHT sighed. He had no energy LEFT. 'I am going RIGHT to bed,' he said. 'Anyway, I need to go on a diet, so I might as well start RIGHT now. Isn't that RIGHT, dear?'

Author unknown

Statues

Statues is best played to music. As the music plays students move gracefully about the room. When the music stops they must freeze like statues and anyone who talks, giggles or moves is out. This is so simple and so much fun, especially when students catch sight of one another and can't help giggling. Start the music again and continue until there is one statue left. If you have time play it again.

Silent charades

On pairs of small, palm-sized pieces of card write a single word or a short phrase. You will need to have the same number of cards as students in your class. As an example, on the first pair of cards you might write 'ballerina twirling' and 'ballerina twirling', on the next two cards, 'angry elephant charging' and 'angry elephant charging', on the next pair, 'police officer directing traffic' and 'police officer directing traffic' and so on until all the cards are filled. Now you're ready to start!

Place the cards, face down, onto the floor and mix them about. Ask students to take a card one at a time, read it, remember it and place it in their pocket. Tell them not to show or tell anyone what they have on their card. This is just for them to know. On 'go' students spread out around the room silently acting out the cue on their card. The idea is for each student to find another who appears to be acting out the same charade as theirs. When they find that person they both sit down on the floor together, but at this point they do not speak or show each other their cue card. Watching the rest of the group finding one another is great fun.

After everyone has found who they believe is their match, and is sitting down, ask students to reveal their cards to the person they believe is their identical partner. There will be giggles of success, and gasps of surprise to find how an 'anteater eating ants' and 'a child licking an ice cream' could get so confused!

Power up the electronic whiteboard

Interactive whiteboards have quickly gained affordability and popularity in schools. Their attraction is that they are electronic, fast, hands-on and can tap into an array of purpose-built games, quizzes, puzzles and brainteasers. They have the unique capacity to deliver a fabulous selection of stimulating activities at the touch of the screen. This technology can also access specific, content rich, dynamic lessons to present to students of all ages. Below are a few websites worth exploring for playful energisers and lessons. In fact some of the lessons are sorted into age group and curriculum areas!

http://eduscapes.com/sessions/smartboard/

www.bristolvaschools.org/mwarren/SBActivities.htm

http://its.leesummit.k12.mo.us/smartboard.htm

www.juliethompson.com/SMART.html

www.amphi.com/departments/technology/whiteboard/eleminteractivesites.html

www.learningbox.com

Conclusion: mood lifts and energising possibilities are limitless

My advice is to experiment with the ideas you feel comfortable with and think will work most easily. Select an idea, play with it, modify it, discard it or keep it based on its merit, and progressively expand to new ideas. Never underestimate the scope of mood lifts when it comes to switching the mood of the class, raising their engagement or helping everyone recover from an unfortunate experience. In the final analysis, however, it is not primarily how novel or playful they are, or how much fun any of the energisers evoke: what tips the balance is the quality of relationship that carries the energiser.

Worksheets

25   My happy face collector

Refer to p. 192 for useful websites and further reading.

Mentorship
An insight into the transformation of tough kids

This chapter describes a unique school-based mentoring programme adopted by a number of South Australian Catholic primary and secondary schools over the last four years. While the programme is not a panacea to the complex mix of problems students and staff in schools face, it certainly adds value to the positive influences we have on kids. It has earned a reputation as a means to build staff capacity, better staff and student connections, and improve the well-being of kids who respond to higher level personal care. It invites staff to take a close and personal journey with a young person. Those who accept the invitation learn something often missed in the hustle and bustle of the classroom. They learn how kids really think, and how the clumsiness of their emotion and behaviour has less to do with innate badness, and much more to do with inexperience, exploration and discovery.

> Just as we are learning to value and conserve the air we breathe, the water we drink, the energy we use, we must learn to value and conserve our capacity for nurture. Otherwise, in the name of human potential, we will slowly but surely erode the source of our humanity.
>
> (Heffner 1978)

Four years ago the Behaviour Education Team asked if I would design and present workshops to train staff in schools to become mentors to students in need of a little extra care and encouragement.

I agreed in a heartbeat!

Being part of a transforming process for kids where the value of relationship is placed first was enticement enough. To me, few things are as compelling as the opportunity to be an agent of change in the lives of young developing human beings. Too often in schools the focus is on the action: busy classrooms, packed curriculum, rapid exchanges between teachers and students, back-to-back learning tasks and the quest for immediate and measurable learning outcomes. Schools by their very nature are hectic places and because of this the subtle beauty of relationship that encompasses ongoing personal connections, a sharing of ideas and new futures can easily become overshadowed. As adults, most of us can recall a person who had a big impact on the way we saw ourselves and viewed the world. Most of us can remember that someone who did a little more than just teach us as part of a group. A significant person who delved a little deeper into what our world was like and shared some insights from their world with us. Someone who took the time to follow up, to see how we were incorporating new information, how we were interacting and progressing.

Since the inception of the programme, an array of staff – teachers, educational support officers, school counsellors, principals, assistant principals, office staff, librarians and grounds personnel – have been trained in the art of mentoring students. This programme has become the quiet achiever.

Overview: mentorship

Mentorship has a rich history within many cultures and is identified when a more experienced person, or group, offers guidance to a younger person or less experienced group. The idea of a mentor began to unfold in Homer's classic *The Odyssey*, when Odysseus entrusted the care and education of his son to a friend named Mentor. Mentor accepted the responsibility of caring for Telemachus while Odysseus was always at war. He became a coach, counsellor, advocate and protector for the boy. Mentorship was also deeply embedded in the age-old elder system used by indigenous Australians and Torres Strait Island peoples. Its purpose was to pass on wisdom, establish spiritual attachments, contribute to family and community, maintain artistic and dance expertise, and develop respect for the rights and property of others. Mentorship was a means to enrich the young and guide the destiny of communities. In the 1970s, sociologist E. Paul Torrance noted that the terms 'sponsor' or 'coach' were insufficient to describe the depth of a mentoring relationship (Torrance 1984). Since then mentorship has become an essential part of education, the commercial world and the public sector, as a change agent (Wright and Wright 1987). It is now recognised as a potent method to transfer professional, technical and management skills. In fact, over the last twenty-five years, formal and informal mentoring programmes have played a critical role in increasing advancement opportunities for women in many work situations (Blake-Beard 2001). These days plenty of well developed mentorship programmes have emerged in communities with clearly defined purposes: mentoring students from school to career, mentoring of refugees, indigenous mentoring, youth mentoring, mentorship of at-risk youth, mentoring children of prisoners, resilience mentoring, mentorship of fatherless boys, university transition mentoring programmes, women's mentoring networks, mentorship as a student retention initiative, mentoring students with disabilities, nurse and health workers mentorship, peer mentoring, job opportunities mentoring networks, business and corporate mentorship, school volunteer mentoring, young parents mentoring programmes and so on. There has long been the belief that mentorship works, but only recently has empirical evidence of this emerged (Beltman and MacCallum 2006; Du Bois *et al.* 2002; Herrera *et al.* 2007; Koerner and Harris 2007; Philip and Hendry 2000; Quarles *et al.* 2005; Rhodes *et al.* 2000).

Does mentoring work in schools?

The introduction of mentorship programmes in schools is comparatively new, and by and large, the initiative has been a compassionate response to guide and support students (Jucovy and Garringer 2007; Lee and Cramond 1999; Royse 1998). These days the designs of mentoring programmes in schools are remarkably diverse. Some draw on mentors from the community to support students, others encourage older students to mentor younger students and a few have taken the initiative to draw on staff members to mentor students. From time to time these programmes gain media attention and are touted as a universal remedy for the problems faced by our youth. Without the media hype it is fair to say that a series of credible studies gauge the value of mentorship as potentially one of the most developmentally important relationships an adolescent might engage in (Johnson 1999; Levinson *et al.* 1978; MacCallum and Beltman 2002). Results from Tierney *et al.*'s longitudinal mentorship study that involved 959 young adolescents concluded positive impacts in all of the areas explored: improved school attendance, higher academic performance, better school retention, talk of positive futures, and less participation in high–risk behaviours (Tierney *et al.* 1995). Studies with a focus on mentoring primary-school aged students have indicated improved levels of emotion, increased personal resilience and the building of positive relationships (Arwood *et al.* 2000). Increasingly this very special relationship where a mentee sees their mentor believing in them and valuing them is being recognised as a steadying, revitalising treatment for students dealing with learning problems, anxiety, social issues, behavioural difficulties, disadvantage, disability and immaturities (Teese and Polesel 2003).

Where do the benefits lie?

What has emerged from our programme mirrors much of the evidence-based literature on school-based mentoring programmes (Hall 2003; Herrera *et al.* 2007). That is, there are the benefits to everyone involved: the mentee and their families, the mentor and the culture of the system.

> Any student would benefit from the program, but the student who struggles to make sense of how the system works, whether it is the family system, the school system or the friends system finds great benefit from the program. One of the greatest advantages is for a student to be able to retell events, look at them a different way, re-story with a wise guide and gain a new look at themselves and the world.
>
> (Mary Carmody, Senior Behavioural Education
> Consultant at CEO, South Australia)

Student feedback

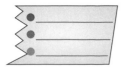

- 'My mentor and I talk about how I could do better. That makes me want to try.'

- 'I didn't think I was important enough (to have a mentor).'

- 'I like my mentor. She has helped me to sort things out at school and with my future.'

- 'My mentor sat with me and my teacher to work out problems I was having. That really helped.'

- 'I call my mentor my second chance. Before we started to make plans I was thinking about leaving school.'

Parent feedback

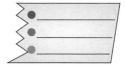

- 'Since he's started with his mentor he's talking about what he might do in the future, instead of everything being too hard, too bad or no way.'

- 'The mentor calls every so often. Just talking to her has helped me sort things out at home. She's as important to me as she is to my son.'

- 'My son's mentor takes an interest in my child's schoolwork and how he is working in class. He really likes to make his mentor proud.'

- 'As soon as my daughter and her mentor started talking about her friendship problems they started to untangle.'

- 'He is more motivated and happier with things at school now.'

Staff feedback

Make no mistake. Mentoring does not just raise the performance of kids!

- 'Mentoring has rekindled my belief about the real influence we have on kids. It's reminded me of why I chose to be a teacher.' (Sam, teacher)

- 'Mentoring wasn't as easy as I'd anticipated. The gift of mentorship is being able to walk alongside our youth, seeing and feeling the issues they face and sending the critical message that we care.' (Lisa, Educational Support Officer)

- 'By taking the time to understand [my mentee's] world I have become far more sensitive to the hidden obstacles children in my class likely face.' (Chris, teacher)

- 'Mentorship has not been a one-way process. I have received as well as given. I will forever treasure the moments when each of the boys have accepted me into their confidence, shared ideas, asked what I thought or whether I could help. I also marvel about how much these young adolescents know and how much more they have to learn.' (Pamela, Educational Support Officer)

Initially our mentoring programme was offered to teachers, but it didn't take long for the ripples of interest to reach administrative and ancillary staff. They wanted to be involved as well and have eagerly embraced the programme's spirit to help kids of all ages build positive images of themselves and reach for better futures. A comment repeatedly made by participating mentors relates to positive attitudinal changes they see in parents towards the school and those who work in it. As the mentor and mentee relationship grows, so do levels of communication and trust between mentee, mentor and parents (Rhodes 2008).

The programme

The programme has a psychosocial bias where a respectful relationship is geared towards promoting the emotional, social and academic well-being of students. This programme is a one-to-one (school staff member to student) encouragement programme for boys and girls. It occurs at school during school hours and volunteer staff are asked to commit to the student for at least one year, although in situations where the relationship has delivered obvious benefits extensions are encouraged. The student (the mentee) and teacher (the mentor) meet in face-to-face meetings each week to review the week, to plan for what is up and coming, to monitor progress and to discuss issues they may be experiencing. Essentially, the forum allows an exchange of ideas and insights through healthy discussion. Most mentors find that meeting with their mentee for one 30- to 40-minute period each week works well.

Who is it for?

Students of all ages are eligible for inclusion.

The one thing most have in common is that they are usually considered to have unique needs. Candidates are selected because they may lack confidence, be anxious, have learning difficulties, social troubles, emotional control problems or they may be coping with a difficult home circumstance. They are students who would benefit from the friendship and encouragement of a caring, stable adult working within the school system.

Our experience and data indicates that many mentees are young males whose parents have separated and they no longer see much of their father. We are also finding that a substantial number of students are battling issues, sometimes in combinations, such as: learning difficulties, fetal alcohol syndrome, ADHD, autism spectrum disorders, anxiety, oppositional defiance disorder, social isolation and disadvantage.

Case study

'*Mentoring wasn't as easy as I'd anticipated.*'

I began to mentor Cooper a year ago. At the time he was in Year 8 and had been identified with ADHD and oppositional defiance disorder. Prior to this I had worked with him in my role as an educational support officer.

He had recently started to live with his father, with whom he had had limited contact over the preceding years. This had been a momentous decision and one he had not taken lightly. How many thirteen-year-olds find themselves in a position of having to leave their mother, younger sister, older brother and new beloved puppy, 'Sophie', in order to develop a long awaited relationship with their father? Cooper was on his best behaviour in his new home with dad and was showing some of his most defiant at school. He was challenging to all. Cooper's speciality was to sabotage activities he did not want to participate in and make sure whatever he did had a big impact on the class as well.

After enlisting the support of Cooper's parents, his home class teacher and my line manager, our first official mentoring session began. I decided to keep our first few sessions fairly casual as I wanted to get to know him. Right from the start, despite my best intentions, Cooper was disinterested in sessions. Sometimes he wouldn't speak. Nevertheless, I persisted. Sessions gradually became easier, and we even started to share a laugh occasionally. Soon we were able to establish a few ideas to help him overcome his frustrated class behaviours. Some success was achieved. To help Cooper feel as though he owned the sessions we set up a 'teach me something' time and he taught me how to play Sudoku. He proved to be poised, patient and chatty when dealing with something he liked and felt confident about. This set the tone for our mentoring sessions. Flexibility and discussing ideas over an activity was the key to our relationship.

As we picked our way through Cooper's talk of being victimised by teachers he also began sharing his knowledge of gardening. Soon we were striking plant cuttings and producing window boxes that he nurtured throughout the year. We shared recipes and would go ingredient shopping and bake, always making sure there were leftovers to take home. We played Mastermind and Uno and we were competitive! In fact, we kept a scorecard of all our games so we could establish an overall champion at the end of the year. I introduced a questionnaire we each filled in through the eyes of the other: favourite colour, worst fears, hopes for the future, best foods, dislikes, loves and so on. My hope was to encourage Cooper to see outside his fairly rigid world. Throughout these activities Cooper's chatting intensified. He became more animated and spoke freely about weekend adventures with mum or dad, his likes and dislikes and we were able to freely discuss options to deal with problems as they predictably cropped up at home and at school.

As the year moved on, Cooper and I recognised a few similarities in one another. We are both highly justice based, competitive, practical and did not suffer fools gladly. Admirable qualities perhaps, but we also agreed on their limitations. Despite this bond, Cooper is not my friend and nor me his. Mentoring is a special example of how a relationship can flourish within the usual constraints of school boundaries. For us, mentorship wasn't about exchanging personal stories, nor should it be in my opinion, or an attempt to 'fix' Cooper. Like any solid relationship, it grew slowly. A mutual respect ensued and because Cooper's relationships with adults had been unstable and fragmented in the past it, was a privilege to provide him with an example of a healthy one.

We celebrated our last session for the year by going ten pin bowling. Cooper beat me because of an unfair advantage. You see, he was able to concentrate for longer periods than I. On our walk back to school he asked if I'd like to meet his dad. We found his father parked in the school car park, waiting to pick Cooper up. Cooper's father thanked me for my contribution and impressed on me just how much Cooper had enjoyed our sessions. I was touched that Cooper wanted to share someone he loves with me.

Mentoring wasn't as easy as I'd anticipated. The gift of mentorship is being able to walk alongside our youth, seeing and feeling the issues they face and sending the critical message that we care.

My other legacy from Cooper is that I complete a Sudoku puzzle every night in bed before I sleep!

Lisa, educational support officer

What is the role of a mentor?

A mentor straddles between being a role model, a sponsor, an encourager, an advisor, a guide, a coach and a counsellor. Whether the mentor's style is supportive and nurturing, or challenging and stretching, a mentor cares about their mentee. Ideally, they lead by example, helping their mentee to find ways to sort through difficulties, to set goals, to achieve them and to see things from different perspectives. While there is no fixed ideal about the traits required to become an effective mentor it appears the following qualities are valuable (Herrera 1999, 2005; Herrera *et al.* 2002):

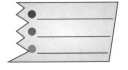

- a wish to see young people develop and find success;

- ability to establish a quality relationship;

- the capacity to listen, guide conversations and reflect back the mentee's thinking;

- a willingness to share personal experiences appropriate to the mentee's development;

- someone who avoids lecturing or giving too much advice;

- able to formulate shared goals and willing to work on them;

- can present honest feedback;

- able to forecast likely outcomes from particular actions;

- prepared to advocate for the mentee;

- can evaluate progress, make adjustments and celebrates wins;

- a desire to be a role model and a motivator.

Mentors are not expected to replace the professional input of psychologists, counsellors, psychiatrists and so on. Nor are they intended to replace a parent's input and responsibility. Above all else, the mentor's role is to contribute to the emotional stability of the mentee's situation.

What is the goal of the programme?

Most of all, this is an encouragement programme to stimulate the confidence, abilities and aspirations of young people. The programme's goal is not to 'fix' students or arrest difficult behaviours. Indeed, surprising and unexpected improvements may come about, but the focus remains on the provision of a trusting relationship.

Mentors can work towards improving a student's school experience by designing opportunities:

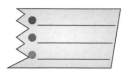

- for the student to debrief and be listened to;

- to deliver feedback on their performance;

- for students to recognise their learning or behavioural barriers;

- to help students function more successfully in the classroom by setting up improvement plans;

- to increase their persistence and raise their self-awareness;

- for work on learning and skill building;

- to link students to appropriate sources of support or to helpful agencies;

- to introduce students to inspirational people (in person or via the net) who may be a source of encouragement to them;

- to explore career paths;

- for organisational support, such as checking in with them to review the week, make planning adjustments, check timetables and organise for what is upcoming;

- to help them sort out issues with teachers, students and parents;

- for peer tutoring. It may be as simple as designing a time for an older student to work on an academic task selected by the younger student.

Case study

'I have learned much from you.'

We met as Kon started Year 8 and our journey continued throughout high school. The first step was getting to know him and that proved to be easy because he felt lost and needed connections. The relationship strengthened quickly and by the third week he asked if I could come with him to the orientation camp. I couldn't, but he offered to take me in his bag!

Besides having individual time together I worked in classes supporting his learning. Kon had been identified with a serious learning difficulty and ADHD. Organisationally and academically, he needed a lot of modification and support. The schoolyard also presented problems as he often misread situations and would overreact. His reasoning and perceptions were very immature. A few students revelled in baiting and teasing him knowing they would always get their reaction. I remember a very angry Kon bursting into my room at the end of lunch saying he wanted to get a student because they had punched him. Investigation proved that the student had not punched him at all, but had pushed his way through a busy, crowded corridor and his hand had made firm contact with Kon's upper arm. There were many incidents like this, but on the positive side, they were each an opportunity to refocus his social understandings.

In Year 10 there was another camp and this time I attended. To my horror it featured rock climbing. I carefully watched Kon and his group on day one. Like most, they struggled to use the ropes and equipment correctly, but by the last day had mastered it. Then it was my turn. I remember putting on the equipment, buckling up and starting to climb. The scared little voice in my head did not allow me to reach the top. Later, I decided to have another shot at it. As I started up the rock face again Kon and his friends appeared and gently coached me up the monster cliff. They told me where I could find foot and hand holds, they held the rope firm when I thought I would fall and before I knew it I was at the top.

Did Kon finish high school? Yes! I was thrilled to be present at graduation night. There was Kon formally dressed, just as all the Year 12 students were, collecting his certificate from the principal. He did not have the academic ability to attend university, but he found a fabulous way forward into an apprenticeship.

Kon had problems to work through. So have the other boys I have mentored at school. However, mentorship has not been a one-way process. I have received as well as given. I will forever treasure the endless moments when each of the boys have accepted me into their confidence, shared ideas, asked what I thought or whether I could help. I also marvel about how much these young adolescents know and how much more they have yet to learn.

Thank you boys, I have learned much from you. Each of you has enriched my life.

Pamela, educational support officer

Which mentoring approach is best?

Mentoring occurs in all manner of ways, from unplanned chats to running a comprehensively tailored plan where outcomes are measured, recorded and celebrated. The most influential element is the continuation of a quality relationship. Right from the outset most mentors have a sense about how the process will work best for themselves and the mentee. The best advice is to do a little homework about your mentee, talk to others, observe and gather up pertinent information. Then respond using your instinct and experience.

Essentially, there are three approaches our mentors move between.

Informal

This sees the relationship operating quite spontaneously. The essence of this model is the development of a vibrant, safe relationship where the mentee values the mentor's support and is keen to discuss issues as they arise. The mentee in this situation uses the mentor as a sounding board to find improvements and solutions.

Planned

This approach offers more formality. Energy is directed towards acknowledging the mentee's challenge, or a particular goal they wish to reach. The relationship develops an orientation where mentor and mentee play with ideas to help the mentee achieve what they want. In this model the mentor takes on the role of a guide and encourager, allowing the mentee to experiment new ideas, develop new understandings and build new skills.

Goal oriented

In this approach the mentee and mentor decide to target a very specific goal. This insists that an individual 'improvement plan' or similar is designed. For information on how to build an 'improvement plan' read the section in Chapter 5 called 'Designing an improvement plan' (p. 107). The most effective plans identify a behaviour that is not working for an individual and finds a way to replace it with a behaviour that should work. It also relies on a visually engaging way to track improvements so it is obvious when the goal is achieved.

Case study

'*You must be the only person who thought I was worth anything.*'

After discussions with the school principal, Rio's teacher, his mum, and of course Rio himself, I was ready to give mentoring a go. Rio was thirteen years old and would leave our primary school to start at high school at the end of the year. He was an unusual lad. In the playground he seemed quiet and aloof. He tended to hold back and circulate on the edge of peers. His mother and teacher described him as a good kid, but unmotivated, detached and disinterested.

Rio and I struck an arrangement to meet once a week for 40 minutes. Looking back I must admit that it was a tentative start, but there was goodwill on both our parts and while engaging in a few challenges over the computer we found a way to exchange ideas. Surprisingly quickly I saw that this boy wanted to talk. That was a shock because my prediction, and the prediction of everyone else, was that he'd probably be hard to engage and I'd have to guard against sessions becoming me asking a hundred questions to get a hundred one-word answers.

As our relationship opened up Rio, with a little prompting, picked up on the same concerns his mother and teacher had mentioned. He wanted closer ties with friends, but said it didn't work. He also revealed that he'd regularly go to bed after midnight because he got carried away with online computer games, then he'd wake up feeling tired and found it hard to get to school. Forgetting to brush his teeth, to shower, to do his hair and refusing to wear deodorant were all a part of his morning lethargy. As you'd imagine, we discussed the obvious reasons why he needed to get to bed earlier and how improvements in his hygiene were linked to how he felt about himself, and how other kids felt about him. We also talked about his transition from primary school to the secondary school next year. Rio's worries about moving to high school concerned students spreading 'bad rumours' about him to other kids and then not being accepted. Halfway through the term he shared that he was not liked by any of the teachers at school. I recall him saying, 'You must be the only person who thought I was worth anything'. Hearing him say this brought the meaning of mentorship into focus for me.

As I got to know Rio I decided to use a planned mentoring approach. I took the role of encourager and suggested ways to experiment with ideas that might give him a sense of accomplishment. I kept his mother in the loop and she appreciated knowing the sort of things we were working on together. Rio and I developed simple ways to measure progress towards the goals we set together. From one week to the next we discussed and recorded how the experiments with friendships were working out and how getting to bed earlier was going. And, there were small improvements. While we were sitting together late in the year Rio leapt up from his seat and thrust his armpit at my nose.

'Do you like the smell of my deodorant?' he asked.

He continued to shoot questions, 'And, what about my hair? I've been using mud. Looks good doesn't it?'

I smiled and asked, 'So, what's happening with the teeth?
How did the experience affect me? It was utterly refreshing and the unexpected ingredient was the pleasure I received from working far more personally with a student. By taking the time to understand his world I have become far more sensitive to the hidden obstacles children in my class likely face.

Chris, teacher

Who volunteers?

Everyone who participates in this programme is a volunteer. Typical volunteers include class teachers, educational support officers, grounds staff, librarians, deputy principals, clerical staff, ICT staff, specialist subject teachers, special education coordinators, deputy principals and principals – any staff member who has a willingness to invest a little time and care in a student.

Mentoring is not overly complex, but it demands common sense and intuition. It is important for a prospective mentor to grasp this, otherwise an incredible concept, with wonderful potentials, can be killed off early as a mentor realises they have bought into more than they want to deal with.

A question often asked by volunteering teachers is whether it is wise to mentor a student who is in their class. The answer is not clear-cut. This has, on occasions, worked very well. Success is determined by the depth of the student and teacher's relationship, the mentee's temperament and the purpose of the relationship. As an example, it may work perfectly well to mentor a student around anxiety or social issues, yet prove to be far more problematic mentoring a student who flexes an explosive temper in the classroom. Mentoring relationships often prove effective because mentors do not have to be authority figures.

'A rejuvenated boy'

Nathan is eight years old. He is an only child and is raised exclusively by his father. He deals with a turbulent and disadvantaged home life.

He began at our school bringing a reputation of multiple suspensions for thoughtless and reactive schoolyard behaviours. By the end of his first term the early signs were not good, and the consequences Nathan continued to receive for poor schoolyard behaviour were not altering his patterns of behaviour. As I considered becoming his mentor I asked my principal to take on the role of contact person whenever behavioural issues arose. I didn't want to compromise my mentoring relationship by continuing as the disciplinarian.

To start with I had no idea where our mentoring relationship would take us. All I knew is that I had a desire to give this a good try. At our first meeting I remember being conscious to create a relaxed tone. My aim was to build a relationship. We scheduled a time each week to meet, although Nathan knew he could catch up with me between times if he wanted to.

I quickly learned that Nathan adored tennis, football and his PlayStation. We spent a lot of time talking about these things and he soon realised my passion for all things sport as well. We met in a variety of settings around the school: the ICT room, resource centre, basketball courts, gymnasium, on the play equipment and out on the school oval. In each session I consciously delivered one or two positive messages to Nathan. To my way of thinking he had received a barrage of negative messages from school in the past. I wanted to change this and provide him with recognition and feedback that might boost his esteem and sense of belonging.

About a month after the commencement of our mentorship I evaluated Nathan's choices in the schoolyard and concluded that not a lot had changed, so I decided to raise this with him in our next session. He listened and I proposed an idea. It was to invite a Year 7 school leader to become a yard buddy for him. Nathan instantly warmed to the suggestion because he saw Rosco as a student to be admired. Together we constructed a yard plan that provided him with structure and clear choice. At the beginning of the week in our session Nathan chose three or four yard activities to participate in during the week. The understanding was that he would remain in a selected area for all of lunch. For example, if he chose tennis at lunchtime on Monday then he would need to remain at the tennis courts for the entire 20-minute lunch period. Nathan's yard buddy would check in to see if he remained in his chosen area and would monitor his play success. Rosco would offer him a score out of ten, based on a code of respectful yard behaviour Nathan designed with us. At the end of the week Nathan, Rosco, and I evaluated the week. Rarely did Rosco have to justify his scores out of ten. Nathan just knew Rosco liked him and wanted to make this work, and I'm sure this helped to tip the scales in his favour. A copy of Nathan's plan was sent home for dad, who could also acknowledge his improved efforts.

I must admit to being hesitant about introducing such a prescriptive plan because I had decided sessions would be quite unstructured. I'm pleased we tried this because after experiencing several weeks of success in the schoolyard Nathan was like a rejuvenated boy. His new behaviours were noticed by other kids and staff, and most importantly he was having fun in the yard. He had learned how to play with others and was enjoying it. Nathan also made a friendship with Rosco, and this in turn led to connections with other students. After six weeks we decided to do away with Nathan's formal yard plan. There was no turning back for him!

I can't tell you how much I enjoyed being a part of Nathan's transformation.

Joe, deputy principal

What about training and support?

The workshop

Prospective mentors are asked to come along to a one-day workshop with a possible mentee in mind. The reason behind this is to add a personal dimension for each participant. The day's workshop is essentially the information contained within this chapter, and by the end of the day participants are poised to begin a mentoring relationship with a student in their school. Following the workshop participants are invited to join an ongoing cluster group.

Cluster meetings

One cluster meeting each term is offered to mentors for twelve months. They are scheduled after school and run for about an hour. These meetings provide opportunities for mentors to share what they are doing, share resources and contacts, exchange ideas, ask for advice, strengthen professional relationships with one another, celebrate successes and develop expertise.

Further avenues of support

Mentors are also encouraged to meet with someone in their leadership team back at school on a regular basis. It makes sense to keep leadership connected to what they are doing, and the bonus is that when a niggling issue arises leadership is already in the picture. Support and advice is also available from the behaviour education consultant attached to each school and from the workshop trainer.

What should I do if I hear worrying information from my mentee?

Very occasionally a mentor will receive information that is contentious or illicit from their mentee. Such information can never be kept as a secret between mentor and mentee. In this circumstance the mentor is committed to follow the protocol always required of them as a staff member working within a school. Our experience has shown that in rare instances when a mentor has had to responsibly share sensitive information with appropriate personnel, or make a mandatory notification, the outcome has been helpful. The overriding motive is to deal with the issue compassionately and constructively. Thankfully, for the most part, mentors are rarely confronted by weighty, controversial issues.

How is a match between a mentor and mentee made?

There is always the challenge of supply and demand when matching willing mentors with potential mentees. Often staff members who would make great mentors are those already doing so many other things. Even so, it is surprising how often a staff member and a student will independently initiate a mentoring relationship. Alternatively, once colleagues and parents know a staff member is available to mentor, advances begin to occur quite naturally.

Is this another programme asking more of school staff?

This programme has flourished on the basis that the school principal or leadership team commit to find a creative solution to release the staff member from a duty or responsibility so they can have their weekly mentoring session with their mentee. The advice we give prospective mentors is if they cannot find support from leadership, then it is best to give the idea away for the time being.

A number of schools support mentors by providing opportunities:

- to access professional readings;

- for further training;

- to debrief to leadership;

- to discuss the programme with colleagues and encourage others to become mentors;

- to develop a small budget to cover minor costs.

Case study

'... so I went about setting up a broad-based mentoring programme at our school'

In my role as school counsellor I'm constantly faced with the challenge of providing children with opportunities to reach their potential, despite adversity in their life.

Yet, I can only stretch myself so far. Much of my plate is filled with the kids who display the classically angry and challenging behaviours and those who show low self-esteem, sadness, friendship issues and are caught up in mild family disturbances are often hard to get to. I've always had a commitment to make some inroads and reach this silent, struggling group.

About a year ago I became enthused by the mentoring programme: a simple concept to benefit students by linking them to a caring, significant adult in their school life. I felt mentorship may prove to be a vehicle to assist a greater number of students, so I went about setting up a broad-based programme at our school. What has evolved is unique and very special.

Firstly, with the unconditional support of the special education coordinator, I ran a series of development sessions with all staff to introduce the notion of what such a programme running throughout the school might look like, and what we might offer. We worked together to identify students who would be advantaged by inclusion into the programme. Typically, so many of the students with learning issues and disabilities are challenged by emotional and behavioural issues.

What we have developed to date are seven teachers who volunteer to mentor students from the mainstream school population. They meet with their mentee for a 30-minute session each week and negotiate activities based on the interests and needs of the student. We have students making gardens, cooking, sewing, learning to dance, developing sporting skills and producing wonderful art and craftwork under the guidance of their mentors. And, within the context of this carefully planned structure mentors and mentees talk and exchange ideas about all manner of things. It is not unusual to see the mentee bring along a friend as this often helps to elevate their social status. To facilitate the programme I release each of the seven teachers so they are able to work with their mentee in another location. During this time I work with their class on sessions based around communication and social skills. The Special Education students are mentored by their school assistant for 10 minutes every day.

The anecdotal evidence to this point suggests significant improvements in the confidence and happiness of the students being mentored. There has also been a decrease in the reactive and explosive types of behaviours, despite a number of the students in the programme having been identified with ADHD, oppositional defiance disorder and autism. Perhaps their calmer approach reflects a stronger sense of connection and a better grasp on their school world. We are not sure, but we like what we are seeing.

The mentoring programme at our school has been a fabulous and enriching experience for my colleagues and me. It has provided a compassionate energy that has strengthened our school culture and staff relationships. Beyond benefiting my own practice, mentorship has given teachers the chance to relate with students more personally. There are many success stories, but what continues to motivate our mentoring team is the look on the faces of students, and the reassurance in their voices, when they describe what is happening between them and their mentor. That's priceless!

Sharon, school counsellor

What if the relationship is not working out?

This happens from time to time, but realistically an initial perfect match between mentor and mentee is near impossible to find. Try to be patient and give the relationship a chance to grow. However, if there is a strong sense that the relationship will not positively develop then bring it to a close.

To conclude the relationship safely make sure that no blame is apportioned to anyone. A well designed programme offers a no-blame clause right from the start and a clear closure procedure so that no one feels hurt or carries a loss of dignity (Shea 1997). It is a wise option to include the student's parents in the closure process so that they truly understand why the relationship has run its course. The student may benefit from knowing that a new mentor wants to work with them should they wish to take up the offer again.

Sample mentoring agreement

We, _____ (mentee's name)

and _____ (mentor's name)

are starting a mentoring relationship. We want this relationship to be a positive experience. We plan for our time together to be valuable. The main goal is to make improvements in the mentee's life.

- Commencement date:
- Period the mentoring programme is intended to run:
- Date the programme is likely to finish:
- Frequency of meetings:
- Where meetings will take place:
- Length of each meeting:
- Mentoring activities decided on:
- Initial goal(s):
- Possible future goal(s):

We have discussed and filled this agreement together. We have talked about and agreed on a 'no-blame' understanding just in case our relationship doesn't work out and needs to end early.

Mentee's signature: _____   Mentor's signature:_____

Date: _____   Date: _____

Parent/caregiver's   Principal's

signature: _____   signature: _____

Date: _____   Date: _____

'Thank you for helping the other girls to like me.'

Madi's class teacher, and others involved with her at school, wondered whether mentorship may be an optimistic way to guide her on how to interact with peers more successfully. While eleven-year-old Madi was considered a gifted student, her rigid, obsessive and reclusive nature put other kids right off. Her parents were convinced that the reason she did not interact with her peers was that she was too clever for them.

I knew that getting to know Madi would be a challenge, and it was. First, Madi and I have contrasting personalities. My bubbly nature really annoyed her. However, with the confidence of hindsight, this was exactly what she needed. Madi's interests included *Star Wars*, karate and horses, horses, horses, horses and more horses, and she was not at all interested in getting to know anything about me. This was her style and it was plain to see why she had no friends. Curiously, she complained about being lonely. I quickly discovered that she saw herself as superior to her classmates.

I worked out the best way forward in sessions was to keep Madi busy while we chatted. So early on we eased into cooking, played computer games and I encouraged her to tell me about *Star Wars* and the horses. While somewhat of a bond formed between us, every week was a challenge. It seemed I had to gain her trust all over again. I found this extremely frustrating and often wondered if the match between us was suitable.

Madi and I created a photo story about horses and presented it to her class. The class was completely silent during her presentation. They were mesmerized by her knowledge, passion and by the fascinating stories she told. What also took them by surprise was Madi actually giving her time and herself to them. This was new! After this Madi and I made a pact about our sessions needing to work in the same way healthy relationships do. She could talk about 'her stuff', but she also needed to ask questions about me and look like she wanted to listen. So of course she continued and tested my knowledge on *Star Wars* and horses. I would share my upcoming wedding plans, things about my basketball team and what I was doing on the weekend. Madi didn't seem to have a natural inclination for this, but she persevered. We always finished the sessions with a five-minute boogie. At first Madi just watched me in utter disbelief and would not join in. That gradually changed. The end of the year came and we agreed to keep working together in the first term of the new year.

Madi returned to sessions in the new year surly and withdrawn. It took four weeks for Madi to start to relate to me as she did late the year before. The upside was that Madi seemed more connected to peers in class and had a great relationship with her new classroom teachers. This was a wonderful step in the right direction. As the term came to an end I felt it was time to bring our sessions to a close. To be honest I felt sure she wouldn't mind at all. I was wrong. Madi cried when I initially broke the news to her. So I learned an amazing lesson. Madi may have looked and sounded like she didn't value mentorship, but these sessions had meant a great deal to her. At our last session Madi made a card for me. It said . . .

'Thank you for liking me and helping the other girls to like me. Say hello when you see me in the yard.'

Mel, educational support officer

Parental consent

The mentee's parent or guardian must consent to the student taking part in the programme.

Sample mentoring consent form

Dear Parent/caregiver

Our school is pleased to offer an innovative mentorship programme.

_____ (Mentor's name)

has agreed to mentor your child. Their aim is to develop a trusting relationship that is likely to support your child in both the classroom and playground.

What is a mentoring programme?

This programme is a personalised encouragement approach.

With the help of their mentor, the programme supports students to develop skills, find confidence and to discover new ways to interact, learn and work.

What is involved?

The mentor will work on a one-to-one basis with your child.

They will meet for about 30 minutes each week at school at a mutually convenient time over the remaining school year.

We seek your permission for (student's name) to be involved in the programme. Your child's mentor will contact you once the consent form below is filled in, signed and returned to school.

Yours sincerely,

Principal's signature: _____

I give permission for _____

to be involved in the 'in-school mentoring programme'.

I understand that this will take him/her from the classroom on a weekly basis for a short time and that the information shared during this time will be kept confidential.

Parent/caregiver's signature: _____

Date: _____

Orientation: tips to get mentors off to a great start

- Once you have decided to mentor a student, start to plan. Think about what this relationship might be like? How might it work best? What is likely to be the upside? What's likely to be the more difficult edge?

- Give yourself adequate time for preparation. Consider when and where you will meet? The location needs to offer privacy, but also needs to ensure your professional security.

- Speak with your principal or leadership team about your interest in developing a mentoring relationship with a student. Remember, you require their support. Without it, do not proceed. They play a pivotal role in promoting the programme to staff and parents, releasing you from other responsibilities so you can work with your mentee, prepare, take part in information sessions and evaluate the process.

- Meet with the mentee's class teacher or home group teacher. They will be able to provide a wealth of background information, as well as discussing convenient release times for the student to meet with you.

- Inform colleagues at the next staff meeting. Tell them who the student is that you intend to work with. Listen to what they have to say. Their collective background knowledge may be invaluable.

- Next, it's time to talk to your prospective mentee or make contact with their parents about what you have in mind. Usually, for older students you know, it is best to float the idea directly to them. If they show the anticipated interest follow up by contacting their parents.

- When contacting parents personal contact is best. However, due to time constraints first contact is often initiated by phone. The quality of this first contact is crucial, so prepare for it. Introduce yourself, explain the programme and actually ask permission for their son or daughter to participate. Keep the details simple. Ask about their child's interests and ways they would like you to support their son or daughter. Convey your enthusiasm and offer your school contact phone number and school email address, and assure them that you'll regularly update them.

- Finish up this initial conversation by letting them know that you will send a letter that will include a brief explanation of the programme, a consent form and an idea of what you hope to achieve. If you haven't already spoken with the student, mention that it would be a help if they could share a little about you and the mentoring programme with their child before you follow up at school.

- Now it's time to think about how you should introduce yourself to your mentee, after all, first impressions are important! It is a good idea to explain how the programme will work and what the objectives could be, but keep it brief. Discuss with your mentee the sorts of things they might like to do with you in sessions – a board game, a computer game, a quiz, a card game, art, craft, construction, a chance for them to teach you something, origami, kicking the football, throwing the basketball, cooking or just talking and planning. Plan 'a getting to know one another' activity for the first session. Make it a thoroughly engaging session and leave them wanting more. Make a follow-up phone call to your mentee's parents to let them know how the first session went (Du Bois *et al.* 2002). In addition, be sure to keep your mentee's class teacher or home group teacher in the loop.

- Take one step at a time. As you get to know one another, begin to work towards identifying areas your mentee identifies as challenging. Discover whether they would like a little support by building a targeted programme together. Find out what sort of support might help. Think about some simple ways you could measure changes as your mentee inches their way towards a goal. Allow for sessions to change as your relationship develops and new considerations unfold. Look for opportunities to reward your mentee when goals are achieved or the relationship comes to a close: participation certificate, acknowledgement at an assembly, etc.

- The best mentors develop clear objectives and hold themselves thoroughly accountable (Grossman 1999). They resist the temptation to rely on 'feel-good data'. Instead, they develop a logbook to collect, analyse and crystallise their thoughts. They use it to record pre-tests completed with their mentee, to plan, review, to write anecdotal stories and to evaluate. Maintaining a logbook is a hallmark of a skilled mentor. It takes mentorship beyond the 'feel good' to documentation that explains what has been designed and achieved. Moreover, it helps to justify the investment the school and system is contributing to the programme.

Case study

'Don't kiss Courtney, or you'll get girl germs'

'I think you'd be really good at this. There's a conference coming up about mentoring students and I've booked you in,' said my principal. It sounded appealing. After all, I thought, it would be a day's break from the classroom, there would be those little sandwiches at lunch, plus I had a mild interest in the idea of mentoring.

At the workshop I remember Mark saying, 'If you have just started teaching or you are about to get married then the timing to start a mentoring relationship with a student may not be right for you.'

I ticked both boxes. I was new to teaching and was soon to marry Courtney. Considering most tell me I'm oppositional in nature, it was game on for me. It helped that I'd come along with a particular student in mind as this allowed me to think about how I might begin the process back at school with Jed. Jed was in Year 5 and was a real handful to manage. He had recently been diagnosed with a learning difficulty, Asperger syndrome, ADHD and oppositional defiance disorder. He hated reading and writing. Jed rarely made eye contact with others and loathed being touched, although he was quick to push or hit others when frustrated or angry. He always preferred to play on his own or with his hand-held computer.

On my return to school I spoke with Jed's classroom teacher and the principal. We found a way for me to be released twice a week for 30 minutes to catch up with Jed. Just prior to our first meeting I saw him in the schoolyard and I asked if he knew how to play a particular computer game. I told him how much difficulty I was having getting past level 3. He grunted, 'Urggh that's easy. I'll show you when I see you.'

Sessions went well and we were surprisingly comfortable together, however, I did stress a bit over making sure the activity was right and the focus of the conversation moved in the directions I wanted. Each time a session ended we shook hands, saying see you next time and looking each other in the eye. These sessions with him made me appreciate just how hard it was for Jed to take on board the social stuff that most of us find so easy. We met regularly throughout the year and our relationship grew. I actually looked forward to sessions with him. Over a game or sharing sports cards or photos from home we talked about what was happening for him at school and in life generally. He loved to talk and was prepared to try new things to ease his frustrated behaviours in the classroom. The feedback was that his behaviour was less reactive when things went wrong. That was a bonus!

Just before I went on leave for my wedding in October, Jed made a surprise visit to my classroom. He walked up to me, looked me in the eye and handed me a wedding card. He shook my hand saying 'Good luck, Mr Veitch'. He turned and walked away. I opened the card and he had written 'Don't kiss Courtney, or you'll get girl germs'. As I looked up he was on his way out the door waving and smiling. After a few dabs with a tissue and some very deep breaths, I composed myself and acted as though nothing had happened in front of my class. Who was I kidding?

Mentoring has rekindled my belief about the real influence we have on kids. It's reminded me of why I chose to be a teacher. By doing not much more than spending time with Jed, talking, sharing and planning, a rewarding relationship grew for both of us, and Jed's emotion became steadier at school.

Sam, teacher

Conclusion: evidence of care

The best way to close is to ask:

Who helped you find *your* compass?

Who inspired any one of *your* transformations?

Every so often an adult will tell how a significant person's guidance and support made a world of difference to them. Their mentor may have been a teacher at school, or mentoring may have taken place outside school through a sporting coach, a friend or relation. What appears consistent is that the mentee felt their mentor believed in them, and was able to help them find a way forward as they discovered a little more about themselves. In some instances the mentoring relationship was brief, but the mentor's belief underscored a belief they held somewhere within themselves about their possible future. As a result, their world felt steadier and more predicable, and in turn they became steadier and more predictable.

At this time a significant group of inspirational staff who embrace the notion of inspiring transformation in the young are quietly taking special care of some of the most vulnerable students. How revitalising and healing it is for kids to see, hear and feel the evidence of their care. The hope is that gradually, more and more kids will be supported by the amazing ripple radiating from this deeply humane programme.

> The impact that any individual has on our lives cannot easily be measured. But the benefits of having a mentor . . . someone who has given freely of his or her own time, can last a lifetime.
>
> (Ivan Lewis, Australian Parliamentary Undersecretary of State for Young People and Adult Skills 2002)

Refer to p. 192 for useful websites and further reading.

Close

Teaching Tough Kids is a practical design to improve the school experience for all students and educators. Its focus has been concerned with an ever-increasing and challenging group of students warmly referred to as 'tough kids'. These are the kids who are not yet under the influence of robust executive functioning. They display poor capacity to listen, to filter out distractions, to remember, to keep pace, adapt to changes in routine and multitask. We watch them struggle to maintain concentration, stay engaged, problem solve, remain emotionally poised, work within groups and self-regulate.

Some are identified with a number of developmental problems, psychological disorders and disabilities: Asperger syndrome, specific learning difficulties, ADHD, oppositional behaviours, ADD, auditory processing difficulties, epilepsy and cerebral palsy to mention a few. Others have endured too much anxiety or trauma in their lives and as a result also display the classic symptoms of hyperactivity, hyper vigilance, impulsive behaviours and mental health problems. Too many of these kids spend too much of their day in an over-aroused state, scanning the social horizon for the next emotional or physical threat. One thing is for sure; the way they think, express emotion and behave tells us they are not able to deal with the world as we would hope. These kids make more than their share of poor and awkward judgments and as a consequence their life is so much tougher.

What is the most fundamental issue when working with the 'tough kids'? To me, it is how we ride the inevitable emotional bumps and behavioural glitches with students. How we respond to our feelings of disappointment or frustration when things do not go so well, how we celebrate success, how we present care and whether we bring an optimistic approach into the classroom is the essence of what is most helpful. As we learn more about our emotional self and how it influences our conscious and unconscious behaviour, schools will become better places for everyone. That's right, our character and mindset are responsible for making what happens in the classroom much better or worse for kids, not another new programme, a government initiative or the promise of funding.

A recurring theme in this book has been the notion of influencing transformation in young developing human beings. To me, few things are as compelling as the chance to be an agent of optimism and change for kids. I subscribe to seeing them as whole healthy human beings capable of having a future with promise, rather than seeing these kids as broken, damaged or deficit.

Cracked pot

An elderly Chinese woman had two large pots, each hung on the ends of a pole, which she carried across her neck. One of the pots had a crack in it while the other pot was perfect and always delivered a full portion of water. At the end of the long walk from the stream to the house, the cracked pot arrived only half full.

For a full two years this went on daily, with the woman bringing home only one and a half pots of water. Of course the perfect pot was proud of its accomplishments. But the poor cracked pot was ashamed of its own imperfection, and miserable that it could only do half of what it had been made to do.

After two years of what it perceived to be bitter failure, it spoke to the woman one day by the stream.

'I am ashamed of myself, because this crack in my side causes water to leak out all the way back to your house.'

The old woman smiled, 'Did you notice that there are flowers on your side of the path, but not on the other pot's side? That's because I have always known about your flaw, so I planted flower seeds on your side of the path, and every day while we walk back, you water them. For two years I have been able to pick these beautiful flowers to decorate the table. Without you being just the way you are there would not be this beauty to grace the house.'

Each of us has our own unique flaw, but it's the cracks and flaws we each have that makes our lives together so very interesting and rewarding.

You've just got to take each person for what they are and look for the good in them.

Author unknown

Cracked pot reassures us that we are all made of the same stuff. We each have talents, hopes, fears and frailties, but the difference for the tough kids is that their search to find who they are is far more demanding on themselves and those around them. Our job is to offer care and direction as they search to see the world as their world, and as a world worth engaging with. They have a lot more to contend with and remind us that life really is a work in progress, for them and for us.

Sometimes the best we can do is to provide a soft place for them to fall. For some of the tough kids school is the only place they receive security, consistent care and hear the kinds of messages kids need to receive. School may be the only place contributing to a healthy future.

For me, the tough kids are also the inspirational kids. They present us with the greatest challenges and in doing so prompt our personal and professional growth. They challenge us to think about what we are doing and why we are doing it, and whether our actions are helpful. These inspirational kids dare us to break away from our comfort zone, to try new ideas and teach in different ways. They prevent us from becoming complacent and believing that it is adequate to teach in the same way, with the same programme and same attitude year after year. In those moments when something clicks for them, or a few years later when we hear about their success, it reminds us that we are all in this together. They teach us about the value of relationship, connectedness and the depth of human spirit. They teach us to scratch below the surface of behaviour and understand the uniqueness of their functioning.

We are the first generation of educators to appreciate the complexities of deficit, delay, disorder and syndrome, frequently aggravated by unfortunate life forces. We are also the first to know the influence we have on the future well-being of students. In the end each of us will be judged on a single question.

How strong was my desire to make a difference?

Finding a way forward with any child or adolescent is absolutely reliant on our will to participate with them in the good and not so good times.

Useful websites and further reading

2 A restorative spirit

www.boysforward.com/school-reforms.asp

www.circlespeak.com.au

www.essentialresources.com.au

www.hansberryec.com.au

www.inyahead.com.au

www.maristyc.com.au/restorative.htm

www.oars.org.au/restorative_justice.htm

www.plotpd.com.au

www.realjustice.com.au

www.restorativepractices.org

www.teachers.tv/search/node/restorative+justice

http://rcrp.blogspot.com/

www.thorsborne.com.au

www.tomkins.org

www.youtube.com (use a range of search terms with 'restorative justice' and 'schools')

Hansberry, W., 2009, *Working Restoratively in Schools: A guidebook for developing safe and connected learning sommunities*, Inyahead Press, Queenscliff, Victoria.

Hopkins, B., 2004, *Just Schools: A whole school approach to behaviour management*, Jessica Kingsley Publishers, London.

Stutzman Amstutz, L. and Mullet, J.H., 2005, *The Little Book of Restorative Discipline for Schools*, Good Books, Intercourse, PA.

Thorsborne, M. and Vinegrad, D., 2007, *Restorative Practices and Bullying: Rethinking behaviour management*, Inyahead Press, Queenscliff, Victoria.

Barkley, R. and Murphy, K., 2006, *Attention Deficit Hyperactivity Disorder: A clinical workbook* (3rd edn), Guilford, New York.

3 Inspiration to improve concentration and task completion

www.add.org
www.add.about.com/health/add/library
www.addaq.org.au/treatment/behavioural/?arid=22
www.chadd.org/attention
www.ericec.org/digests/e569.html
www.familyvillage.wisc.edu/lib_adhd.htm
www.goaskmom.com/that_works_adhd_inattentive/focus.html
www.helpforadd.com/info.htm
www.russellbarkley.org

Barkley, R., 2005, *Taking Charge of ADHD: The complete, authoritative guide for parents* (3rd edn), Guilford, New York.

Green, C. and Chee, K., 2002, *Understanding ADHD*, Doubleday Books, Moorebank, New South Wales.

Jensen, E., Markowitz, K. and Dabney, M., 2006, *A New View of AD/HD: Success strategies for the impulsive learner*, Corwin Press, San Diego, CA.

Nadeau, K.G., 2002, *Understanding Women with AD/HD*, Advantage Books, Lakeland, FL.

Rief, S., 2008, *The ADD/ADHD Checklist: A practical reference for parents and teachers* (2nd edn), Jossey-Bass, San Francisco, CA.

Hoopmann, K., 2009, *All Dogs Have ADHD*, Jessica Kingsley Publishers, London.

4 Strategies to help organisation and memory

Specific learning difficulties
www.bdadyslexia.org.uk
www.dyslexia.com/library/classroom.htm
www.dyslexia-inst.org.uk
www.dyxi.co.uk
www.hreoc.gov.au/disability_rights/standards/standards.html
www.iamdyslexic.com
www.ldinfo.com
www.ldonline.org
www.ninds.nih.gov/disorders/dysgraphia/dysgraphia.htm
www.speld.org.nz
www.speld-sa.org.au/links.html

Organisation
www.4ormore.co.uk/organise/time.htm
www.chartjungle.com
http://ineedmoretime.com/Organize_Kids.htm
www.mdx.ac.uk/www/study/Timetips.htm
http://organizedhome.com/content-59.html

A fun website for teachers
www.jigzone.com

Gold, M., 2003, *Help for the Struggling Student: Ready-to-use strategies and lessons to build attention, memory, and organizational skills*, Jossey-Bass, San Francisco, CA.

Moss, S. and Schwartz, L., 2007, *Where's my Stuff?: The ultimate teen organizing guide*, Zest Books, San Francisco, CA.

Pinsky, S., 2006, *Organizing Solutions for People with Attention Deficit Disorder: Tips and tools to help you take charge of your life and get organized*, Fair Winds Press, Gloucester, MA.

Springer, S. and Alexander, B., 2005, *The Organized Teacher: A hands-on guide to setting up and running a terrific classroom*, McGraw-Hill, New York.

5 Creating the best start for challenging kids

www.aacap.org
www.aacap.org/cs/root/facts_for_families/children_with_oppositional_defiant_disorder
www.addadhdadvances.com/ODD.html
www.betterhealth.vic.gov.au/bhcv2/bhcArticles.nsf/pages/Oppositional_defiant_disorder
www.conductdisorders.com/aboutus.htm
http://jamesdauntchandler.tripod.com/
www.mayoclinic.com/health/oppositional-defiant-disorder/DS00630
www.mentalhealth.com/dis/p20-ch05.html
www.psychology.org.au

Leaman, L., 2005, *Managing Very Challenging Behaviours*, Continuum International, London.

Maughan, B., 2000, *Conduct Disorders in Children and Adolescents*, Cambridge University Press, London.

Easton, L., 2008, *Engage the Disengaged*, Corwin Press, Thousand Oaks, CA.

Kazdin, A., 2008, *The Kazdin Method for Parenting the Defiant Child: With no pills, no therapy, no contest of wills*, Houghton Mifflin, Boston, MA.

6 Ideas to enrich social and emotional connections

Autism and Asperger syndrome
www.autismaus.com.au
www.autismeducation.net
www.autismsa.org.au
www.autism-society.org/site/PageServer
www.cesa7.k12.wi.us/SPED/autism/05/visualexamplesindex.htm
www.education.gov.ab.ca
www.health.gov.au
www.iidc.indiana.edu/index.php?pageId=32

www.macswd.sa.gov.au
www.polyxo.com
www.teachers.tv/search/node/autism
www.thegraycenter.org
www.tonyattwood.com.au
www.udel.edu/bkirby/asperger
www.users.dircon.co.uk/~cns
www.vicnet.net.au/~asperger

Peer mediation
www.conflictsolvers.com.au/school-survey.html
www.cruinstitute.org

Attwood, T., 2007, *The Complete Guide to Asperger's Syndrome*, Jessica Kingsley Publishers, London.

Faherty, C., 2000, *Asperger's: What does it mean to me?* Future Horizons, Arlington, TX.

Haddon, M., 2003, *The Curious Incident of the Dog in the Night-time*, Random House Children's Books, Oxford.

Hoopmann, K., 2009, *All Cats Have Asperger Syndrome*, Jessica Kingsley Publishers, London.

Purkis, J., 2006, *Finding a Different Kind of Normal: Misadventures with Asperger syndrome*, Jessica Kingsley Publishers, London.

Winter, M., 2003, *Asperger Syndrome: What teachers need to know*, Jessica Kingsley Publishers, London.

7 Designs to lift moods

http://classroom-activities.suite101.com/article.cfm/icebreaker_energizers
www.eslflow.com/ICEBREAKERSreal.html
www.eslkidstuff.com/Classroomgamesframe.htm
www.group-games.com
www.icebreakers.ws
www.teampedia.net/wiki/index.php?title=Main_Page
http://wilderdom.com/games/

Bordessa, K., 2006, *Team Challenges: 170+ group activities to build cooperation, communication and creativity*, Zephyr Press, Chicago, IL.

Cole Miller, B., 2004, *Quick Team-building Activities for Busy Managers: 50 exercises that get results in just 15 minutes*, AMACOM, New York.

Nason McElherne, L. and Lisovskis, M., 2006, *Quick & Lively Classroom Activities Book & CD-ROM: Meaningful ways to keep kids engaged during transition time, downtime, or anytime*, Free Spirit Publishing, Minneapolis, MN.

Pike, B. and Solem, L., 2000, *50 Creative Training Openers and Energizers*, Pfeiffer Publishers, San Francisco, CA.

8 Mentorship

www.bigbrothersbigsisters.org.au
www.coachingnetwork.org.uk/Default.htm
www.creativeideasforyou.com/Mentor_Teacher_1.html
www.creativeideasforyou.com/Mentor_Teacher_3.html
www.decs.sa.gov.au/mentoring/
www.dsf.org.au
www.mentoring.org
www.thesmithfamily.com.au
www.youthengagement.sa.edu.au/pages/mentoring/CommunityMentoring/
www.youthmentoring.org.au

Ambrose, L., 2008, *Common Sense Mentoring*, Perrone-Ambrose Associates, Deerfield, IL.

Maxwell, J., 2008, *Mentoring 101*, Thomas Nelson, Nashville, TN.

Sweeny, B., 2007, *Leading the Teacher Induction and Mentoring Program* (2nd edn), Corwin Press, Thousand Oaks, CA.

Zachary, L., 2005, *Creating a Mentoring Culture: The organization's guide*, Jossey-Bass, San Francisco, CA.

References

Adler, A., 1929, *The Practice and Theory of Individual Psychology*, Routledge & Kegan Paul, London.

Adolphs, R., Sears, L. and Piven, J., 2001, 'Abnormal processing of social information from faces in autism', *Journal of Cognitive Neuroscience*, 13: 232–240.

AlphaSmart Direct Inc., 2008, *Renaissance Learning*, www.alphasmart.com (viewed 15 December 2008).

Amen, D.G., 2002, *Healing ADD: The breakthrough program that allows you to see and heal the 6 types of ADD*, Berkley Books, New York.

American Psychiatric Association, 1994, *Diagnostic and Statistical Manual of Mental Disorders (DSM-IV)*, 4th edn, APA, Washington, DC.

Appelbaum, M., 2008, *How to Handle the Hard-to-Handle Student, K-5*, Corwin Press, Thousand Oaks, CA.

Ardila, A., 2008, 'On the evolutionary origins of executive functions', *Brain and Cognition*, 68 (1): 92–99.

Armstrong, T,. 2000, *Multiple Intelligences in the Classroom* (2nd edn), Atlantic Books, London.

Arwood, S.B., Jolivette, K. and Massey, G., 2000, 'Mentoring with elementary-age students', *Intervention in School and Clinic*, 36 (1): 36–40.

Ask Oxford: Oxford Dictionary, 2008, *Compact Oxford English Dictionary*, www.askoxford.com (viewed 17 December 2008).

Attwood, T., 1998, *Asperger's Syndrome: A guide for parents and professionals*, Jessica Kingsley Publishers, London.

Attwood, T., 2007, *The Complete Guide to Asperger's Syndrome*, Jessica Kingsley Publishers, London.

Axup, T. and Gersch, I., 2008, 'The impact of challenging student behaviour upon teachers lives in a secondary school: teacher's perceptions', *British Journal of Special Education*, 35 (3): 144–151.

'Bad behaviour', 2008, *Life at 3*, television broadcast, ABC Television, 9 October.

Baker, J., 2001, *Social Skills Picture Book: Teaching play, emotion and communication to children with autism*, Future Horizons, Arlington, TX.

Baker, J., 2006, *Social Skills Picture Book for High School and Beyond*, Future Horizons, Arlington, TX.

Barekat, R., 2006, *Playing it Right! Social skills activities for parents and teachers of young children with autism spectrum disorders, including Asperger syndrome*, Autism Asperger Publishing Company, Shawnee Mission, KS.

Barkley, R., 1997, 'Inhibition, sustained attention, and executive functions: constructing a unifying theory of ADHD', *Psychological Bulletin*, 121: 65–94.

Barkley, R., 2006, *Attention Deficit Hyperactivity Disorder: A handbook for diagnosis and treatment* (3rd edn), Guilford, New York.

Baron-Cohen, S., 2004, *The Essential Difference: Men, women and the extreme male brain*, Penguin Books, London.

Barton, J., Cherkasova, M., Hefter, R., Cox, T., O'Connor, M. and Manoach, D., 2004, 'Are patients with social developmental disorders prosopagnosic? Perceptual heterogeneity in the Asperger and socio-emotional processing disorders', *Brain*, 127: 1706–1716.

Baumeister, R., 2002, 'Rejection massively reduces IQ', *New Scientist*, March, www. newscientist.com/article/dn2051-rejection-massively-reduces-iq-.html (viewed 21 December 2008).

Beltman, S. and MacCallum, J., 2006, 'Mentoring and the development of resilience: an Australian perspective', *International Journal of Mental Health Promotion*, 8: 17–28.

Bender, W., 2007, *Differentiating Instruction*, Corwin Press, Thousand Oaks ,CA.

Bender, W. and Larkin, M., 2003, *Reading Strategies for Elementary Students with Learning Difficulties*, Corwin Press, Thousand Oaks, CA.

Berthoz, S. and Hill, E., 2005, 'The validity of using self-reports to assess emotion regulation abilities in adults with autism spectrum disorders', *European Psychiatry*, 20: 291–298.

Biddulph, S., 1994, *Manhood*, Finch Publishing, Lane Cove, NSW.

Bird, R., 2008, *The Dyscalculia Toolkit*, Corwin Press, Thousand Oaks, CA.

Blake-Beard, S.D., 2001, 'Taking a hard look at formal mentoring programs: a consideration of potential challenges facing women', *Journal of Management Development*, 20 (4): 331–345.

Bouck, E. and Bouck, M., 2008, 'Does it add up? Calculators as accommodations for sixth grade students with disabilities', *Journal of Special Education Technology*, 23 (2): 17–32.

Boyle, J., 2008, 'Reading strategies for students with mild disabilities', *Intervention in School and Clinic*, 44 (1): 3–9.

Bradshaw, J., 2001, *Developmental Disorders of the Fronto-Striatal System*, Psychiatric Press, Philadelphia.

Braithwaite, J., 1989, *Crime, Shame and Reintegration*, Cambridge University Press, Cambridge.

Brown, T., 2008, 'AD/HD and the challenges of early adulthood', *LADS Newsletter*, 74: 4–6.

Bryan, T., Burstein, K. and Bryan, J., 2001, 'Students with learning disabilities: homework problems and promising practice', *Educational Psychologist*, 36 (3): 167–180.

Burrows, L., 2007, *Recreating the circle of wellbeing: A professional development resource to support learners with learning and emotional difficulties*, State of South Australia, Department of Education and Children's Services, Adelaide.

Buzan, T., 2003, *Mind Maps for Kids*, Harper Collins, New York.

Byrnes, M., 2008, 'Writing explicit, unambiguous accommodations', *Intervention in School and Clinic*, 44 (1): 18–24.

Cahill, H. (ed.), 2000, *School matters: Mapping and managing mental health in schools*, Commonwealth of Australia, Canberra.

Cahill, H., Shaw, G., Wyn, J. and Smith, G., 2004, *Translating Caring into Action*, Australian Youth Research Centre, Melbourne.

Cameron, J. and Pierce, W.D., 1994, 'Reinforcement, reward, and intrinsic motivation: a meta-analysis', *Review of Educational Research*, 64: 363–423.

Cameron, J. and Pierce, W.D., 1998, *The Debate about Rewards and Intrinsic Motivation. Readings in educational psychology* (2nd edn), Allyn & Bacon, Columbus, OH.

Cameron, L. and Thorsborne, M., 1999, 'Restorative justice and school discipline: mutually exclusive? A practitioner's view of the impact of community conferencing in Queensland schools', presented to the reshaping Australian institutions conference, Australian National University, Canberra.

Carlisle, J.F., 2002, *Improving Reading Comprehension. Research-based principles and practices*, York Press, Timonium, MD.

Carter, N., Prater, M.A., and Dyches, T.T., 2009, *Making Accommodations and Adaptations for Students with Mild to Moderate Disabilities* (What every teacher should know about series), Merrill/Pearson, Upper Saddle Road, NJ.

Cerderlund, M. and Gillberg, C,. 2004, 'One hundred males with Asperger syndrome: a clinical study of background and associated factors', *Developmental Medicine and Child Neurology*, 46: 652–661.

Clinch, R., 2000, *Secret Kids' Business*, Hawker Brownlow Education, Moorabbin, Victoria.

Cohen, V.L. and Cowen, J.E., 2008, *Literacy for Children in an Information Age*, Thomson Wadsworth, Australia.

Conroy, M., Dunlap, G., Clarke, S. and Alter, P., 2005, 'A descriptive analysis of positive behavioural intervention research with young children with challenging behaviour', *Topics in Early Childhood Special Education*, 25 (3): 157–166.

Cremin, H., 2007, *Peer Mediation*, Open University Press, Buckingham.

Cullen, J. and Richards, S., 2008, 'Using software to enhance the writing skills of students with special needs', *Journal of Special Education Technology*, 23 (2): 33–43.

Dalton J. and Boyd, J., 1992, *I Teach: A guide to inspiring classroom leadership*, Elanor Curtain Publishing, Australia.

Darby, P., 2002, 'ADD/ADHD and autism: new directions in treatment', *Classroom*, 22 (4): 16.

Dinkmeyer, D. and Dreikurs, R., 2000, *Encouraging Children to Learn*, Brunner-Routledge Group, Philadelphia, PA.

Dodd, S., 2005, *Understanding Autism*, Pro-Ed, Austin, TX.

Dreikurs, R., Brunwald, B., Bronia, P. and Floy, C., 1998, *Maintaining Sanity in the Classroom: Classroom management techniques* (2nd edn), Taylor & Francis, Levittown, PA.

Dreikurs, R. and Soltz, V., 1989, *Children: The challenge*, Hawthorn/Dutton, New York.

Du Bois, D.L., Holloway, B.E., Valentine, J.C. and Cooper, H., 2002, 'Effectiveness of mentoring programs for youth: a meta-analytic review', *American Journal of Community Psychology*, 30 (2): 157–197.

Eber, L., Breen, K., Rose, J., Unizycki, R. and London, T., 2008, 'Wraparound as a tertiary level intervention for students with emotional/behavioural needs', *Teaching Exceptional Children*, 40 (6): 16–22.

Elliot, J. and Thurlow, M., 2006, *Improving Test Performance of Students with Disabilities*, Corwin Press, Thousand Oaks, CA.

Evers, W., Tomic, W. and Brouwers, A., 2004, 'Burnout among teachers', *School Psychology International*, 25 (2): 131–148.

Fabes, R.A., Fultz, J., Eisenburg, N., May-Plumber, T. and Christopher, F.S., 1989, 'Effects of rewards on children's prosocial motivation: a socialization study', *Developmental Psychology*, 25: 509–515.

Forlin, C., Keen, M. and Barrett, E., 2008, 'The concerns of mainstream teachers: coping with inclusivity in an Australian context', *International Journal of Disability, Development and Education*, 55 (3): 251–264.

Franklin Electronic Publishers, 2008, *Speaking Language Master*, www.franklin.com/estore/dictionary/LM-6000B/ (viewed 15 December 2008).

Frith, U., 2001, *Autism and Asperger Syndrome*, Cambridge University Press, Cambridge.

Gardner, J., Grant, J. and Webb, P., 2003, *Autism for All Teachers: A teacher's guide to working with students with ASD*, KLIK Enterprises, Western Australia.

Gillon, G., 2005, *The Gillon Phonological Awareness Training Program*, Canterprise, Christchurch.

Ginott, H., 2003, *Between Parent and Child* (revised edn), Random House, Canada.

Giorcelli, L., 2000, 'Wrap around', *ACTIVE Newsletter*, June 2000, Hyperactive Children's Association of Victoria, Yarraville, Victoria.

Glaser, D., 1969, *The Effectiveness of a Prison and Parole System*, Bobbs-Merrill, Indianapolis, IN.

Glen, H.S. and Nelson, J., 1989, *Raising Self-reliant Children in a Self-indulgent World*, Rocklin Publishing & Communication, Prima, CA.

Goldberg, E., 2001, *The Executive Brain: Frontal lobes and the civilized mind*, Oxford University Press, New York.

Gray, C., 2000, *The New Social Story Book: Illustrated edition* (2nd edn), Future Horizons, Arlington, TX.

Gray, C. and White, A., 2002, *My Social Stories Book*, Future Horizons, Arlington, TX.

Green, J., 2008, 'Thinking differently about thinking differently', *Perspectives on Language and Literacy*, 34 (3): 7.

Grossman, J., 1999, *Contemporary Issues in Mentoring*, Public/Private Ventures, Philadelphia, PA.

Gutstein, S., 2001, *Solving the Relationship Puzzle: A new developmental approach that opens the door to lifelong social and emotional growth*, Future Horizons, Arlington, TX.

Haddon, M., 2003, *The Curious Incident of the Dog in the Night-time*, Random House Children's Book, Oxford.

Hall, J., 2003, *Mentoring and Young People: A literature review by the SCRE centre*, University of Glasgow, Glasgow.

Hannell, G., 2004, *Dyslexia: Action plans for successful learning*, David Fulton, London.

Hastings, R. and Bham, M., 2003, 'The relationship between student behaviour patterns and teacher burnout', *School Psychology International*, 24: 115–127.

Hattie, J., 2009, *Visible Learning: A synthesis of over 800 meta-analyses relating to achievement*, Routledge, New York.

Hedley, D. and Young, R., 2003, 'Social comparison and depression in thirty-six children and adults with a diagnosis of Asperger syndrome', *Autiser* (Autumn): 3–4.

Heffner, E., 1978, *Mothering: The emotional experience of motherhood after Freud and feminisim* (1st edn), Doubleday (Anchor Books), New York, Chapter 1.

Hendley, S., 2007, 'Use positive behaviour support for inclusion in the general education classroom', *Intervention in School and Clinic*, 42: 225–228.

Herrera, C., 1999, *School-based Mentoring: A first look into its potential*, Public/Private Ventures, Philadelphia, PA.

Herrera, C., 2005, *School-based Mentoring: A closer look*, Public/Private Ventures, Philadelphia, PA.

Herrera, C., Vang, Z. and Gale, L.Y., 2002, *Group Mentoring: A study of mentoring groups in three programs*, Public/Private Ventures, Philadelphia, PA.

Herrera, C., Baldwin-Grossman, J.T., Kauh, J., Feldman, A., McMaken, J. and Jucovy, L.Z., 2007, *Making a Difference in Schools: The big brothers big sisters school-based mentoring impact study*, Public/Private Ventures, Philadelphia, PA, www.ppv.org/ppv/publications/assets/220_publication.pdf (viewed 17 December 2008).

Holverstott, J., 2005, '20 ways to promote self-determination in students', *Intervention in School and Clinic*, 41 (1): 39–41.

Howley, M. and Arnold, E., 2005, *Revealing the Hidden Social Code: Social stories for people with autistic spectrum disorders*, Jessica Kingsley Publishers, London.

Ilot, G.A., 2005, *In the Deep End*, Queensland University Publishing Unit, Queensland.

Inspiration Software, 2008, *The Leader in Visual Thinking and Learning*, www.inspiration.com (viewed 15 December 2008).

Jackson, L., 2002, *Freeks, Geeks and Asperger Syndrome: A user guide to adolescence*, Jessica Kingsley Publishers, London.

James, F. and Kerr, A., 2004, *On First Reading: Ideas for developing reading skills*, Belair Publications, New South Wales.

Janzen, J., 2003, *Understanding the Nature of Autism*, Therapy Skill Builders, Psych Corporation, San Antonio, TX.

Johnson, A., 1999, *Sponsor a Scholar: Long-term impacts of a youth mentoring program on student performance*, Mathematical Policy Research, Princeton, NJ.

Johnson, D. and Johnson, R., 1989, *Leading the Cooperative School*, Interaction Book Company, Edina, MN.

Jucovy, L. and Garringer, M., 2007, *The ABCs of School-based Mentoring*, North West Regional Education Laboratories and the Office of Juvenile Justice, Portland, OR.

Kim, W.C. and Mauborgne, R., 2003, 'Fair process: managing in the knowledge economy', *Harvard Business Review*, January: 127–136.

Kingsley, E.P., 1987, 'Welcome to Holland', www.our-kids.org/Archives/Holland.html (viewed June 2009).

Knowles, E., 2001, *The Oxford Dictionary of Quotations*, 5th edn, Oxford University Press, New York.

Koerner, C. and Harris, J., 2007, 'Inspired learning: creating engaged teaching and learning environments for university and school mentor programs', *International Education Journal*, 8 (2): 354–364.

Lannie, A. and McCurdy, B., 2007, 'Preventing disruptive behaviour in the urban class-room: effects of the good behavior game on student and teacher behaviour', *Education and Treatment of Children*, 30 (1): 85–98.

Laycock, D., 2007, *Teacher's restorative booklet*, The Centre for Restorative Justice, Adelaide.

Lee, J. and Cramond, B., 1999, 'The positive effect of mentoring economically disadvantaged students', *Professional School Counseling*, 2 (3): 172–179.

Le Messurier, M., 2004, *Cognitive Behavioural Training: A how-to guide for successful behaviour*, Hawker Brownlow Education, Moorabbin, Victoria.

Lepper, M.R., Keavney, M. and Drake, M., 1996, 'Intrinsic motivation and extrinsic rewards: a commentary on Cameron and Pierce's meta-analysis', *Review of Educational Research*, 66: 5–32.

Levinson, D.J., Darrow, C.N., Klein, E.B., Levinson, M.A. and McKee, B., 1978, *The Seasons of a Man's Life*, Knopf, New York.

Lewis, I., 2008, 'Closing the gap in a generation: health equity through action on the social determinants of health', Conference on Closing the Gap in a Generation, 6–7 November, Department of Health, London.

Lillico, I., 2004, *Homework and the Homework Grid*, Tranton Enterprises, Western Australia.

Lock, R., 2008, 'Create effective teacher–paraprofessional teams', *Intervention in School and Clinic*, 44 (1): pp. 41–44.

Lord, C. and McGee, J., 2001, *Educating Children with Autism*, National Research Council, Washington, DC.

Lubliner, S., 2005, *Getting into Words: Vocabulary instruction that strengthens comprehension*, Brookes Publishing, Baltimore, MD.

Maag, J.W. 2001, 'Rewarded by punishment: reflections on the disuse of positive reinforcement in schools', *Council for Exceptional Children*, 67 (2): 173–186.

Maag, J.W., 2008, 'Rational-emotive therapy to help teachers to control their emotions and behavior when dealing with disagreeable students', *Intervention in School and Clinic*, 44 (1): 52–57.

MacCallum, J. and Beltman, S., 2002, *Mentoring in Schools*, The Community Centre for Curriculum and Professional Development, Murdoch University, Perth.

MacDermott, S., Williams, K., Ridley, G., Glasson, E. and Wray, J., 2007, 'The prevalence of autism in Australia. Can it be established from existing data?', *Journal of Paediatrics and Child Health*, 44 (9): 504–510.

Marron, J.A., 2002, 'Way to go: positive reinforcement programs for your child with attention deficit/hyperactivity disorder (ADD/ADHD)', *Exceptional Parent Magazine*, July: 68–70.

Marshall, P., Shaw, G. and Freeman, E., 2002, 'Restorative practices: implications for educational institutions', Third International Conference on Conferencing, paper presented at Dreaming of a New Reality, August 2002, Circles and other Restorative Practices, Minneapolis, Minnesota.

Martinussen, R., Hayden, J., Hogg-Johnson, S. and Tannock, R., 2005, 'A meta-analysis of working memory impairments in children with Attention-Deficit/Hyperactivity Disorder', *Journal of the American Academy of Child & Adolescent Psychiatry*, 44 (4): 377–384.

Meltzer, L., 2007, *Executive Function in Education: From theory to practice*, Guilford Publications, New York.

Miller, A., 2008, 'Sam's world: providing stability in a precarious reality', *Autism Spectrum Quarterly* (Autumn): 25–27.

Morrison, B., 2007, *Restoring Safe School Communities: A whole school response to bullying, violence and alienation*, Federation Press, Sydney.

Moxon, J., Skudder, C. and Peters, J., 2006, *Restorative Solutions for Schools: An introductory resource book*, Essential Resources Educational Publishers, Invercargill.

Mulrine, C.F., Prater, M.A. and Jenkins, A., 2008, 'Attention deficit hyperactivity disorder and exercise: the benefit of classroom movement activities throughout the day', *Teaching Exceptional Children*, 40 (5): 16–22.

Nathanson, D.L., 1992, *Shame and Pride, Affect, Sex and the Birth of the Self*, W.W. Norton & Company, New York.

Nathanson, D., 2004, *Managing Shame, Preventing Violence: A call to our clergy*, Silvan Tomkins Institute, Philadelphia, PA.

National Institute of Mental Health, 2000, 'Multimodal treatment study of children with Attention Deficit Hyperactivity Disorder', US Department of Health and Human Services, www.nimh.nih.gov.

Nelson, J., 1987, *Positive Discipline*, Ballantine, New York.

Pavey, B., 2007, *The Dyslexia-Friendly Primary School*, Corwin Press, Thousand Oaks, CA.

Petersen, L. and Adderley, A., 2002, *Stop, Think, Do Social Skills Training: Primary years of schooling ages 8–12*, ACER, Camberwell, Victoria.

Petersen, L. and Le Messurier, M., 2006, *STOP and THINK Friendship DVD Package*, Lindy Petersen, Adelaide.

Pfiffner, L.J., Rosen, L. and O'Leary, S., 1985, 'The efficacy of an all positive approach to classroom management', *Journal of Applied Behaviour Analysis*, 18: 257–261.

Philip, K. and Hendry, L.B., 2000, 'Making sense of mentoring or mentoring making sense? Reflections on the mentoring process by adult mentors with young people', *Journal of Community & Applied Social Psychology*, 10: 211–223.

Prizant, B.M., 2008, 'Straight talk about autism: on recovery', *Autism Spectrum Quarterly* (Summer): 39–42.

Prosser, B., 2006, *ADHD Who's Failing Who*, Finch Publishing, Sydney.

Purkis, J., 2006, *Finding a Different Kind of Normal: Misadventures with Asperger syndrome*, Jessica Kingsley Publishers, London.

Quarles, A., Maldonado, N. and Lacey, C., 2005, 'Mentoring and at-risk adolescent girls: a phenomenological investigation', paper presented at the annual meeting of the American Educational Research Association, 11–15 April 2005, American Education Research Association, Montreal, CA.

Rankin, J. and Reid, R., 1995, 'The SM rap: or here's the rap on self-monitoring', *Intervention in School and Clinic*, 30: 181–188.

Raskind, M., Goldberg, R., Higgins, E. and Herman, K., 1999, 'Patterns of change and predictors of success in individuals with learning disabilities: results from a twenty-year longitudinal study', *Learning Disabilities Research and Practice*, 14 (1): 35–49.

Reid, R., 1996, 'Self-monitoring for students with learning disabilities: the present, the prospects, the pitfalls', *Journal of Learning Disabilities*, 29: 317–331.

Reid, R. and Harris, K.R., 1993, 'Self-monitoring of attention versus self-monitoring of performance: effects on attention and academic performance', *Exceptional Children*, 60: 29–40.

Reiter, A., Tucha, O. and Lange, K., 2005, 'Executive functions in children with dyslexia', *Dyslexia*, 11: 116–131.

Reynhout, G. and Carter, M., 2008, 'A pilot study to determine the efficacy of a social story intervention for a child with autistic disorder, intellectual disability and limited language skills', *Australasian Journal of Special Education*, 32 (2): 161–175.

Rhodes, J., 2008, 'Improving youth mentoring interventions through research-based practice', *American Journal of Community Psychology*, 41 (1): 35–42.

Rhodes, J., Grossman, J. and Resch, N., 2000, 'Agents of change: pathways through which mentoring relationships influence adolescents', *Child Development*, 91: 1662–1671.

Robison, J.E., 2007, *Look Me in the Eye*, Bantam, Sydney.

Rockwell, S., 2007, *You Can't Make Me*, Corwin Press, Thousand Oaks, CA.

Rogers, B., 2003, *Behaviour Recovery: Practical programs for challenging behaviour*, ACER, Melbourne.

Royse, D., 1998, 'Mentoring high-risk minority youth: evaluation of the big brother project', *Adolescence*, 33 (129): 145–158.

Russell, P., 2008, 'Building brighter futures for all our children: a new focus on families as partners and change agents in the care and development of children with disabilities or special educational needs', *Support for Learning*, 23 (3): 104–112.

Salimpoor, V., 2006, 'Techniques for remediation of executive dysfunction in children with developmental disabilities', *Autism and Asperger's Digest* (February): 32–35.

Savner, J. and Smith-Myles, B., 2000, *Making Visual Supports Work in the Home and Community: Strategies for individuals with autism and Asperger syndrome*, Autism Asperger Publishing, Shawnee Mission, KS.

Seligman, M., 2002, *Authentic Happiness: Using the new positive psychology to realize your potential for lasting fulfilment*, Free Press, New York.

Shea, G., 1997, *Mentoring* (revised edn), Crisp Publications, Menlo Park, CA.

Sicile-Kira, C., 2008, 'I is for individualized', *Autism Spectrum Quarterly* (Summer): 12–13.

Silins, H., Mathews, C., Lokan, J. and Hudson, M., 2007, *Developing Mentally Healthy Children*, The Australian College of Educators, South Australia.

Smith-Myles, B. and Tapscott-Cook, K., 2000, *Asperger Syndrome and Sensory Issues: Practical solutions for making sense of the world*, Autism Asperger Publishing, Shawnee Mission, KS.

Snow, P., 2008, 'Oral language competence in childhood and adolescence: the missing link in mental health promotion?', Keynote presentation, joint conference between New Zealand speech language therapists association and speech pathology Australia, Reflecting connections, Auckland.

Snow, P.C. and Powell, M.B., 2008, 'Oral language competence, social skills, and high risk boys: what are juvenile offenders trying to tell us?', *Children and Society*, 22: 16–28.

Snowling, M., 2000, *Dyslexia*, Blackwell Publishers, Oxford.

Stanley, F., 2008, 'Risking our kids', *Future Makers and Rymer Childs and Thunderbox*, television broadcast, ABC Television, 7 October.

Stevenson, B., 1967, *The Home Book of Quotations*, 10th edn, Dodd, Mead and Company, New York.

Sugai, G. and Horner, R.H., 1999, 'Discipline and behavioral support: preferred processes and practices', *Effective School Practices*, 17: 1–22.

Swindoll, C.R., 1982, *Strengthening your Grip: How to live confidently in an aimless world*, Thomas Nelson/W Publishing Group, Nashville, TN.

Szatmari, P., 2004, *A Mind Apart*, Guilford Press, New York.

Teese, R. and Polesel, J., 2003, *Undemocratic Schooling: Equity and quality in Mass Secondary Education in Australia*, Melbourne University Press, Carlton.

Tierney, J.P., Grossman, J.B. and Resch, N.L., 1995, *Making a Difference: An impact study of big brothers big sisters*, Public/Private Ventures, Philadelphia, PA.

Thornton, S., 2008, 'Wellbeing', *Professional Educator*, 7 (2): 24–27.

Thorsborne, M. and Vinegrad, D., 2002a, *Restorative Practices in Classrooms: Rethinking behaviour management*, Inyahead Press, Queenscliff, Victoria.

Thorsborne, M. and Vinegrad, D., 2002b, *Restorative Practices in Schools: Rethinking behaviour management*, Inyahead Press, Queenscliff, Victoria.

Torrance, E.P., 1984, *Mentoring Relationships: How they add creative achievement, endure, change, and die*, Bearly Press, Buffalo, NY.

Trent, F. and Slade, M., 2001, *Declining Rates of Achievement and Retention: The perceptions of adolescent males*, Australian Government, Department of Education, Science and Training, www.dest.gov.au/archive/highered/eippubs/eip01_6/default.htm (viewed 17 December 2008).

Tullemans, A., Dixon, R.V. and Marman, R., 2005, *How to Stop your Words Bumping into Someone Else's and Other Really Useful Social Stories: A guide for young children with Autism Spectrum Disorder*, Seachange Publications, Victoria, Canada.

Wachtel, T. and McCold, P., 2001, 'Restorative justice theory validation', in G. Elmar, M. Weitekamp and H.-J. Kerner, *Restorative Justice: Theoretical foundations*, Willan Publishing, Devon.

Weare, K., 2004, *Developing the Emotionally Literate School*, Paul Chapman, London.

Webster-Stratton, C., Reid, J. and Hammond, M., 2004, 'Treating children with early-onset conduct problems: intervention outcomes for parent, child and teacher training', *Journal of Clinical Psychology*, 33 (1): 105–124.

Weiner, B., 1998, *History of Motivational Research in Education: Readings in educational psychology* (2nd edn), Allyn & Bacon, Columbus, OH.

Wiersma, U.J., 1992, 'The effects of extrinsic rewards in intrinsic motivation: a meta analysis', *Journal of Occupational and Organizational Psychology*, 65: 101–114.

Williams, R., 2008, 'Individualised funding: a summary review of its nature and impact, and key elements for success', *Interaction*, 22 (1): 5–25.

Wing, L., 1981, 'Asperger syndrome: a clinical account', *Psychological Medicine*, 11: 115–130.

The World of Asperger's, 2008, Catalyst, television broadcast, ABC Television, 28 August.

Wright, C.A. and Wright, S.D., 1987, 'Young professionals', *Family Relations*, 36 (2): 204–208.

Young, R., 2009, 'Transition training', *SERUpdate*, 19 (1): 4–5.

Zehr, H., 2002, *The Little Book of Restorative Justice*, Good Books, Intercourse, PA.

Zito, J., Safer, D., Dosreis, S., Gardner, J., Boles, K. and Lynch, F. 2000, 'Trends in the prescribing of psychotropic medications to preschoolers', *Journal of the American Medical Association*, 283: 1025–1030.

Zito, J., Safer, D., Dosreis, S., Gardner, J., Soeken, K., Boles, K., Lynch, F. and Riddle, M., 2003, 'Psychotropic practice patterns in youth: a 10 year perspective', *Archives of Pediatric & Adolescent Medicine*, 157: 17–25.

Worksheets

think strip

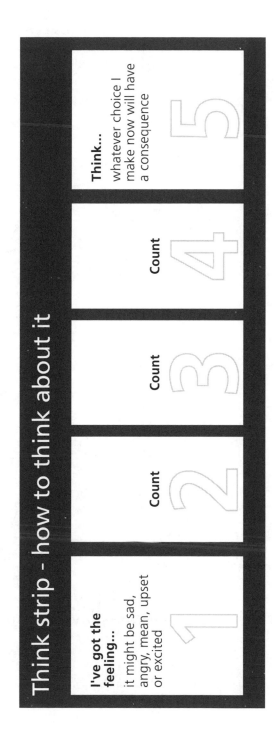

Think strip - how to think about it

I've got the feeling…
it might be sad, angry, mean, upset or excited

1

Count
2

Count
3

Count
4

Think…
whatever choice I make now will have a consequence

5

star chart

When you track changes good things happen!

When you are trying to replace an old behaviour with a new, better one you need a way to keep track of your successes. Each time you do it, colour in or place a sticker on a star.

Start date ....

Finish date ....

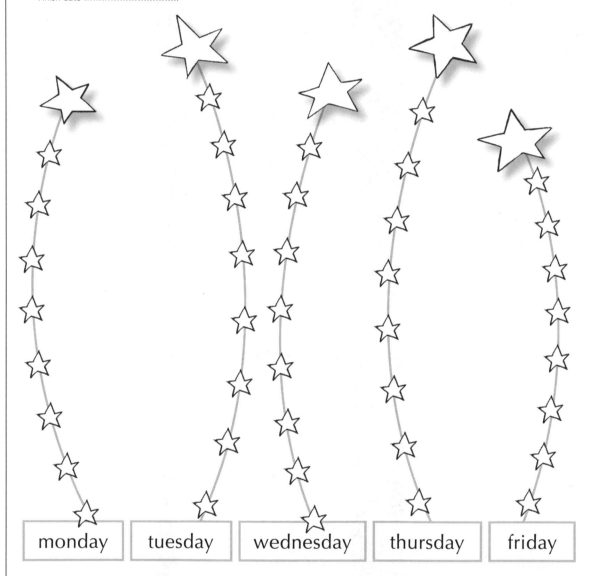

| monday | tuesday | wednesday | thursday | friday |

The new better behaviour I'm trying for is...

The reminder I'd like my teacher(s) to use is ....

My reward or incentive when I make it to the BIG STAR each day is ....

My reward or incentive when I make all five BIG STARS for the week is ....

Teaching Tough Kids, Routledge © Mark Le Messurier 2010

catching helpful behaviours

Sometimes when I catch YOU smiling, helping someone, being organised and ready, listening well, having a neat desk or showing wonderful cooperative skills I'll ask YOU to place a sticker in the square next to your name.

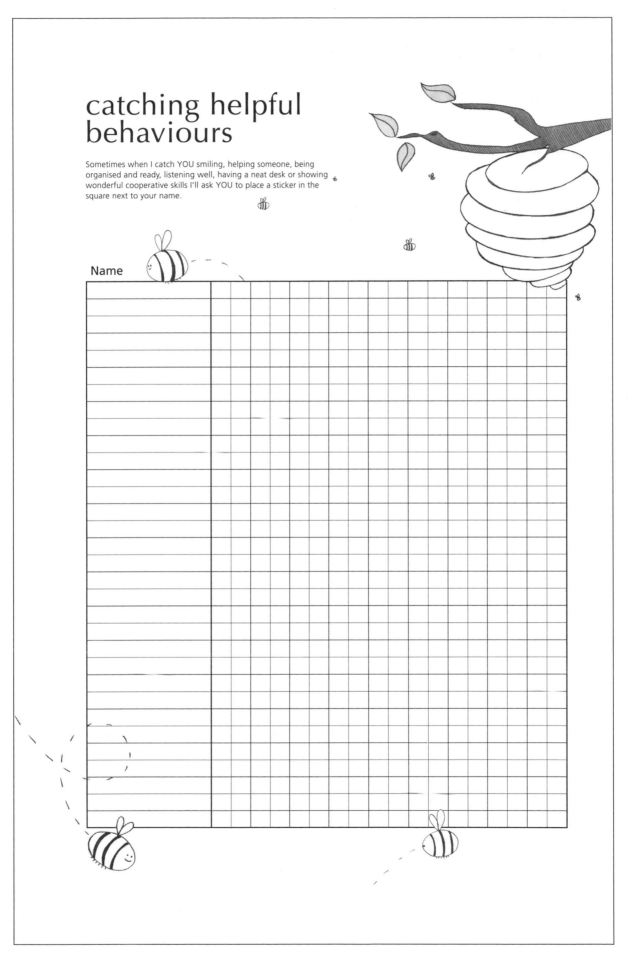

Name

student monitoring

student ....

date ....

teacher ....

Please answer the items below based on your observations of this student or feedback you have received during the past week.

Note: higher scores indicate better functioning

	Not at all	A little	A lot	Too much
Fidgets in seat	4	3	2	1
Wanders around the classroom	4	3	2	1
Hard for teacher(s) to get along with	4	3	2	1
Talks too much	4	3	2	1
Distracts others	4	3	2	1
Argumentative with other students	4	3	2	1
Gets easily distracted	4	3	2	1
Doesn't finish work	4	3	2	1
Trouble maintaining attention	4	3	2	1
Does careless/quick work	4	3	2	1
Does not listen very well	4	3	2	1
Has difficulty remembering what to do	4	3	2	1

	Not at all	A little	A lot	Really great
Is 'having a go' at things	1	2	3	4
Is following class rules	1	2	3	4
Is trying to get along with peers	1	2	3	4
Seems willing to discuss and compromise	1	2	3	4

Is the student better in the morning or the afternoon?   Which one? ....

Place an 'X' on the line below to indicate the percentage of work the student completed in class over the past week:

```
0     10     20     30     40     50     60     70     80     90     100
```

The quality of work completed by the student this week was:

very poor   poor   satisfactory   good   very good

Did this student hand in all assigned work? This includes homework requirements. Specify the assignments that were missing:

Please include any other comments or observations you believe are important:

Based on the information collected, do you believe further adjustments or interventions need to be considered?

  Teaching Tough Kids, Routledge © Mark Le Messurier 2010

chunking tasks

Here's one way to keep an eye on the time. As you begin a task, record in each balloon when the smaller parts of the task should be started.

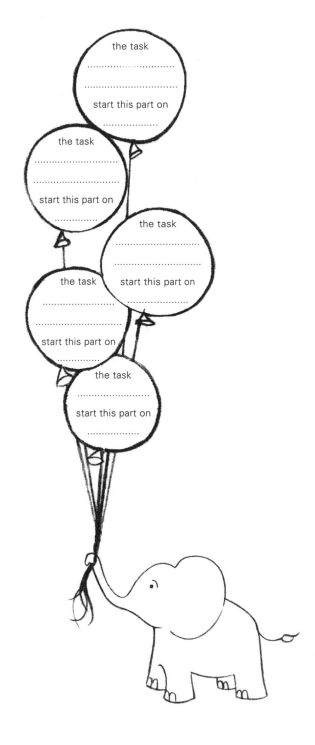

the task
....
....
start this part on
....

the task
....
....
start this part on
....

the task
....
....
start this part on
....

the task
....
....
start this part on
....

the task
....
start this part on
....

mini daily timetable

Know what's on for the day with your
mini daily timetables.

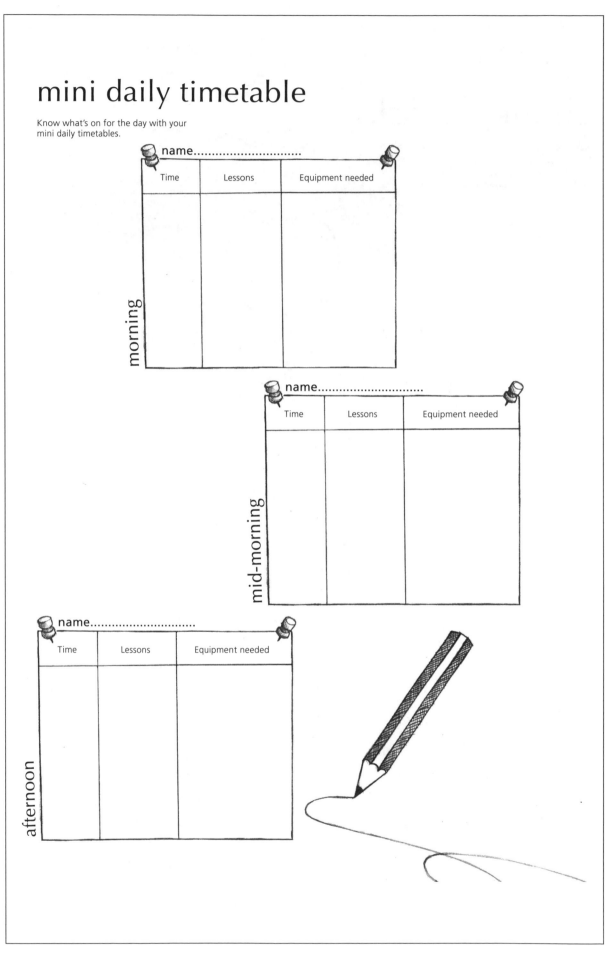

name...............................

Time	Lessons	Equipment needed

morning

name...............................

Time	Lessons	Equipment needed

mid-morning

name...............................

Time	Lessons	Equipment needed

afternoon

Teaching Tough Kids, Routledge © Mark Le Messurier 2010

name..............................

after school timetable

Fill in each of the half hour time slots. Record regular weekly activities:
TV programmes, dance lessons, scouts, karate and so on. You will see that
certain times of each day lend themselves to homework.

time	mon	tue	wed	thur	fri	sat/sun
4:00 – 4:30						
4:30 – 5:00						
5:00 – 5:30						
5:30 – 6:00						
6:00 – 6:30						
6:30 – 7:00						
7:00 – 7:30						
7:30 – 8:00						
8:00 – 8:30						
8:30 – 9:00						

name..............................

my weekly planner

A planner helps you to remember what to do AND when to do it! Fill in the planner so you will know when to: tidy your schoolbag, do homework, do your chores, watch TV, go to bed, go to karate, clean your teeth, finish a school assignment, etc.

time	mon	tue	wed	thur	fri	sat/sun
8:00 - 9:00						
9:00 – 10:00						
10:00 – 11:00						
11:00 – 12:00						
12:00 – 1:00						
1:00 – 2:00						
2:00 – 3:00						
3:00 – 4:00						
4:00 – 5:00						
5:00 – 6:00						
6:00 – 7:00						
7:00 – 8:00						
8:00 – 9:00						

Teaching Tough Kids, Routledge © Mark Le Messurier 2010

name.............................

my four week planner

Fill in the planner with the things that are up and coming, like: family outings, catching up with friends, school assignment due dates, special events and so on.

week	mon	tue	wed	thur	fri	sat/sun
one						
two						
three						
four						

progress charts

Here are two charts to help keep track of your progress.

Choose one of the charts below and then colour a section on the thermometer or a spot on the giraffe's neck each time you complete part of the task. When all of the sections or spots are coloured you'll know the task is finished.

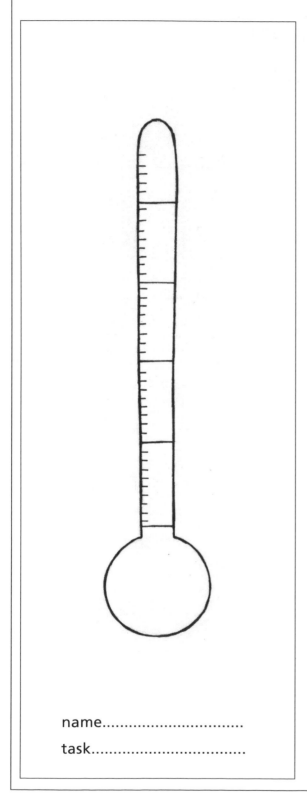

name.............................

task.............................

name.............................

task.............................

Teaching Tough Kids, Routledge © Mark Le Messurier 2010

name............................

date started...................

progress train

Work out how many small bits you can break the task into. Write the name of each part of the task onto each of the carriages. As you finish each part of the task, colour in the carriage or put a sticker on it. Doing one thing at a time helps to keep you moving in the right direction!

my checklist

Checklists are great reminders. They can also be used to break a task down into smaller steps. Put the checklist where you will see it and can update it everyday.

name...........................

☐

☐

☐

☐

☐

☐

☐

☐

☐

☐

☐

Teaching Tough Kids, Routledge © Mark Le Messurier 2010

the islands of competence inventory

What are your talents or interests? We want to know.

Can you share what sports, clubs, associations or activities you enjoy doing outside school?

What do you enjoy? It's time for us to learn what you do!

name.............................

What is it?

Where?

What can you do?

What is it?

Where?

What can you do?

What is it?

Where?

What can you do?

What is it?

Where?

What can you do?

inspired by Loretta Giorcelli's thinking

success plan
go for the cup!

When you are trying to replace an old behaviour with a new, better one you need a way to keep track of your successes. Each time you are successful, colour in or place a sticker on a spot.

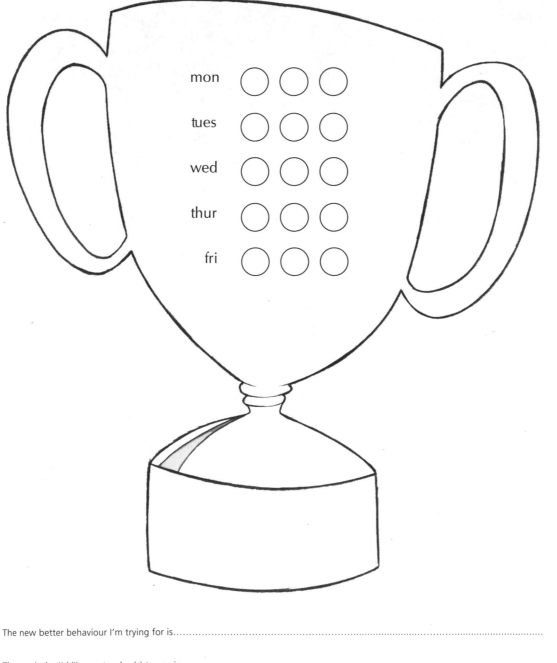

The new better behaviour I'm trying for is...

The reminder I'd like my teacher(s) to use is ....

My reward or incentive when I make three spots a day is ....

My reward or incentive when I make most of the spots (negotiate a number) for the week is ....

Teaching Tough Kids, Routledge © Mark Le Messurier 2010

ABCs of behaviour
assessing behaviour to improve functioning

Behaviour happens for a reason.
Find out why.

behaviour
Describe it...

consequence
What happens after the behaviour?

How intense is it?

1   2   3   4   5   6   7   8   9   10

Low intensity $\longrightarrow$ High intensity

reason
Why does the behaviour start?

timing
When does the behaviour start?

my new way to do it

Keeping track of my progress:
tick or place a sticker in a circle for each successful day

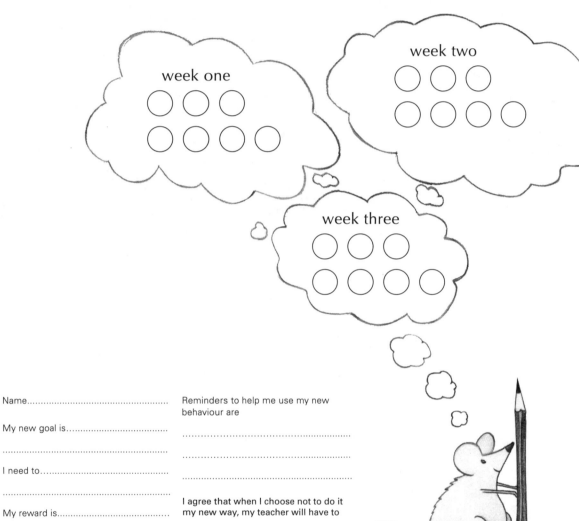

Name..

My new goal is......................................

....

I need to..

....

My reward is...

....

I can earn my reward by........................

....

My teacher can help me by ....

....

Reminders to help me use my new
behaviour are

....

....

....

I agree that when I choose not to do it
my new way, my teacher will have to

....

....

Mum/dad's signature.............................

My teacher's signature..........................

My signature..

  Teaching Tough Kids, Routledge © Mark Le Messurier 2010

blast off! tracking chart

My goal is...
....

Reminders my teacher can use to help me get to each goal are

....

....

....

Small rewards for landing on the stars are

....

Larger rewards for landing on the planets are

....

My big reward for finishing is

....

Each time you reach your goal for the morning, the afternoon or the day, colour in or put a sticker on the next star or planet. Finally, when you finish your space journey you will receive your biggest reward.

go and fly your kite!
tracking chart

Each time you reach your goal for the morning, the afternoon or the day, colour in or put a sticker on one of the pieces of the Kite's tail. Finally, when you arrive at the Kite, you will receive the special reward.

My goal is...

....

Reminders my teacher can use to help me get to each goal are

....

....

My small reward for arriving at each small piece on the Kite's tail is

....

My larger reward for arriving at each larger piece on the Kite's tail is

....

My special reward for finishing up on the Kite is

....

LET'S START!

   Teaching Tough Kids, Routledge © Mark Le Messurier 2010

name...............................

you can count on Winston's segments! tracking chart

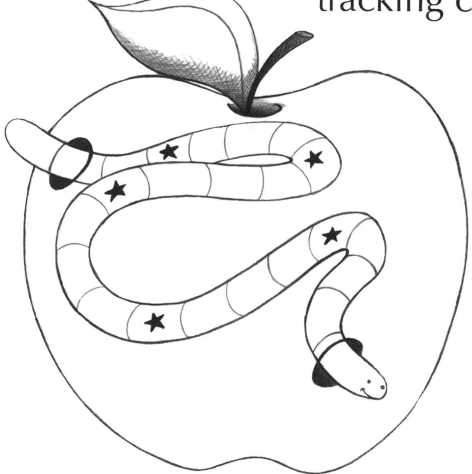

Each time you reach your goal for the morning, the afternoon or the day, colour in or put a sticker on one of Winston's segments. When you finally arrive at Winston's head you will receive the special reward you have been aiming for.

My goal is...
....

Reminders my teacher can use to help me get to each goal are

....
....
....

Small rewards for landing on each of Winston's segments with a star on it will be

....

My special reward for finishing up on Winston's head will be

....

LET'S START!

name.............................

staying on track with my dragon tracking chart

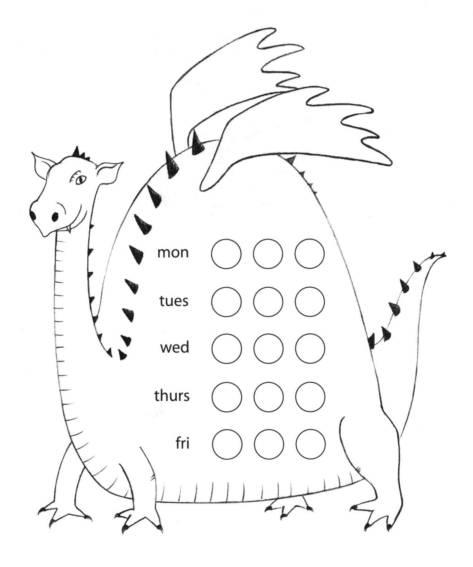

When you are trying to swap an old behaviour with a new, better one your dragon chart can help you to stay excited about your goal! Each time you do it – in the morning, in the afternoon and in the evening – colour in a spot.

My dragon chart goal is.........................

....

Reminders my teacher can use to help me are

....

....

My special reward for colouring in 12 or more dragon **spots** for the week is

....

My 'super' special reward for achieving my goal for 4 weeks is

....

Teaching Tough Kids, Routledge © Mark Le Messurier 2010

name.................................

staying on track with my duck tracking chart

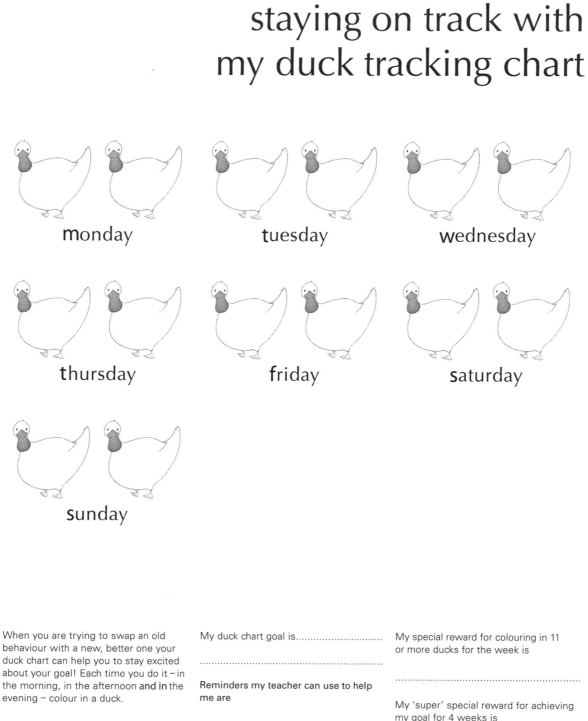

monday   tuesday   wednesday

thursday   friday   saturday

sunday

When you are trying to swap an old behaviour with a new, better one your duck chart can help you to stay excited about your goal! Each time you do it – in the morning, in the afternoon **and in** the evening – colour in a duck.

My duck chart goal is.............................

....

Reminders my teacher can use to help me are

....

....

My special reward for colouring in 11 or more ducks for the week is

....

My 'super' special reward for achieving my goal for 4 weeks is

....

....

being different is ok

Find out how old you were when you did these things.

Colour the graph to show the results.

What's normal is that every one of us does things differently and at different speeds.

What matters most? To understand and accept differences.

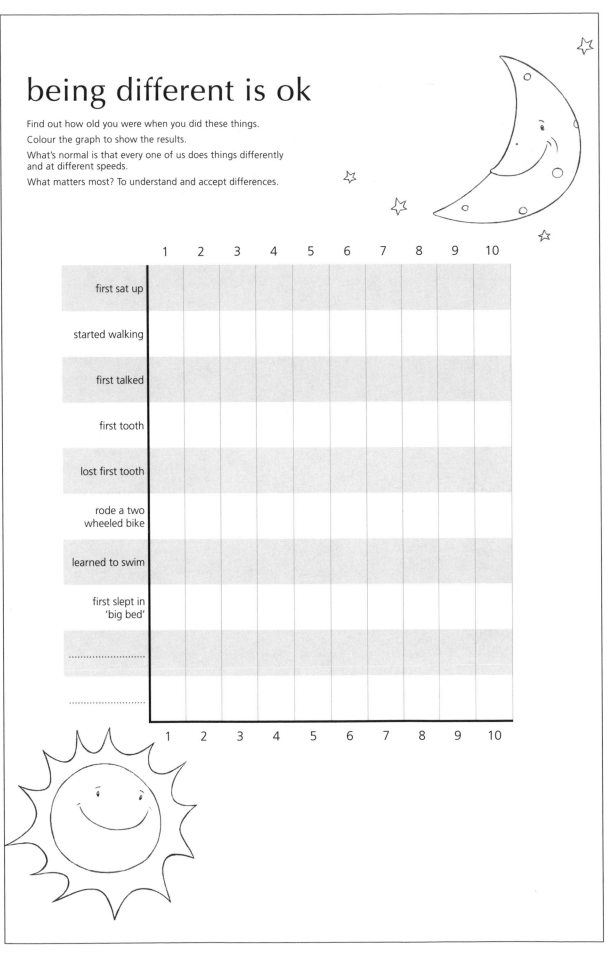

	1	2	3	4	5	6	7	8	9	10
first sat up										
started walking										
first talked										
first tooth										
lost first tooth										
rode a two wheeled bike										
learned to swim										
first slept in 'big bed'										
....										
....										

| | 1 | 2 | 3 | 4 | 5 | 6 | 7 | 8 | 9 | 10 |

Teaching Tough Kids, Routledge © Mark Le Messurier 2010

my team

Build a team that can help you.

Think about what you need and who you can help you.

Select people you trust!

name.............................

Who? ....

Their role ....

you

Who? ....

Their role ....

Who? ....

Their role ....

Who? ....

Their role ....

A break card allows you to move from the classroom when you are feeling stressed and go to the safe person or safe place we have agreed on.

This break card entitles ………..................... to take a break when it's needed. When taking a break remember to:

-
-
-

Teaching Tough Kids, Routledge © Mark Le Messurier 2010

name.............................

my happy
face collector

Listen to your teacher to find out what
they are looking for, and then remember
to do it. When your card becomes full
of stamps or stickers from your teacher,
you win!

FRANKLIN SQ. PUBLIC LIBRARY
19 LINCOLN ROAD
FRANKLIN SQUARE, N.Y. 11010

OCT   2009